IN THE WAKE OF THE *EREBUS*

ABOUT THE AUTHOR

John Ramsland OAM is Emeritus Professor at the University of Newcastle NSW and a well-regarded historian with broad interests including Aboriginal studies, sport, child social welfare and marine history. He is an author of several books and many articles. *Children of the Backlanes, Custodians of the Soil* (now translated into French), and *Remembering Aboriginal Heroes* (co-authored) are considered classics in their field. *Brave & Bold. Manly Village Public School 1858 – 2008,* also published by Brolga, Melbourne, won a prestigious NSW Writer's Centre award.

His most recent books are *The Rainbow Beach Man* (2009) and *Cook's Hill Life Saving & Surf Club* (2011).

Published by Brolga Publishing Pty Ltd
PO Box 12544 A'Beckett St Melbourne Australia 8006
ABN 46 063 962 443
email: sales@brolgapublishing.com.au
web: www.brolgapublishing.com.au

Front cover image: 'The Erebus & Terror amongst the ice floes in a gale,' watercolour by J.E. Davis
Back cover image: Alexander John Smith, MLA

National Library of Australia Cataloguing-in-Publication entry:
   Ramsland, John, 1942-
   From Antarctica to the Gold Rushes: in the wake of the *Erebus*
   9781921596926 (pbk.)
   Smith, Alexander.
   British Antarctic Expedition (1839–1843)
   Gold mines and mining—Victoria—Castlemaine—History.
   Men—Australia—Biography.
   920.710994

Printed in China
Cover design by David Khan
Typesetting and design by Imogen Stubbs

From
Antarctica
to the
Gold Rushes
in the wake of the *Erebus*

Alexander Smith RN,
Polar voyager, astronomer & goldfields commissioner
1812 – 1872

John Ramsland

Fabulous voyagers! What histories
Are there behind your deep and distant stare!
Show us the treasures of your memories,
Those jewels and riches made of stars and air.

Charles Baudelaire, 'Voyaging'

IN MEMORY OF
ROMA MEREDITH FFLOYD THOMSON (née Chomley)
(1923 – 2008)

**The unfailing keeper of the papers of
Commander Alexander John Smith R.N.**

CONTENTS

ACKNOWLEDGEMENTS

Merilyn Pedrick, a descendent of Commander Alexander Smith RN, came across the author's article in *Australian Heritage* and liked the immediacy of his style and his approach to the writing of history. She contacted him, inviting him to write about her ancestor and his largely unrecognised contributions to the British Empire and to the colonial Castlemaine community. He eagerly accepted the challenge.

As well as preparing typed transcripts of Smith's regular and numerous letters to family members in England between 1830 and 1872, and those from friends in England like Sir Joseph Hooker, Merilyn gathered together much of the family historical material that was available from relatives in urban and country Victoria. She also provided for scrutiny photocopies of the original documents held privately by family members. Merilyn typed early drafts of most of the chapters from the handwritten versions of the book. Without such assistance, the book could not have emerged.

Ian Hockley, an astute local researcher and member of the Castlemaine Historical Society, conducted a thorough search of the Society's archives and unearthed contemporary documents, some of a legal nature, about Alexander Smith's position and status within the Castlemaine community as well as the property he owned. Ian took photographs of relevant graveyard evidence in the Castlemaine Cemetery.

While the responsibility for the text and its interpretation is the author's alone, he wishes to recognise the assistance of archivists and other staff of the Mitchell Library, Sydney, the La Trobe State Library of Victoria and the National Library of Australia.

His wife, Dr Marie Ramsland, contributed by making electronic searches of contemporary newspapers and official government sources, by typing and editing the several advanced drafts of the text.

*Shipwreck at Night – HMS **Thetis**,*
painting by Alexander John Smith RN,
oil on a piece of the ship's wreckage (Private Collection)

1

Prologue

A Miraculous Escape

Three days after his eighteenth birthday, midshipman Alexander John Smith aboard HMS *Warspite* took up his pen on 23 December 1830 to write to his family about the terrible events that had befallen him. He gave an eye-witness account of the wreck of HMS *Thetis*. Many of his comments read like a routine entry, abrupt and exact, as in a ship's log highlighting the basic skills of his naval training. They occasionally, however, become more startling and dramatic:

> ... at 8.10 a.m. on Sunday 5th inst., [of December 1830], we were running with a very strong breeze under double reefed topsails, main top gallant sails Jib driven and four top Mainsails Stud sail with the wind about S E B E steering N E B E running 10/4 knots. Cape Frio by dead reckoning M E B E 28', having had no sun since the morning of the 3rd when we left Rio [de Janeiro]. I was alarmed by hearing sung out

by the Officer of the watch "Hard aport the Helm".
I instantly sprang upon Deck, the hands were turned
up. "Shorten Sail" and all rushed upon Deck; when
I got there I supposed the ship was taken aback in a
heavy squall (for it was blowing very hard), and from
the rear of the surf I thought it was the Ship going
astern, but was quickly convinced to the contrary by a
most dreadful shock that threw every one down. I got
up directly and looking round saw we were close on
board an almost perpendicular shore with a tremendous surf breaking on it (the Helm was instantly put
hard aport, and after the first shock she came to on
the starboard tack and carried away all the Larboard
Topsail and Lower yardarms and again struck with
a tremendous crash and shook stern on to the rocks,
and down came (it is impossible for me to describe
with how dreadful a crash), all the lower masts right
amidships.

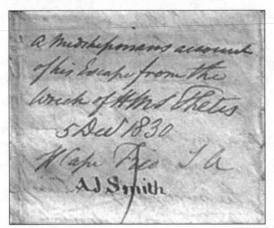

Most miraculously only three men were killed by
them altho' every one was on deck – as for myself I
got as close as possible to the starboard bulwark and
was only slightly touched by one of the shrouds; an
immense number of the people however, were much

injured by the falling of the masts and their rigging. After their fall the Captain ordered what small sails we could get at to the set on the stumps, both fore and Main Mast were carried away within 9 feet of the Deck. We got a Fore Royal and Main T.G. Stud sail set one on each mast and a puff coming off the land, forged her ahead, but she quickly drifted in again and from the heavy swell began beating her starboard quarter in.

I was on the main Deck getting the Pumps and Ports shipped...[1]

Here was a moment or two he would never forget! Seventeen-year-old midshipman Smith found himself on the main deck of HMS *Thetis* amidst the chaos and imminent dangers of shipwreck. The ship was living up to its classical name of a sea nymph that violently changed form. The heavy swell near the rocks of Cape Frio, or Cabo Frio near the coast of Brazil, had begun to smash in the ship's starboard quarter. Rocks came crashing through the side of the main deck; the ship had begun to fill quickly with swirling sea water, despite the frantic efforts a few minutes before of Alexander Smith and others at the pumps below.

Captain Burgess had then called to Smith to send everyone up to the deck to save themselves from drowning. Going down the ladder, Smith sent all hands around him up to the open deck and then courageously attempted to get further down to the men in the lower deck, but did not succeed as it was 'all afloat and every hatch blown up by the force of water'.

Realising there was nothing further he could do by

---

1 A.J. Smith to his family, HMS *Warspite*, 23 December 1830 (Merilyn Pedrick Collection). Hereafter, all unpublished letters cited are from this collection which includes both the originals and the transcriptions of them made by Merilyn Pedrick.

remaining there, he headed up on deck to be faced with a terrible scene, as the most daring were attempting to jump ashore on the rocks below the cliff. As soon as they gripped the rocks on the face of the cliff, many were torn back into the sea by the tumultuous swirling swell and crashing waves. There was nothing 'to hold on by and they were immediately drowned or crushed by the ship chafing her sides against the rocks'. Many of the sailors had not learned to swim. Smith briefly looked on with horror.

From the unstable rocking main deck, Alexander Smith then looked up and saw the mountain looming above, hanging over their heads and appearing almost ready to crush down on them, such was the violent rocking of the deck and the illusion it created. Smith thought that the ship had found its way into a cavern and that 'there was not the slightest chance [now] of saving' his own life. He expected that in a few moments 'everything would be over'. Few members of the crew were able to hold on even to the sides of the vessel as it tilted dangerously. Every lifeboat had been stove to pieces.

But the moment of despair passed quickly for Midshipman First Class Smith; he noticed how every man had behaved in a 'most gallant manner', that not a soul apart from the few invalids aboard had cried out at all. He 'thought only of that'. Such a thought strangely comforted and calmed him. And yet it was to remain a vivid memory for the rest of his life.

He recalled how not a quarter of an hour before the ship struck the coastal rocks, everybody on board was talking of the quick passage they were making back home to England and to loved ones from their long sojourn in the Royal Navy's South American Station.

They had just left Rio de Janiero in Brazil and had only recently since departed from their base on the River Plate or Rio de la Plata in Uruguay near Montevideo and turned north to follow the coast. Cape Frio was always a dangerous promontory for shipping.

Realising by this time that the ship was beginning to 'settle', that is sink fast into the chaos of rocks and swirling swell, Smith took himself aft and stripped off his heavy water-laden shirt to prepare to abandon ship. Looking desperately around, he 'fancied' that he saw a place he might be able to reach, that he might be able to hold on to in the treacherous waves. He sprang from the *Thetis* as far as he could. At the same time, the heavy swell of the sea took him forward and landed him on a rock. Apart from a few bruises, he was unharmed but knocked up.

Another swell suddenly arose sharply and he clung desperately to the rock, but was nearly suffocated by the water breaking over it. This forced him to let go, but he was carried a few feet higher up the rock by the waves of the fast mounting tide where he caught hold and held on desperately for some time with his feet dangling without anything to gain a foothold. This eventually forced him to drop about five feet when his arms became too tired to hang on. He sprang up again with the assistance of the surf and got above the outcrop to find firmer ground to stand on. Struggling to stand, he looked around and could see the wrecked ship floating, almost submerged down to its main deck.

He suddenly realised that the tide was still on the rise and he would soon be washed away. He could see there wasn't a soul near him, no crew member. He scrambled to a slightly higher and safer place on the cliff face above the wild sea. Despondent, he stood there for a few moments with the rain pouring down and the wind beating hard against his face. He felt exhausted after his battle with the sea.

Then he thought he heard someone above call: "Catch hold!". Puzzled, he immediately asked: "of what?". And realised something was hanging down the cliff face – it was a rough rope made of several pairs of sturdy canvas trousers securely knotted together. With some risk of overbalancing into the sea below, he eventually caught the improvised rope as the whipping wind blew it closer.

Gripping tightly, he was thankfully dragged up to a spot where he found to his pleasant surprise fifty able seamen, five midshipmen and two lieutenants huddled together on a ridge of rock.

Before he had heard the call, he imagined he was the sole survivor.

The men milled around him, warmly congratulating him on his narrow escape from the ferocious dangers of the deep. They told him that several others had tried the improvised trouser rope earlier but, except for a dozen or so, all had fallen back into the turbulent waters. They had counted at least fifteen who had died trying the same method of escape.

Nearly all the many trouserless survivors that he met on this higher patch of land had escaped from the ship in its early stages of being wrecked when her quarter had stove in and before she had drifted round the headland to the cavernous place below where he was rescued from – a place where so many had failed to escape and so few had been saved. Alexander Smith appears to have been the last rescued survivor of the entire *Thetis* disaster. After a short lapse of time, knots were undone and trousers were thankfully put back on.

After the excitement settled down a little and the adrenalin stopped flowing as much, the exhausted Smith found that his knees, breast and hands had been severely cut during the final adventure of coming up the cliff face. His own trousers were in shreds. His wounds were bound by part of his neck–kerchief and a piece of frock belonging to one of the men who had survived. Through the whole time, they remained in their place of assembly on the ledge of rock on the cliff face. They could hear through the wild gusts of wind the relentless grinding and crashing of the ship's side and guns against the rocks below them – a despairingly dismal sound.

At length, by a heavy rebound of the swell and surf which furiously rent the vessel against the cliff, the tide took the wreckage of the ship away from the dangerous point into a kind of bight in the coastline where she was caught 'in a regular sort of cradle and sank as far as her Upper Deck, on which was no more than a foot or two of water but with a heavy surf breaking on her'.

After many valiant efforts, the Boatswain, the ship's strongest man, had managed to heave a line to the shore. One seaman who had clambered over the rocks to the shore in the earlier stages of the wreck took hold and secured it. To the end of this line, a stout hawser[2] was bent. One of the men carrying a lighter line went ashore by it. Then a second hawser was sent on shore in case the first should break, which, as events turned out, came in very useful.

Unfortunately for the three men who went first, the rope parted and they all dropped and drowned in the surf.

By daylight, however, most survivors cut off from the shore on the headland were landed. After a painful and difficult walk, the exhausted men found two unoccupied huts which held only 'a few salt fish rather the worse for being kept for too long'. They then had the ill luck to discover they were on an island and not on the mainland. They stayed with the huts for the day distressingly thirsty and hungry. Few could stomach

2   Hawser, a large rope or cable.

the salted fish found there. Their Robinson Crusoe experience began.

About 5pm, a small native canoe came from nearby and the men in it offered to take all the survivors over to a village on the mainland about six miles across the sea for a fee. They requested the rate of eight dollars for each trip. Captain Burgess agreed to this fee and by the next morning 'all hands were got over'.

The village Prago Do Ange consisted of a few 'wretched huts'. On the first day, the shipwreck survivors had plenty of everything as the villagers believed that they had plenty of money to spend. Alexander Smith obtained a pair of trousers as the ones he was wearing at the time of the disaster had been comprehensively shredded on the rocks by the power of the waves and on his climb to safety to his comrades.

Soon after, the villagers turned up in a group to collect payment. Having no cash, Alexander Smith was forced to hand the trousers back and revert to his shredded ones. The native villagers soon became discontented and aggressive about the lack of cash flow and refused the party any further essential supplies. Captain Burgess, however, was able to send a message to his Commandant who replied that if the village headman did not supply them with a few essential things for survival the consequences would be grave.

After this communication, the villagers supplied the survivors with a little fish and Indian corn, but soon after they were entirely abandoned — the native villagers simply disappeared.

On 18 December, the Navy's Man-of-War arrived to the rescue and brought them to safety aboard HMS *Druid*. The death toll, however, was large. Twenty-seven men had lost their lives in the disastrous incident and ninety-five men and officers were badly injured, some having to have legs and arms amputated as a result of being crushed when the rigging fell heavily on them.

* * * * *

But who was Alexander John Smith? This study seeks to know him, to reveal him and follow his professional career and private life to the end of his days.

Born and raised in that great naval establishment of Greenwich, he joined the Royal Navy at the tender age of fourteen as a Midshipman Volunteer First Class and was assigned to HMS *Thetis* at Portsmouth. He served on the *Thetis* for nearly four years and was occasionally based at Rio de Janeiro as part of the Royal Navy's great South American Station.

Midshipman,
engraving by Merks,
after Thomas Rowlandson,
PW4970, NMM, Greenwich

The function of the South American and other British Naval Stations around the world was strategic and militaristic – a demonstration of the nation's growing sea power after the Napoleonic Wars. The duties of the Station involved a role in policies of local and Imperial defence, services to British Colonial governors and their officials, the protection of the lives and property of British subjects in countries beyond British jurisdiction as well as the difficult task of protecting natives as British dependents from abuse, even from British subjects.[3]

In Alexander Smith's initial set of experiences as a midshipman in the British Navy, HMS *Thetis* carried out these duties, in a variety of ways before the ship's disaster, by visiting and patrolling Rio de Janeiro, Buenos Aires, Valparaiso, the Falkland Islands and other coastal places in South America as well as some of the more remote Atlantic islands. Alexander Smith's next assignment was placement aboard HMS *Druid*. In March 1831, he was discharged from the *Druid* and, in January 1832, became a midshipman on HMS *Harrier*. Thus other adventures began to unfold taking him all the way to the vast Indian Ocean and the Royal Navy's station there on the southern coastline of Asia.

---

3   John Bach, 'The Royal Navy in the South West Pacific: the Australia Station 1859-1913', *The Great Circle* Vol. 5, No 2, October 1983, p 117.

2

Formative Greenwich Years
Family & Naval Traditions

Alexander John Smith was born on 20 December 1812 in Greenwich, the birthplace of Henry VIII, Elizabeth I and Mary I. The royal Tudors were born in Greenwich Palace, but Alexander came into being at the more modest Flint House, a rambling old place built of flint and red brick that stood back from the main street near the corner of Royal Hill.

All of the Smith family believed that Flint House had been part of the old palace that had been demolished at the end of the seventeenth century and replaced by Sir Christopher Wren's spectacular Royal Naval Hospital framing the Queen's House, which Wren was prevented from pulling down. Flint House conceivably could have been a residence in the grounds of the old Greenwich Palace as it was close by Wren's buildings, but may have been re-built later.

Be that as it may, Flint House had a spacious front courtyard made private by a row of tall lime trees when the Smith family lived there. For Alexander and his brothers and sisters, the house had a big garden to play in. It was divided longitudinally by a wall with vines growing on its western side with clusters of large delicious purple grapes in season. There were several fine pear trees and a walnut and mulberry tree. It was a favourite place under such trees during the hot summer for the children to sit or play in the shade. A variety of flowers and borders were grown by their father's widowed sister Fanny who turned up every day at Flint House. She threatened the children (who were terrified of her) 'with dire punishment and worse if they dared to touch the flowers or damage the borders'.[1] Apart from this threat, it was a joyous playground for Alexander Smith and his brothers and sisters. Indeed, the garden remained in Alexander John Smith's imagination for the rest of his life. In later years, he recreated such a garden on his property 'Langley' in faraway Victoria, Australia. The love of garden was indelible.

Alexander was the second son and third child of Lord Henry Smith and Jane Mary (née Voase) and was christened into the Anglican faith at Greenwich on 23 January 1813 about a month after his birth. His two elder siblings were Henry Thomas born in 1810 and Jane Mary born in 1811. His young siblings in succession were William Richard born in 1814; Edward James born in 1815; Mary born in 1816; John Peter George born in 1818; Bernhard born in 1820, Emma Anne born in 1822; Fanny Voase born in 1824 and Mary Bate born in 1826 – a robust family of eleven children. Their mother spent many years bearing children from 1810 to 1826.

---

1   Gertrude M. Attwood, *The Wilsons of Tranby Croft*, Hutton Press, Beverley, East Yorkshire, 1988, pp. 22-3.

*   *   *   *   *

The Greenwich connection began with Alexander Smith's paternal grandfather Henry Smith who was born in 1736 and died in 1802, about eleven years before Alexander was born. Henry joined the navy at an early age, saw action in the Seven Year War between 1756 and 1763 – a complex European War partly over struggles between Britain and France in the New World involving the English capture of Quebec. He was badly wounded and thereafter retired from active service.

He found employment as a Lieutenant at the Royal Greenwich Hospital which was established to relieve and support seamen belonging to the Royal Navy who, because of disablement caused by wounds, particularly the loss of limbs (which was commonplace) or those of frail old age, were unable to support or maintain themselves. The institution also aided widows and the children of sailors slain or disabled in the service of the Royal Navy in battles to protect or expand the British Empire.

In early 1770 at the age of about forty-five, Lieutenant Henry Smith RN married Maria Short who was some fourteen years his junior. Their four children were all born in their apartment at Greenwich Hospital. To their second child and eldest son, Alexander's father, they gave the rather unusual name of Lord Henry. Lord Henry grew up in his parents' quarters and eventually entered into a clerical position in the Naval Pay Office, a well-staffed large organisation centred at Greenwich.[2]

The Royal Hospital for Seamen at Greenwich, in which Lieutenant Henry Smith and his wife's apartments were located, was established in 1694 by King William and Queen

2   Attwood, *The Wilsons of*, pp. 20-2.

Mary. It was situated five miles from London Bridge on the southern bank of the Thames, elevated on a terrace 865 feet in length, looking towards the river and with 'four distinct piles of buildings': King Charles', Queen Anne's, King William's and Queen Mary's Quarters. The whole presentation, it was argued in 1820 eight years after Alexander Smith's birth, was 'the most magnificent and beautiful *coup d'oeil* that can be imagined':

> In the centre of the grand square stands a beautiful statue of his late Majesty King George the Second [1688-1760] executed by the famous Rysbrack,[3] and carved out of a single block of white marble, which weighed eleven tons. This block was taken from the French by Admiral Sir George Rooke, and being a statue that was presented by Sir John Jennings Knt., at that time Master and Governor of the Hospital, as a mark of his respect and gratitude to his Royal Master.[4]

Such icons and magnificent buildings represented to the young boy Alexander Smith the patriotic naval spirit, a sense of duty and adventure. In growing up at Greenwich, he was mentally engulfed by it all – one of the major factors in his enlistment in the Royal Navy at a young age. Everyday life for him as a child was densely surrounded by such deeply influential British Empire iconography. Service to King and Country was a persistent call of the sirens.

The Royal Hospital for Seamen at Greenwich was bounded

---

3   John Michael (Joannes Michiell) Rysbrack (1693-1770), an important sculptor born on the continent, studied in Antwerp, went to England in 1720. Many of his works are in Westminster Abbey.

4   *A Description of the Royal Hospital for Seamen at Greenwich*, W. Winchester and Sons, London, 1820.

by the Royal Observatory erected on an eminence in the Royal Park in August 1679 by order of Charles II. King Charles' building on the Hospital grounds was on the west side of the great square, its eastern part a residence for Charles based on and after the design concept of the famous Indigo Jones and made of Portland stone with a middle tetra-style portico of the Corinthian order. The pavilions were also Corinthian, surmounted by an Attic order with a balustrade with sculptures of two figures representing 'Fortitude' and 'Dominion of the Sea'. Elsewhere there were sculptures representing 'Mars' and 'Fame'. The western side of the King Charles building, finished in 1813 a year after Alexander Smith was born, contained accommodation for ten sailor pensioners.

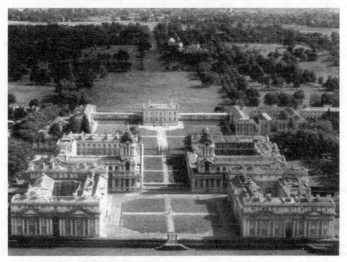

The Royal Hospital for Seamen, Greenwich

The King William building from the Thames behind the King Charles building had a great hall, vestibule and dome with a circle of stately columns designed and erected by Sir Christopher Wren. It carries a dedication to the glorious death of the iconic naval hero Lord Horatio Nelson combined with a sculpture of Britannica.

In such 'beauty, solidity and magnificence' by about 1820, the buildings on the site held nearly 3,500 persons including its governor, principal officers, pensioners and nurses, retired naval officers and their families together with their servants. It was an institution on a large, prominent and public scale, unique in British society of the time.[5]

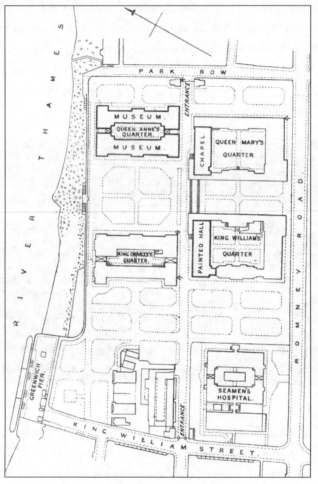

Plan of the Royal Hospital for Seamen

5   *A Description of the Royal Hospital for Seamen*, pp. 2-11.

The funds employed in the building and maintenance of the Hospital were derived by an annual subscription of £2,000 by the reigning monarch as well as subscriptions from the great officers of State, from Parliament and from wealthy individual private citizens. Money grants were derived from fines levied on smugglers and a duty of sixpence a week paid out of the wages of all Royal Navy seamen.

The first pensioner-sailors were received in 1705 and by 1814 had reached and sustained its highest compliment of 2,710 men while Alexander Smith was still an infant at nearby Flint House. The sight of uniformed sailors going backwards and forwards on the pathways and streets was commonplace to the Smith family children.

From 1763, out-pensions were granted from Hospital funds. In the early 1800s, government grants supplemented other funding sources because of the rapidly increasing number of internal and external pensioners, especially during the Napoleonic Wars. Later in the nineteenth century, numbers progressively decreased after the impact of the Napoleonic Wars lessened.

While Alexander Smith was primarily educated at home at Flint House, for a shorter time he probably attended the Greenwich Hospital School nearby which, over the first half of the nineteenth century, housed a thousand or so sons of seamen and mariners. The School was supported by Hospital funds.[6]

It had been erected near the Hospital in a two-storey building that absorbed just about two hundred boys. While

---

6   *Descriptive Catalogue of the Portraits of Naval Commanders, Representations of Naval Actions and of the Relics, &c. Exhibited in the Painted Hall and the Royal Naval Museum at Greenwich Hospital*, printed for her Majesty's Stationery Office, Eye and Spottswoode, London, 1900, pp. 3-5.

Alexander was probably a day student, the upper storey was a dormitory 'fitted with hammocks for the boys to sleep in' just as though they were on a ship. To enter the School, the boys had to be sound of mind and body and able to read. As an educational institution, it was under the management of the directors of the Greenwich Hospital.

It was a kind of pre-apprenticeship scheme. The boys had to be under twelve years of age. The curriculum consisted of reading, writing and navigation. After three years at the School, the boys were usually 'bound out for seven years of sea service'. At the age of fourteen, Alexander Smith became a Volunteer Midshipman in the Royal Navy because of his genteel social class background. Other boys became Able Seamen. Some rose through the ranks of the Royal Navy to become officers.

At the Greenwich Hospital School, the boys wore a naval-style uniform consisting of jacket and formal breeches, (with extra leather breeches to wear on weekdays), blue serge waistcoat, checked shirts and black velvet stocks (collars similar to a clerical collar as part of the formal uniform), a small round hat and blue worsted stockings.

When they were bound out to sea-service, they were furnished with two suits of clothes, a hat, two pairs of shoes, three pairs of worsted stockings, three checked shirts, two black silk handkerchiefs and a worsted nightcap, flock bed and pillow, two blankets, a coverlet, two checked pillow-biers 'and such religious and nautical books and instruments as judged expedient'.[7]

When the Admiralty introduced automatic pensions (or superannuation) for officers and warrant officers from 1836 and from 1856 for ratings, the numbers of Greenwich Hospital

---

7   *A Description of the Royal Hospital for Seamen at Greenwich*, p. 45.

Greenwich Hospital Pensioners in a local tavern,
painting by Isaac Cruikshank 1791

pensioners began to diminish rapidly and the original function of the institution eventually disappeared.

By 1873, just after Alexander Smith's death in Australia, the complex of buildings became the Royal Naval College where officers from all over the world trained in the naval sciences. In autumn 1999, the University of Greenwich began teaching there and was joined in October 2001 by Trinity College of Music.[8]

But Greenwich was a different world when Alexander Smith grew up there between 1813 and 1824 – a world that gloried in Horatio Nelson's defeat of the combined French and Spanish fleets at the Battle of Trafalgar in 1805.

Throughout Alexander's childhood in Greenwich, both his grandmothers visited regularly and were eagerly awaited. Grandmother Smith appeared to have the warmer nature according to Attwood's study of the Smith family life. Even

8   Tom Wood, 'Early charitable naval pensions', *Practical Family History*, No 64, April 2003, pp. 5-7.

in extreme old age she remained a handsome vibrant woman. Greenwich had played a significant part in her life. She would frequently sit in the dining room of Flint House watching the children at play in the garden. She wore lavender-coloured dresses in silk or satin with a black silk apron on top and a white net cap. In her apron pocket was a little horn box which always contained sugar plums as rewards for the children when they spelt a word correctly. She 'would also carefully peel an apple in a single long swirl, which before the admiring eyes of her grandchildren immediately become a swan. Paper hats and boats were always being created from sheets of newspaper'. She was a grandmother who had a strong influence on her grandchildren. She 'taught the children to love all things, and never to inflict pain'.[9]

At Flint House when the children were little, a large playroom opened out from the dining room. At Christmas time, even when Grandmother Smith was eighty years of age, she would lead the children in games like "Thread the Needle" and "Puss in the Corner". Their father Lord Henry would present magic lantern shows to entertain the children with pictures like the Eddystone lighthouse with a ship sailing by.[10]

In her account of domestic life at Flint House, Attwood derived much of her information from an unpublished memoir written by Emma Anne Smith, one of Alexander Smith's young sisters, written at Mentone circa 1882-1884 and edited by her brother John Peter George.[11] With two siblings recalling their experiences of childhood, there is no reason to doubt their authenticity. Emma Anne, who never married, was to

---

9   Attwood, *The Wilsons of*, p. 23.

10 Attwood, *The Wilsons of*.

11 Attwood, *The Wilsons of*, Footnote I, p. 36.

become, for Alexander Smith in Australia, one of his main correspondents with his extensive family in the motherland right up to his death in 1872.

One of the Smith family joys was to stroll together in the Greenwich Park at the rear of the Royal Greenwich Hospital which stretched back to Blackheath. It was the oldest of London's Royal Parks having been developed and enclosed in 1433 and had been opened to the public in the eighteenth century. It contained the original Royal Observatory.[12]

On Sundays, the favourite walk for the children was down the river bank towards Woolwich more generally known as Woolwich Arsenal which was more military than naval, a place where munitions were produced for the British armed forces. While there was a stench from the river at low tide and the decaying bloated carcasses of drowned dogs floating in the shallows, there were also the gibbets that fascinated the children. Here, bodies of executed pirates hung for months and even years. They swung in the wind and shed tarsal and metatarsal bones which the boys searched for and collected. There were still shreds of clothing attached to the skeletons that fascinated and excited the children on their walk.

Shortly after the Duke of Clarence became Lord High Admiral in 1826, he saw the gibbets as he sailed down the river. Being a sensitive man, he ordered their removal. This was about the time that Alexander John Smith joined the navy as a Volunteer Midshipman.

Lord Henry Smith, the children's father, dominated the family scene while they lived at Flint House, Greenwich. He was omnipresent – an attractive dignified and handsome

---

12 John Ayto & Ian Crofton (compilers), *Brewer's Britain & Ireland*, Weidenfeld & Nicolson, London, 2005, pp. 492-3.

The Smiths of Greenwich

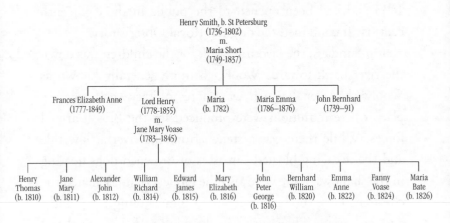

Henry Smith, b. St Petersburg
(1736-1802)
m.
Maria Short
(1749-1837)

| Frances Elizabeth Anne (1777-1849) | Lord Henry (1778-1855) m. Jane Mary Voase (1783–1845) | Maria (b. 1782) | Maria Emma (1786–1876) | John Bernhard (1739–91) |

| Henry Thomas (b. 1810) | Jane Mary (b. 1811) | Alexander John (b. 1812) | William Richard (b. 1814) | Edward James (b. 1815) | Mary Elizabeth (b. 1816) | John Peter George (b. 1816) | Bernhard William (b. 1820) | Emma Anne (b. 1822) | Fanny Voase (b. 1824) | Maria Bate (b. 1826) |

Lord Henry Smith   Jane Mary Voase

paterfamilias who could be flamboyant, even theatrical. He behaved as a gentleman and had been well educated in the elite Westminster School situated close to Westminster Abbey and founded in 1560 by Queen Elizabeth I. The School produced poets (William Cowper, John Dryden), philosophers (John Locke) and historians (Edward Gibbon) and provided an intensely classical education of a superior sort. Such an elite education rubbed off on Lord Henry Smith as he was an avid reader and had a broad general knowledge that he imparted constantly to his children.

He was devoted to his wife Jane Mary, but had an easily provoked temper. The children overheard occasional lively rows (as children tend to do). Nevertheless, he was kind-hearted and proud of his eleven children. When they were little, he frequently seemed abrupt and could speak sharply if they interfered with what he was doing or if they made too much noise.

> As he grew older, he enjoyed a nap after the five o'clock dinner. The servant would put out the lamp, and the family would draw their chairs into a half circle round the fire, father and mother opposite to each other, and nearest the blaze. The children had to whisper together, and if one of them laughed aloud, their father would always wake up and admonish the offender. This they feared. After his nap the bell would be rung and the lamp relit.[13]

Unlike the usual habits of the gentry in the early nineteenth century, Lord Henry Smith drank and ate in moderation, but could be volatile about bad cooking. 'God Almighty sends good meat, but the Devil sends cooks', he would frequently exclaim at the family dinner table.

---

13 Attwood, *The Wilsons of*, p 23-4.

On Sunday mornings at St Alphage's Church where Alexander and his siblings were mainly christened, Lord Henry was insistent on their good docile behaviour. Nevertheless, if the sermon dragged on and on he would look at his watch and proclaim audibly how many minutes the preacher had exceeded his schedule. If the sermon continued, he would begin to shake and rattle his seal and chain. He was also known for disciplining school children in front of the pulpit by pointing out the wrongdoer with a stern finger[14] until the wrongdoing ceased.

Lord Henry Smith was the first son of Lieutenant Henry Smith RN and born in a naval officer's married quarters of the Royal Hospital for Seamen at Greenwich on 16 September 1778 (or 1779). As a young man, he had a business in Russia where his father had been born in St Petersburg. He returned to England later to become a wine merchant for a period.

At the time of his marriage to Jane Mary Voase on 1 January 1806, he held a position in the Naval Pay Office at Greenwich having returned to the place of his birth. They took up residency of Flint House. Jane Mary Voase was the daughter of John Voase and Judith (née Holmes), a wealthy prominent Yorkshire family, and was born on 5 January 1783. All of their children were born in Greenwich.

In the Naval Pay Office, Lord Henry Smith did not get on well with his superior who was pompous, opinionated and un-popular with staff. With his talent for drawing (which many of his children inherited), he drew a caricature of his superior but was found out. The subject of his drawing complained to his superior officer and the artist and his accomplice in the joke were suspended from their work for a week and docked

14 Attwood, *The Wilsons of,* p 24.

a week's salary. Both angry, they resigned from the office. Maybe they considered clerical work deadly boring.

John Voase, Jane Mary's father, had made a fortune in the wine trade and Lord Henry Smith decided to do likewise. He was soon disillusioned and pulled out before he lost everything. During this time, Lord Henry and Jane Mary had created their large family at Flint House.

In 1828, Lord Henry was declared bankrupt which forced the family to leave Greenwich. (Lord Henry had stood surety for a Mr Whitelock for £4,000 which was all the capital he had. Whitelock was a clergyman and postmaster at Bath – a friend of a friend. Suddenly Whitelock defrauded and disappeared. As surety, Lord Henry was forced under law to pay the debt which Whitelock had undertaken. He was unable to do so completely and was thus bankrupted because of his generosity of spirit and trust in another who was not known to him personally. They were then forced to live on Jane Mary's inheritance of £400 a year). As Flint House was expensive to run, the family headed north to East Riding in Yorkshire close to members of the wealthy Voase family[15] – but that's another story.

As Leo Tolstoy put it in his opening sentence of his famous novel *Anna Karenina*: 'All happy families resemble one another, each unhappy family is unhappy in its own way'.[16] Alexander Smith certainly grew up in a most happy large family despite its sudden financial troubles that had forced them to leave Greenwich.

For the rest of his life, Alexander remained in regular correspondence with members of the family, throughout his seventeen-year naval career in many different cultures and

15 Attwood, *The Wilsons of*, pp. 24-25.

16 Leo Tolstoy, *Anna Karenina*, translated by Louise & Aylmer Maude, Folio Society, 2008, p.3.

places and in his subsequent life until his death. Such letters flowed from one end of the world to the other full of affection, playfulness and the drive to share life's experiences of both joy and sorrow. Such letters are full of exuberant domestic detail.

Be that as it may, the family had had a happy and fulfilling time at Flint House at Greenwich where Alexander John Smith had grown up under the overwhelming influence of the great British naval traditions. In the Gallery of the Greenwich Hospital, the iconography of naval adventure and achievement must have done much to stir his youthful imagination and shape his ambition for a career in the Royal Navy. The famous battle scenes were displayed there and he would have gazed at them on many occasions. They soon became embedded in his boyhood dreams of exciting adventure.

As the impressionable boy Alexander Smith wandered on many occasions through the gallery, he would have paused at the six views of the burning of the *Luxembourg*, a galley commanded by Captain William Kellaway which caught fire at sea on 25 June 1727. A significant disaster at sea, twenty-three of the crew escaped in one of its lifeboats. After twelve days of suffering, seven of them survived to reach Newfoundland.

One of the survivors, Captain William Boyes, eventually became Lieutenant Governor of Greenwich Hospital. Such images prefigured Alexander Smith's own adventure in the wrecking of HMS *Thetis* in early December 1830 on the coast of South America where he narrowly escaped with his life.

He may have viewed the heroic and romantic portraits of James, Duke of York, afterwards King James II, and Admiral Edward Vernon. James was appointed Lord High Admiral on the Restoration of the monarchy. He commanded the Fleet in person at the defeat of the Dutch Fleet in June 1665 and also in the Battle of Solebay in May 1672.

Vernon was appointed Captain in 1706 and Vice Admiral in 1739. He was in command of a squadron in the same year and captured the defenceless Porto Bello. He was in command of the Fleet in the attack upon Carthagena in 1741 and was made Admiral in 1745. In his career, he served in the Mediterranean, the West Indies and in the Baltic Sea.

Alexander Smith would have also come across paintings and drawings of the French Fire Ships defeated by Admiral Sir Charles Saunders at the Siege of Quebec on 28 June 1759; Lord Howe's victory over the French Fleet on 1 June 1794 and the defeat of the Spanish Fleet by the British Fleet commanded by Admiral Sir John Jervis on 14 February 1797 as well as other deeds of dramatically heroic dimensions.[17] Such images fired the boy's imagination.

He dreamt of sailing the seas in a beautiful frail wooden edifice surrounded by water and in the invariable presence of companionable others with adventurous spirits. Alexander Smith's childhood was a trajectory into the Royal Navy which was all around him in picturesque Greenwich on the Thames.

Some of the male children of Lord Henry and Jane Mary were drawn like Alexander to the navy. Alexander's older brother Henry Thomas enlisted in the Royal Navy and advanced to the rank of Lieutenant. He died at the age of forty in December 1850. Alexander John himself rose to the rank of Commander and died at the age of fifty-nine in 1872. William Richard also joined the navy and died unmarried in November 1851 at the age of forty-seven. The grandfather of these three boys, Henry Smith, was also a lieutenant in

---

17 *Descriptive Catalogue of the Portraits of Naval Commanders*, pp. 9-63.

the Royal Navy until his death in the Greenwich Hospital in February 1802.

Like Patrick O'Brian's fictitious but authentic characters in his novel *Master and Commander*,[18] Lieutenant Henry Smith cruised the Portuguese and Spanish coasts constantly giving chase to enemy ships. He was appointed to a frigate, the *Blonde*, on 27 August 1760 and the following January sailed with her to patrol the French and Portuguese coastline for a year. They captured several French ships after battle and sent them to Lisbon under prize crews. The most significant of these occurred on 11 and 12 February 1762. These were recorded in the ship's log:

> Chased a large French ship and came up to her in spite of having lost main top mast. Proved to be the *Boutin*, mounting 20 guns and 189 men, laden with coffee and pepper. Put prize crew on board and continued in company to Lisbon.[19]

There is no doubt that the naval tradition was a strong magnetic force in the family of Alexander John Smith. His grandfather must have been a compelling role model.

Such adventurous stories filtered down to Alexander John Smith and convinced him about a life on the ocean waves. As soon as he turned fourteen, he was to join the adventurous wooden world of the Georgian Navy as an enthusiastic Volunteer Midshipman and his practical nautical education began. The regulations:

> … required a candidate for a commission to pass an oral examination in seamanship, to serve six years at

---

18 Patrick O'Brian, *Master and Commander*, Folio Society, London, 2008.

19 Cited in entry 16 on Lieut. Henry Smith, 'Modified Register for Bishop John Smith' transcript (Merilyn Pedrick Collection).

sea, and two of those in the Navy in the ratings of midshipman or master's mate ... long sea service was indispensable. In both cases the necessary experience had to have been gained as a rating. Gentleman or no, every officer had begun his career on the lower deck ... In practice he was growing in years and knowledge, taking on more responsibilities and behaving more and more like the lieutenant he hoped one day to be.[20]

20 N.A.M. Rodger, *The Wooden World. An Anatomy of the Georgian Navy*, Folio Society, London, 2009, pp.235-6.

HMS *Thetis* in full sail (British School), 18th century graphite, brown wash (PU8508, NMM, Greenwich)

Intermezzo
The South American & East Indian Stations

But the true voyagers set out to sea
Just for the leaving's sake; heart lift aloft,
Nothing dissuades them from their destiny,
Something beyond their knowing cries, "We're off!"

Charles Baudelaire, 'Voyaging'

Alexander Smith arrived in Portsmouth after leaving Flint House, his family home, with the intention of joining the Royal Navy. He was a tender almost but not quite, fourteen years of age. He was to become part of the grand tradition of boys 'being bred up to the sea life, almost as apprentices to their masters'[1].

While Alexander Smith was from the gentry class as a volunteer, there was many a boy drawn from the Greenwich Hospital School or from Christ's Hospital for orphans. Some were poor waifs from the streets. Alexander was, however, a young gentleman aiming for the quarterdeck and had great expectations for a prominent career in the Royal Navy as an officer. He saw his childhood dreams of adventure in foreign parts as about to be fulfilled. The regulations stated that naval

---

1   Rodger, *The Wooden World*. p.13.

officers' sons might not be younger than eleven, nor others younger than thirteen at the time of enlisting. Alexander, then, was the correct age as a volunteer. There were also occasionally noblemen's sons amongst the recruits. Such boys and youths altogether made up between six and ten per cent of a typical ship's company in the Royal Navy.

The actual work of a young gentleman like Alexander Smith might bear only a fragile relationship with his nominal rating as a midshipman. At various times, he would work with the seamen 'including working aloft which was regarded as an important part of a future officer's training' and learn navigation from the schoolmaster, if there was one, or from the master if there wasn't. At a suitable age, the young man would be allowed to walk on the quarterdeck as a young gentleman, and, if he was favoured, to mess with the lieutenants in the ward room. Some young midshipmen could be assigned for a period to various officers as valets or servants. The whole process was an educative one through practical experience and a good degree of watchful mentoring by seniors.

Alexander Smith entered the Royal Navy on 18 December 1826 as a First Class Volunteer Midshipman at Portsmouth two days before his fourteenth birthday. On his arrival there, he discovered a city and a port on the Hampshire coast on the eastern side of Portsmouth Harbour, about twenty-four kilometres (15 miles) south east of Southampton. Even by the thirteenth century, Portsmouth had become an important naval station. A royal dockyard was established there by Henry VII in 1496. He also had the world's first dry dock constructed by engineers. By the time Alexander Smith appeared on the scene, Portsmouth had consolidated its position as Britain's principal naval base.[2] Like Greenwich, naval traditions,

2   Ayton & Crofton, *Brewer's Britain & Ireland*, pp. 892-3.

training and activities were all around the young man.

Alexander was assigned at Portsmouth aboard the frigate HMS *Thetis* which was soon to be bound for Britain's South American Station in Rio de Janeiro. A naval frigate was a warship next in line and size to a ship of the line. As a sail-rigged sloop of between sixteen and eighteen guns, the *Thetis* was a fifth or sixth rate cruising warship with two internal decks, the lower unarmed and the upper mounted with the main battery.[3]

In the South American Station, the *Thetis* was a hard-working cruiser that spent the majority of its time at sea, patrolling the South American coastline in the 'Domination of the Seas' for King and Country. At sea, all men-of-war were required to keep two watches.

Each section of the ship was divided into two parties, the starboard and larboard watches and no less than one watch was on the deck at all times, night and day. Each watch lasted four hours, except for the two two-hour dogwatches between four and eight in the evening which made the number of watches in the day an odd number, thus the duties of each watch varied continually. The ship's bell was rung at the end of each half-hour (a half-hour sandglass was used as a time measure). At eight bells, the watch changed.

In the whole cycle of the sea day, the seven watches began at noon when the officers took their sights and plotted the ship's position. This meant the calendar at sea was always twelve hours ahead of that ashore.

At four o'clock in the morning, the whole ship's crew was roused. At sea, all those in night watches had only four hours sleep at the most and were liable to be woken at any moment in the event of a crisis. On the *Thetis* as well as on most Royal

---

3 Rodger, *The Wooden World*, p. 342.

Navy sea-going vessels, lack of sleep was a constant hardship of life for everybody.

At sea in South America, life aboard the *Thetis* was arduous. The work involved much pulling and hauling as all manoeuvres depended on manpower. Work aloft was ceaseless. Certain tasks required the united strength of all seamen, such as weighing anchor.

The time not occupied in essential work of the ship was employed for Alexander Smith and other midshipmen in training and education in seamanship and navigation, both practical and theoretical. Formal instruction in seamanship was necessary for boys and youths. The boatswain and his mate could teach the young essentials like knotting and splicing. The senior officers taught navigation and the mathematical calculations related to it. The work aloft could only be learnt in practice by imitating the experienced seafarers. Admiralty orders required boys and youths to be exercised aloft on a daily basis. Sometimes this could even be done while in port, but it was best at sea under real conditions. For young gentlemen like Alexander Smith, it was considered indispensable to work aloft with the topmen. The aim was to end up with 'finished seamen' who knew what they were ordering their men to do.[4]

Alexander Smith served on the *Thetis* for nearly four years making frequent cruises to Buenos Aires, Valparaiso and the Falkland Islands. As recounted, the *Thetis* was shipwrecked on 5 December 1830 at Cape Frio in a violent storm after leaving Rio de Janeiro in Brazil bound for the motherland to end their tour-of-duty. Smith was most fortunate to survive.

He returned to England aboard HMS *Druid* and was discharged in the ensuing March. In December 1831, he was appointed midshipman of HMS *Harrier*, a newly-launched

4   Rodger, *The Wooden World*, pp. 23-30.

sloop of eighteen guns built at Pembroke in 1830-31. Then in January the following year, he left Plymouth headed for the faraway East Indies Station.

They arrived at St Helena where Napoleon had been exiled on 9 July 1832 and then sailed across to the Cape of Good Hope, South Africa. Alexander gave a vivid account in a letter to his family of the *Harrier*'s arrival at the Cape before they entered into the vastness of the Indian Ocean. The bay where they anchored was entirely land-locked and about fifteen miles deep with high hills surrounding it. Simon's Town

'For a midshipman like Alexander Smith it was considered indispensable to work aloft with the topmen', lithograph, W. Sharp after John Hayter, c. 1850, PU3702, NMM, Greenwich

consisted of about seventy houses. He immediately noticed that the Admiral's house on a hill was 'very pretty' set amongst bowers of vines and orange and lime trees, with a 'most beautiful garden'. The other houses of the town were also attractive with their whitewashed exterior walls contrasting with an abundance of green trees. Alexander found there were two regiments of troops assigned to the town, the 72nd and the 73rd. He found the Governor Sir Lowry Cole to be very much liked 'by all hands', a great sporting character with two packs of hounds. He hunted twice a week to the 'very great amusement of the Dutch' who, Alexander noted, 'were on very good terms' with the English. Cole and the other English gentlemen of the town hunted the native jackal (rather than the fox). Other game was in abundance about six miles outside the town: partridge, hare, deer and impala as well as pheasants. Enormous quantities of fish were also taken: Roman, Hottentot, Red, Broad Noses, Spate, Rock Cod and Garnet.

Alexander and two other midshipmen accepted an invitation from relatives of the ship's captain to stay with him for a couple of days in Cape Town, six miles away. They all went on an enjoyable hunt on horseback and saw some of the countryside.[5]

The *Harrier* then ventured into the Indian Ocean arriving in Trincomalee on 17 July 1832. The following day, they sailed for Madras. The 25th of September found them in Ceylon. They then sailed for Bengal, reaching it on 8 October. They returned to Trincomalee on 5 November via Madras and then made the return journey. They refitted their vessel on the Prince of Wales Island from 10 January 1833. By May that year, they were in Batavia and then found themselves in Singapore on 23 April before cruising on to Madras again arriving there on 5 June. They returned to Singapore on 31 July 1833 and then sailed for Malacca. Alexander's ship also visited Negapore Heads, Bombay and Mauritius.

Alexander Smith was employed, amongst other things, in the suppression of piracy in the Straits of Malacca. He took part in two major conflicts which culminated in the destruction of the pirate settlements of Poulo Arroa and Poulo Sujee. The monsoons of the East Indies of Asia modified cruising conditions, but Alexander Smith visited many places on cruises of the Indian Ocean between 1832 and 1835. The *Harrier* eventually returned to England to be paid off. Alexander had gained much experience and came back a seasoned sailor.

On arrival back in England in Portsmouth Harbour,

---

5   Letter circa July 1832, Alexander Smith to his family.

Alexander, now aged twenty-three, wrote to his mother at Cottingham near Hull on 23 July 1835. He was delayed aboard the *Harrier* while giving evidence in the court marital of the ship's Acting Master for repeated acts of drunkenness. He had been summoned by the Judge Advocate along with others to give evidence for the prosecution. Alexander found it a 'great nuisance' as it delayed his leave and he had no idea how long the court martial would last. He provided his mother with details of the situation and other recent events in the Royal Navy together with the possibilities of placements aboard other ships.

He then wrote of his arrival at Portsmouth after four years on cruises in the Indian Ocean:

> We came into Portsmouth Harbour yesterday evening. We weighed about 4 o'clock blowing very strong as much sail as we could stagger under double Reefs and topsails, the wind dead on end up the Harbour, never was a Ship beaten in in more beautiful style as fast as the yards were round the Helm was down again my Father must recall the narrowness of the Harbour, made more so now by the number of yachts. We made about 11 tacks in about 18 minutes, thousands of people looking at us. When at last just after shortening sail and the Dr.yard … had run out a Warp to haul alongside the Hulk the Old Britannia just ahead of us, we unfortunately canted with the tide on top of her, her Bowsprit took out our Mizzen topsail and MsTops mast rigging away and there we hung for a few minutes when another warp was run out and we landed clear and once more lashed alongside the … Hulk doing nothing, for as yet, strange to say, we have not received any order to prepare for paying off.[6]

6   Alexander Smith to his mother, HMS *Harrier*, 23 June 1835, Portsmouth Harbour.

And so Alexander writes on. Whether his mother was able to cope with all the technical terms is doubtful, but his pure enthusiasm for his work as a seafarer does come through in every line of his letter!

On 4 July 1835, it was reported that the court martial had been cancelled. The *Harrier* was paid off on 13 July. Alexander was free to take home leave.

He had passed his oral examination on 5 August 1834 finalising his training apprenticeship as a midshipman. He could now receive an appointment as mate on one of His Majesty's ships. In December 1835, he joined HMS *Cove* in the capacity of Mate sixth rate, his first promotion.[7] Smith was fortunate to have as his captain the esteemed experienced polar navigator James Clark Ross who was already famous in naval circles.

Born on 15 April 1800, James Clark Ross had joined the Royal Navy before his twelfth birthday in 1812. He was born in London, the third son of George Ross and a nephew of Sir John Ross. James Clark Ross served under his uncle on HMS *Briseis* in the Baltic, then in the White Sea and off the coast of Scotland. He accompanied his uncle on his first Arctic voyage in search of a north-west passage in 1818 and, on his return, joined HMS

Sketch by Alexander Smith

7   Entry 47M on 'Captain Alexander John Smith' in 'Modified Register for Bishop John Smith', p. 10.

Severn cruising in the English Channel. Between January 1819 and 1827, he made four Arctic expeditions under William Edward Parry. During another expedition between 1829 and 1833, again under his uncle, he determined the position of the North Magnetic Pole, at the time located on the Boothia Peninsula in Arctic Canada. This achievement in May 1831, along with his handsome Byronic appearance, won him great popular acclaim in Britain. He became a Georgian celebrity, especially in scientific and Admiralty circles.

On his return from these major expeditions, he also received rapid promotion to post captain and captain of HMS *Cove* in 1834. Aboard ship, he met and became the patron and mentor to Alexander John Smith. Smith voyaged with him aboard the *Cove* to Baffin Bay in search for some missing whalers who had been frozen in the ice pack. On this particularly dangerous voyage, Ross became deeply impressed with Alexander Smith's ability and potential. In his turn, Smith learnt much from Ross' astute and determined captaincy and leadership.

In February 1836, Alexander Smith wrote to his mother about his perilous cruise aboard the *Cove* with Captain Ross demonstrating his marvellous seamanship on that voyage. Alexander emphasised the conditions he underwent of a prolonged hurricane experienced in Davis Strait. Heavy gales with hard squalls of snow and hail seemed to be 'without intermission'. No one on board had ever seen its equal and many were vastly experienced sailors in polar regions. During one watch, Alexander and his companion were lashed to the mizzen rigging with 'a most awful sea breaking over our Starboard Bow'. Lifeboats were dashed 'into ten thousand pieces'. He felt himself almost suffocated with the volume of water that rushed over him. When he opened his eyes, he saw the ship on her broadside, the bulwarks all washed away and, for all appearances, she seemed to be sinking. But as Alexander put it, 'God in his mercy' righted the ship. However, the fore and aft decks were again awash. Captain Ross manoeuvred sails magnificently and brought the ship out of the trouble it was in.

Alexander found it difficult to explain his feelings in such circumstances. Even in the wreck of the *Thetis*, he had never felt so much in peril about the dangers of the deep. He had heard the cries on the lower deck that the ship was going down. It was believed the bows and sides of the *Cove* had been stove in, but that was false. Nevertheless, after the thirty-six hours of the hurricane, the ship looked all but 'a perfect wreck' – the ship's carpenter found damage almost everywhere.

Despite being 'nearly frozen to death', Alexander reported to his family that he had never been in better health. He was of the opinion that Captain James Ross was 'without exception the finest fellow' that he had ever met, 'the most persevering indefatigable man you could conceive'. He was 'beloved by everyone'.

Because of the terrible conditions, the berths of both the officers and the crew were 'most miserable', wet through the many leaks. Alexander argued that 'you cannot keep the wet out of your bed and I expect all my clothes by the time I get home will be rotten'. Everyone, including the captain, Alexander went on, claimed bitterly of the cold, the tremendous winds and the continuous rolling of the ship. It was really 'no joke' to turn out at four in the morning to keep watch. They kept company with large ice bergs and witnessed the Aurora Borealis each night – which was 'splendid beyond description, colours of every description shooting out of the Zenith in every direction'.

They anchored at Stromness Harbour, the Orkneys in the north of Scotland where they were to overhaul for at least a week, perhaps more.[8]

The *Cove* had been hired and specially commissioned on 21 December 1835 by Captain James Clark Ross to sail to Greenland waters to relieve whalers beset by ice in Baffin Bay. Before a perilous and fruitless voyage, facing hurricanes and gales, they had weighed anchor and sailed from the Orkney Isles on 11 January 1836. In August that year, they returned to Hull from where they had originally set

James Clark Ross as a young officer, artist unknown, c.1830.

sail, without having found any of the lost whaling ships due to the impenetrability of the ice of Baffin Bay.

A few days after writing to his mother, Alexander, still aboard the *Cove*, wrote dutifully to his father: 'We are a rum set of coves. My hair is so long that it comes down to my mouth…' His hands were so hard that they were like a piece of mahogany wood. But again he praised the captain as a fine fellow and stated that, aboard the *Cove*, they were most fortunate in all their officers.[9]

With the conclusion of the *Cove*'s voyage back from Baffin Bay, James Clark Ross stood head and shoulders in the Arctic experience above any other officer in the Royal Navy. He

---

8 Alexander Smith to his mother, 18 February 1836, HMS *Cove*, Stromness Harbour.

9 Alexander Smith to his father, HMS *Cove*, 20 February 1836.

had spent eight winters and fifteen navigable seasons in the Arctic regions – an unequalled record. He was then offered a knighthood in recognition of this distinguished service, but he turned it down.[10]

Between 1835 and 1838 while Smith was posted elsewhere, Ross was employed by the Admiralty to make a major and detailed magnetic survey of Great Britain to further acclaim.[11] As a naval careerist, he had almost reached his zenith.

In the meantime, Smith garnered further sea experience by being appointed for a few months as a mate aboard HMS *Salamander*, a steamer on the coast of Spain. He then served for two years amongst the Orkneys in Scotland as an extra mate on HMS *Mastiff*, a surveying vessel. (Temporarily in November 1837, he had taken charge of HMS *Cutter* as its commanding officer until he joined HMS *Mastiff* under the command of George Thomas and, for a short period in March 1837, he served aboard HMS *North Star*.)[12]

As Alexander's career took further shape, Captain James Clark Ross recalled his noticeable potential and ability and marked him down for future possible enterprises. Ross was described by a fellow officer as 'the finest officer I have met with… He is perfectly idolized by everyone'. When British scientists pressed for an expedition to find the mysterious South Magnetic Pole – the 'Magnetic Crusade' – James Clark Ross was the obvious choice to lead it.[13]

10 Ernest S. Dodge, *The Polar Rosses. John & James Clark Ross and their Explorations*, Barnes & Noble, New York, 1973, p. 184.

11 David McGonigal (Chief Consultant), *Antarctica. Secrets of the Southern Continent*, Simon & Schuster, Australia, 2008, p. 280; Raymond John Howgego, 'R27 Ross, James Clark 1818-1849' in *Encyclopedia of Exploration 1800 to 1850*, Hordern House, Potts Point, 2004, pp. 514-5.

12 Alexander Smith to his mother, 13 March 1837 aboard the *North Star* where he discusses their extended family.

13 McGonigal, *Antarctica*, p. 280.

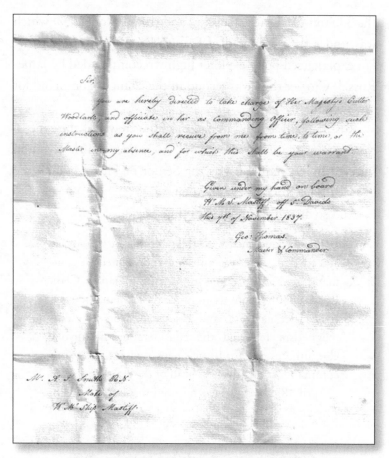

Alexander is given added responsibility by his Master & Commander

In the summer of 1838, a meeting at Newcastle of the British Association for the Advancement of Science discussed in detail the deficiencies in the existing knowledge of terrestrial magnetism and proposed that a major expedition should be fitted out to determine the position of the South Magnetic Pole. In its turn, the proposal was emphatically endorsed by the Royal Society and further encouraged by Lord Melbourne's government. The following year, the Parliament voted the necessary funds. Command of the whole expedition was given to James Clark Ross and two ships were provided, the 370 ton *Erebus* (the flagship) and the 340 ton *Terror* which was under the command of Francis Reardon Moira Crozier (an experienced polar explorer highly recommended by James Ross).[14] Crozier then was second in the chain of command for the expedition.

Ross had a free hand in choosing the crews for the expedition in consultation with Crozier. Alexander Smith was soon selected by Captain Ross as the Senior or First Mate on the *Erebus* under Ross' direct command.

And so an adventure of a lifetime began.

> Everyone concerned with the planning of the voyage agreed that there was only one man suited to command such an arduous undertaking. James Clark Ross's qualifications as an officer, a seaman, an experienced ice navigator and as an expert on terrestrial magnetism rendered the consideration of anyone else unnecessary, for he was equipped to act as both commander and scientific head of the expedition. On 8 April 1839 he received his commission to H.M.S. *Erebus* ...[15]

Alexander Smith's sea trunk (Private Collection)

---

14 Howgego, *Encyclopedia of Exploration 1800 to 1850*, p. 130.

15 Dodge, *The Polar* Rosses, p. 186.

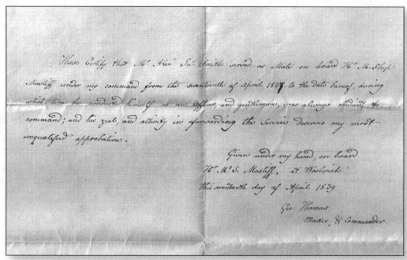

The Captain of HMS *Mastiff*'s report about Alexander Smith

4

The Epic Antarctic Expedition Begins
September 1839 – April 1841

Then a bright star appears – the man whose name will ever be remembered as one of the most intrepid polar explorers and one of the most capable seamen the world has ever produced – Admiral Sir James Clark Ross.

Roald Amundsen,
cited in M.J. Ross,
Ross in the Antarctic, p. iii

James Clark Ross in full dress uniform,
engraving by Henry Cook
after J.R. Wildman, 1840

The Norwegian Roald Amundsen, the ultimate polar explorer of the early twentieth century, greatly admired the Englishman James Clark Ross as the greatest polar explorer of the nineteenth century. In planning, preparation and leadership, he saw him a mirror image of himself. While the ever-confident Amundsen's list of polar achievements never has been, indeed never can be, surpassed, the same was once said of James Clark Ross before the turn into the twentieth century. Amundsen, however, had technological advantages over his nineteenth-century idol because of the Industrial Revolution and the modernisation of sea-going equipment and ship design. Hence Amundsen's estimation of Ross was by no means inaccurate.

Following in the Footsteps

Amundsen served on the ship *Belgica* when it endured the first over-wintering by an expedition in the sea ice off Antarctica (1897-99). This was something that Ross was strict in avoiding so as not to endanger his crew in vulnerable wooden vessels. Amundsen commanded *Gjoa* to make the first single-ship voyage through the North West Passage in 1903-1906 and, on the way, established that the North Magnetic Pole had a new position since James Clark Ross' first discovery of it in 1831.

Ironically, the North West Passage was where Ross' close friend Sir John Franklin and his whole expedition were lost in 1845. They had used the very same ships, the *Erebus* and the *Terror*, as James Clark Ross had done in the triumphal achievements of his Antarctic voyages with Alexander Smith aboard the flagship *Erebus* in the vital position of First Mate.

Ross led an expedition in 1848-49 to find Franklin's expedition to no avail. Like Ross, Amundsen took part in an unsuccessful expedition to recover the expedition of the Italian polar explorer Umberto Nobile in their new airship *Italia* which had crashed on its return flight from the North Pole. Like the *Erebus* and the *Terror* before it, the overloaded *Italia* disappeared without a trace. This occurred on 18 June 1928. These tragic incidents help to underline James Clark

Ross' outstanding judgement in the mid-nineteenth century.

The evidence for the claim that Roald Amundsen was the most successful polar explorer of all time is undeniable. Like James Clark Ross, he was a giant in an enterprise where so many had failed; so many had died through the combination of faulty judgement and the icy unleashed powers of nature. More than anyone in polar history, Amundsen pushed back the known boundaries of the world's highest latitudes both in the Arctic and in the Antarctic.

Roald Amundsen

The fact that he beat Captain Robert Falcon Scott RN to the geographical South Pole is widely known. Equally well known is that Scott and his party all perished on the way back owing to lack of food and bad weather. That Amundsen followed the inspiration of James Clark Ross is, however, relatively little known. By standing on the shoulders of a giant, he achieved something more. In locating the North Magnetic Pole, Amundsen enabled a major scientific discovery about terrestrial magnetism. He led the first team to the South Geographic Pole in the 1911-12 season using dog teams and arriving thirty-five days ahead of Scott's man-hauling team. He was the first to circumnavigate the Arctic Ocean (1918-21). In 1925, he made the northernmost flight by aircraft to 87° 44' North and then miraculously escaped from an impossible position 'on the ice'. With the Italian Umberto Nobile, he was almost certainly the first in 1926 to reach the North

Geographic Pole. Their flight to the Pole from Spitsbergen in the airship *Norge* then continued south until the two men reached the Alaskan coast, the first crossing of the Arctic Ocean – and by its longest axis – from Europe to America. Thus he pioneered new routes, made scientific discoveries and flew the Norwegian flag at both Poles. Like Ross, he had a sea in the Antarctic named in his honour.

The legacy of Amundsen's prodigious achievements lies in his adherence to the principles that James Clark Ross had originally laid down as essentials for any polar expedition. Amundsen put it this way:

> I may say that this is the greatest factor – the way in which the expedition is equipped – the way in which every difficulty is foreseen, and precautions taken for meeting or avoiding it. Victory awaits him who has everything in order – luck people call it. Defeat is certain for him who has neglected to take the necessary precautions in time; this is called bad luck.[1]

Smooth and Efficient Preparations

On the eve of his great Antarctic sea expedition between 1839 and 1843, James Clark Ross most certainly made sure that he had 'everything in order', that he took precautions and carefully anticipated 'every difficulty', drawing from his vast experience of polar exploration in the North. For his time, Ross took all the precautions that could be devised. He had learnt his lessons well. And some seventy-two years later in the early modern world, Amundsen did the same by following his dictums.

Like Roald Amundsen after him, James Clark Ross recognised that polar exploration was a moral discipline and that

---

1   Cited by Pen Hadow in his Introduction to Tor Bomann-Larsen, *Roald Amundsen* (Translated by Ingrid Christopherson), Sutton Publishing, Stroud, 2006, p. xii.

human character might be a more important factor than even kilometres and latitudes as he searched after the earth's best kept secrets.

The choice of crews for the expedition was to him of the utmost importance. From the numerous applicants for the service, Ross chose the following officers and then appointed them[2] to the *Erebus* or the *Terror*:

Erebus	*Terror*
Captain: James Clark Ross	**Commander:** Francis R.M. Crozier
Lieutenant: Edward Joseph Bird John Sibbald James F.L. Wood	**Lieutenant:** Archibald McMurdo Charles G. Phillips Joseph W.Kay
Master: Charles T. Tucker	**Master:** Pownall P. Cotter (acting)
Surgeon: Robert McCormick	**Surgeon:** John Robertson
	Clerk in Charge: George H. Moubray
Mate: *Alexander J. Smith*, 1st Henry Oakeley Joseph Dayman	**Mate:** Peter R. Scott Thomas E.L. Moore William Molloy
Assistant Surgeon: Joseph D. Hooker	**Assistant Surgeon:** David Lyall
Second Master: Henry B. Yule	**Second Master:** John E. Davis
Purser: Thomas R. Hallett	

2   Captain Sir James Clark Ross, *A Voyage of Discovery and Research in the Southern and Antarctic Regions during the years 1839-43*, Vol. 1, August '39-April '41, John Murray, London, 1847 (Facsimile by David & Charles (Holdings) Ltd, Devon, 1989), p.xix.

The complement of each ship was sixty-four persons, mostly experienced and skilled seamen.

Erebus and *Terror* were selected by the Admiralty for the expedition, but James Clark Ross took special care of their refitting and preparation and devoted great attention to strengthening the superstructure of both ships. *Erebus* was 372 tons and *Terror* 326 tons. Both were bomb-vessels which were designed to carry and fire mortars, usually at coastal targets. They were men-of-war and carried one or two heavy mortars.

At times, their mortars were placed on shore and the boats operated as sloops. They were the smallest of the men-of-war class and the most specialised vessels in the fleet. Bomb-vessels were used to a great extent on the Spanish coast in the Napoleonic Wars to bombard military land emplacements or targets.[3]

Terror had been built in 1813 and had seen action in the American War of Independence in 1815. In 1828, she was commissioned again owing to the terrorism of the Barbary pirates in the Mediterranean, but was wrecked near Lisbon and taken to Plymouth for repairs. She was commissioned again in 1836 for service under George Back who had served with Sir John Franklin. Under Back, *Terror* had received a battering in perilous conditions in ice floes and returned to England in poor condition. She had to be completely refitted. *Erebus* was built in 1826 and had seen only two years of service in the Mediterranean from 1828 to 1830.[4]

When the Lord Commissioners of the Admiralty formally appointed Captain James Clark Ross RN on 8 April 1839, he was directed to proceed with the equipping of the expedition

---

3   Rodger, *The Wooden World*, pp. 24, 340; M.J. Ross, *Ross in the Antarctic. The Voyages of James Clark Ross in Her Majesty's Ships Erebus & Terror 1839 – 1843*, Caedmond of Whitby Publishers, Whitby, 1982, pp. 26-27.

4   Ross, *A Voyage of Discovery*.

with a liberal budget unlike Wilkes, the American leader. Ross was forty years of age at the time and in his prime. He received detailed advice from the British Association for the Advancement of Science and the Royal Society. These two learned societies had supported the expedition and its scientific purpose.

Erebus, like others of her class as a bomb ship, was strongly built in the first place and had a 'capacious hold'. It was in relatively new condition. *Terror* had been originally strengthened so that it could contend with ice floes in the Arctic seas where it was used to rescue a number of British whaling ships in Baffin Bay during the winter season of 1836. This action had proved its capabilities in ice floes. The following summer as related, it came under the command of Sir George Back in his 'arduous but unsuccessful attempt to reach Repulse Bay'. *Terror* was heavily damaged during that voyage but repaired and fortified. A month later, she was commissioned under Commander Francis R.M. Crozier as one of the officers especially selected by Ross as his second-in-command for the Antarctic Expedition.

Ross drew extensively on his polar experience in preparing *Erebus* and *Terror*. Like Amundsen in the next century, he left nothing to chance. As Amundsen's metaphor put it, he was indeed the bright star and Alexander Smith had been chosen as part of his galaxy. He made sure he foresaw every difficulty and made sure everything was in order. He made every improvement for the voyage that former experience had suggested. He had a special concern for the health, safety and comfort of his crews – matters that would help to maintain good morale and discipline. He collaborated closely with the Overseer of Chatham Dockyard and Francis Crozier to achieve his goals.[5]

When *Erebus* and *Terror* left the hands of the dockyard workmen, they were as strong as ships could be made in the tradition of generations of northern whalers and explorers. The decks were constructed of two thicknesses of the stoutest planking separated by layers of water-proofed cloth. The bow and stern were fitted internally nearly solid with timber to strengthen them. Externally, all projections were removed and a thick outer skin of planking was incorporated and smoothed down, varying in thickness so as to provide the greatest strength in sections likely to come into direct violent contact with dangerous floating icebergs. The hulls were double coppered and copper was substituted for iron in the fastenings wherever possible.[6]

This was how Mr Rice, Overseer of Chatham Dockyard, described the work at the time:

> The ship is fortified externally by solid chock channels, the spaces between the channels being similarly fitted, tapering at the extremities, so as to form an easy curvature in a fore and aft direction; the side is doubled with six-inch oak plank under the channel increasing to eight-inch at the wale, which is three feet broad; from thence, through a space of five feet, the doubling diminishes to three inches in thickness, of English elm, and the remainder of the bottom to the keel is doubled with three inch Canadian elm. The quarter galleries are removed, and the quarter pieces and stern strongly united by planking; all rails and projections being carefully avoided...
>
> Within-board, the spaces between the bands at the floor-heads, &c., are fitted in with six-inch oak

5   Ross, *A Voyage of Discovery*.

6   Hugh Robert Mill, *The Siege of the South Pole*, Alston Rivers Ltd, London, 1905, pp. 252-3.

plank; the entire surface in the hold being caulked, two thicknesses of 1½ inch African board are then worked diagonally over the bands, &c., at right angles to each other, each layer being also caulked. The thwartship bulkheads of the fore, main, and after holds are wrought diagonally of two thicknesses of 1½ inches African board at right angles to each other, the upper ends rabbetting into the lower deck beams, and the lower ends into four-inch plank, wrought upon the doubling.[7]

And so on.

The ships were provisioned under the naval system for long periods of time at sea. A remarkable feature of food supplies for the time was the large consignment of fresh tinned meats and soups and an enormous quantity of vegetables. The recent Donkin's invention of tinned food was used extensively, chiefly supplied by John Gillon and Company of Leith and Gamble, Cope, Nicol, Cooper and Wells. They were of the highest standard and were conveniently portable and easily and systematically stored. The total weight of food supplies taken aboard the two ships was tabulated by James Clark Ross in his published account.

	Lbs.
Meats	33,484
Vegetables	15,004½
Soups (equal to)	6,140
Gravy	4,808½
Total	59,437

	Tons	Cwt.	Qrs.	Lbs.
or	26	10	2	14[8]

7   Ross, *A Voyage of Discovery*, Appendix No I, by Mr. Rice, Overseer Chatham Dockyard,Chatham, 19 September 1839.

8   Ross, *A Voyage of Discovery*, p. xx.

This included five tons of carrots and four tons of pickles.

In sum, it was about 26 tons of food supplies, representing one of the largest expeditions ever undertaken.

The real cause of scurvy – the lack of vitamin C – was in specific terms unknown until well into the twentieth century, but fresh vegetables, fruit and lemon juice were well-known as preventatives. Ross' experience in Arctic expeditions had shown him the value of fresh meat and game in maintaining good health and good morale and in building up general resistance to scurvy.

Ross had made a study of Eskimo diet. This convinced him of the need for a substantial diet with plenty of fat to promote bodily warmth and resistance to infection. The canned provisions were thus to prove invaluable.[9]

All of those supplies made for cramped conditions for the crew. Rear Admiral M.J. Ross, the great-grandson of Sir James Clark Ross, describes them well in his history of the expedition:

> The whole ship's company lived on the lower deck, the captain aft, officers' cabins outboard and messes amidships. The commissioned officers' mess (the present day wardroom) was then known as the gunroom; the mates, second master and assistant surgeon messed in the 'mates' mess' or 'berth'. The gunner, boatswain and carpenter shared a cabin, and had a separate mess. The rest of the ship's company lived forward of the officers' quarters, with the galley (which catered for the whole ship) amidships. At the foremost end of the deck was the sick berth. The orlop deck and hold contained the spirit room, slop room, sail room, bread room and stowage for coal, stores and provisions.

---

9 Ross, *Ross in the Antarctic*, pp. 28-9.

While the atmosphere would have been close in summer with sixty-four souls aboard each ship all living in the lower deck, a special Sylvester stove with flues was installed at Chatham Dockyard to provide warm air conditioning in the interior of the ships in preparation for the extreme conditions of the Antarctic.[10] This kind of heating did not exist in the ships of the American expedition; thus their crews suffered much more of exposure to the extreme cold.

A list of the articles supplied to Ross' Antarctic Expedition reveals the great leader's expert understanding of the need for variety in food to build general health and morale amongst his two crews. In the tins of preserved meats, there was boiled, roast and seasoned mutton and mutton with vegetables; boiled, roasted and seasoned veal and veal with vegetables and ox-cheek and vegetables. There was soup and bouilli and concentrated gravy soup. Vegetable soups included carrots and gravy and turnips and gravy. There were dressed cabbages, table vegetables, mixed vegetables, carrots, parsnips, beet-root, onions and turnips. Condiments or, as Ross called them, 'medical comforts' included cranberries, mixed walnuts, onion and cabbage pickles as well as mustard and pepper.[11]

Ross made sure that warm clothing 'of the best quality' was available on both ships for when they reached the cold Antarctic regions. This would be then issued to the crew 'gratuitously' while they were 'employed amongst the ice, to protect them from the severity of the climate'.[12]

From the first, the expedition was a highly popular one with the general public. Both crews were volunteers. They would be in receipt of double pay from the time of sailing.

---

10 Ross, *Ross in the Antarctic*, pp. 27-8.

11 Ross, *A Voyage of Discovery*, p. xxi.

12 Ross, *A Voyage of Discovery*, p. xxi.

The officers (including Alexander Smith as First Mate on the *Erebus*) were selected by Ross from a particularly large number of applicants who wished to take part.

Selecting the Crews

The great Antarctic expedition under the command of Ross had magnetic research and not geography as its central object. It originated when Colonel Edward Sabine read a paper on terrestrial magnetism in August 1838 at the British Association at Newcastle that led to a deputation to the government. The lack in knowledge of terrestrial magnetism in the southern hemisphere was viewed as needing research and the collection of data by the expedition observing magnetic direction and intensity in high southern latitudes between the meridian of New Holland (Australia) and Cape Horn. All other discoveries were then to be associated both loosely and tightly to this purpose.

The selection of people for the expedition by Ross all had to be relevant to this purpose: **Francis Crozier** (aside from being an old mess mate of Ross) was an unequalled navigator and collector of scientific data as well as a practised magnetic observer; **Lieutenant Edward Bird** of the *Erebus* was a distinguished Arctic officer highly thought of by Sir Edward Parry and by Ross; **Lieutenant John Sibbald** was a steady capable officer and **Lieutenant James Wood** a good surveyor; **Lieutenant Charles Phillips** of the *Terror* was an enthusiastic active officer and an excellent seaman with good judgement.

Of the Mates, **Alexander Smith** was well-known to James Clark Ross having served under him enthusiastically and impressively in the Davis Strait on board the *Cove*. Ross viewed him as a protégé of great ability and potential. **Henry Oakeley**, the Second Mate on the *Erebus* was also a skilful and capable young officer.[13]

Thomas Moore, the Second Mate of the *Terror* was a young officer endowed with ability, energy and tact. (He later became a Rear Admiral and Governor of the Falkland Islands between 1855 and 1862.) **Dr Robert McCormick** and **Dr John Robertson**, the two surgeons, were to undertake geological and zoological research during the expedition. (Later, **Sir**)

Joseph Hooker, by George Richmond 1855

Joseph Dalton Hooker, Assistant Surgeon aboard the *Erebus*, then a very young man, was a valuable expedition member, especially as a botanist. He later rose to eminence as Director of Kew Gardens and was a close associate and articulate supporter of Charles Darwin. On the *Erebus*, he belonged to the same 'mates' mess' as **Alexander Smith** and formed a life-long friendship with him, particularly due to a mutual interest in plants. They also were of a similar age.

Charles Tucker, the Master of the *Erebus*, was a proven capable and efficient officer and **Henry Yule**, the Assistant Master of the same vessel, was a competent surveyor. **John Davis**, the Second Master of the *Terror* who became a good friend of **Alexander Smith**, was very able, a surveyor and a skilful artist who recorded in watercolour some of the key and exciting events of the three Antarctic voyages. Davis was to provide the charts and drawings for Sir James Clark Ross.[14]

Through his choice of such distinguished officers, Ross was

---

13 Sir Clements Markham, *The Lands of Silence. A History of the Arctic and Antarctic Exploration*. Cambridge University Press, Cambridge, 1921, pp. 410-1.

14 Markham, *The Lands of Silence*, pp. 412-14.

demonstrating a key aspect of outstanding leadership. They were the cream of the Royal Navy. His intention was to weld them together into a remarkably united body so as to better face the perils of the expedition, the considerable dangers of the Antarctic deep.

As well, he knew he had to become perfectly acquainted with the two bomb vessels, their particular ways that required highly skilled seamanship and the dynamics of the sociology of the crews as they became fused in close interpersonal relationships in cramped conditions, particularly as they would be isolated from the outside world. Ross' position as the supreme leader while at sea would require a consistent form of authority, immense technical ability and all the nuances of excellent seamanship that had been obtained in struggle – memories of his dangerous, arduous and vast experience in northern polar expeditions that needed to be translated to the conditions as he found them in the unknown silent world of Antarctica.

Rivals – d'Urville and Wilkes

In 1773, James Cook had been the first to cross the Antarctic Circle, but for much of the nineteenth century, Antarctica remained defiantly baffling. Indeed, its centre – the Pole around which it rotated – was not reached until 1911 by the great Norwegian explorer Roald Amundsen. Cook's record survived until the Russian explorer Thaddeus von Bellingshausen circumnavigated Antarctica in 1813 to 1821. He was then followed by English sealer James Weddell breaking into the Antarctic Circle in 1823. Weddell reached 74° S in the sea named after him.

Weddell made three Antarctic voyages and proposed, incorrectly, that the Pole was surrounded by open sea. This tantalising prospect was to spur other explorers, particularly

James Clark Ross who ventured south in 1839 to 1843.

In 1838, funding became available from the United States Congress to man a polar expedition under the command of Lieutenant Charles Wilkes. Admiral Jules-Sébastien César Dumont d'Urville was soon given a commission by the French government to explore the southern seas, in part as a quick response to the imminent American threat. Incredibly, the two expeditions passed within a 'musket shot' of each other in the vast southern ocean without communication.[15]

Before the British expedition under Ross left England, the siege of the Antarctic had been initiated by other ambitious nations. Both Dumont d'Urville and his French expedition and Wilkes and the United States expedition had already ventured into the Antarctic regions and had retreated to the South Pacific to wait out the polar winter.[16]

Dumont d'Urville commanding the *Astrolabe* and *Zélée* used Hobart in Van Diemen's Land as his base and had sailed south from Hobart on New Year's Day 1840. He traced 150 miles of continuous snow-covered coast which he called Adélie Land, between meridians 136° and 142°. Because of major sickness in his crew, he was forced to return to Hobart on

Jules-Sébastien Dumont d'Urville
(from d'Urville's *Atlas* 1841)

15 Susan Hunt, Martin Terry & Nicholas Thomas, *Lure of the Southern Seas. The Voyages of Dumont d'Urville 1826–1840*, History House Trust of New South Wales, Sydney, 2002, p.45.

16 David McGonigal(Chief Consultant), *Antarctica: Secrets of the Southern Continent*, Simon & Schuster, Sydney, 2008, p.284.

17 February 1840.

Wilkes, commanding a squadron consisting of the sloops USS *Vincennes* and USS *Peacock*, the brig *Porpoise*, the store-ship *Relief* and two pilot boats *Sea Gull* and *Flying Fish*, had also returned from an Antarctic cruise where he had faced a barrier that he named Termination Land. Confronted with this obstacle, Wilkes called a halt to his voyage on 22 March 1840. Later he sailed directly for Sydney. Wilkes, knowing that the British expedition was on its way and as a good-will gesture, wrote a letter to Ross enclosing a tracing of a chart that revealed his course and discoveries made from his flagship *Vincennes* at the Bay of Islands on 5 April 1840 and posted it. Ross did not receive it until his expedition, in due course, reached Hobart. He did not answer it and expressed himself peevishly about the French and American expeditions.[17]

The French had made two attempts upon the South Pole. In early January 1838, d'Urville had taken the *Astrolabe* and *Zélée* south from the Straits of Magellan intending to get closer to the South Pole than anyone before him. He followed in the tracks of Weddell. It was to no avail. Within days of crossing the Antarctic Circle, the expedition ran into severe storms and had to dodge large icebergs. They faced gales and 'marrow-freezing cold'. On 21 January, they attempted to find a path through the pack ice, but by the 23rd they were forced to retreat northwards towards the South Orkney Islands.

A violent storm prevented them from landing for fresh supplies of seal and penguin meat and they sailed south again on 2 February when the weather settled a little. D'Urville showed courage as well as Gallic confidence in their abilities in doing so. They stopped for a while in open water and the crew celebrated, but d'Urville who had been ill for weeks,

---

17 Dodge, *The Polar Rosses*, pp. 193-4; Mill, *The Siege of the South*, pp. 213-14.

wrote: 'I went to bed and heard the rowdy celebrations…
The rashness and impudence [of going south again] unfolded
before my eyes'. He realised that the only way out was by the
way he had gone in.

He sailed the corvette through an opening in the ice, but
before midnight they found themselves trapped – they were
ice-bound and it took five precious days of exhausting labour
to break into open water. There were many hours of hauling
and cutting. Finally, there was a favourable wind change. They
then continued westwards surveying and mapping Graham
Land and the South Shetlands before the ships retreated to
Chile. D'Urville determined in future to have more respect
for the pack ice.[18]

His difficult experiences in the pack ice were a precursor to
those the James Clark Ross expedition was to experience. In
Dumont d'Urville's writings about the experiences of his ice-
bound ships, both frustration and awe are expressed: 'Austere
and grandiose beyond words … filled us with an involuntary
feeling of dread … nowhere else can man feel so strongly the
sense of his own impotence'. He vividly remembered that the
'profound silence reigns over those icy plains and life is only
represented by a few petrels, gliding soundlessly, or by the
whales whose loud, ominous spouting occasionally breaks its
sad monotony'.[19] Alexander Smith was later to recall similar
emotions.

When the French expedition reached Valparaiso on 25
May, two of the crew were dead and seven others soon deserted. But a week later, they set off across the Pacific landing at
many islands on the way up to Guam; they explored the Torres

---

18   McGonigal, *Antarctica*, p.280; Hunt, Terry & Thomas, *Lure of the Southern
Seas*, pp.45-6.

19   Cited in Hunt, Terry & Thomas, *Lure of the Southern Seas*, p.46.

Strait and touched on northern Australia, circumnavigated Borneo, visited Singapore and Batavia, then headed south again, this time for Hobart. In Hobart, d'Urville resolved to make another attempt on Antarctica.

The Lieutenant Governor Sir John Franklin, a leading polar explorer, warmly welcomed d'Urville in Hobart. He was to do the same for the Ross Expedition when it arrived some time later. Franklin provided useful information on food and clothing in polar regions. He warned the French that such regions were zones of optical tricks, and of the danger of snow-blindness. While they were in Hobart, Franklin's interest never flagged. The corvette was repaired and victualled. Many of the French were gravely ill from contaminated water that had been loaded aboard two months earlier in Sumatra. Several died. New replacement sailors were recruited to enhance the depleted crews of the two vessels.

The *Astrolabe* and *Zélée* set sail from the Derwent on New Year's Day 1840. Their commander planned nothing less than to sail due south as far as he could go and to establish the position of the elusive magnetic pole.

On 19 January, they crossed into the Antarctic Circle. On 21 January, they launched a boat from each ship to a tiny islet. The excited boat crews landed, unfurled the French tricolour and collected some granite chips and a few unlucky penguins. They left a message for those who would follow. D'Urville named the area Terre Adélie after his beloved wife. To commemorate the occasion, the officers drank a bottle of Bordeaux to the glory of France. The boats returned to the ships with the granite chips to prove they had landed on land and not on ice.

The two ships followed the Antarctic coast westward, but the prevailing breeze became a blizzard. For two days, they were lost in swirling snow and fog. Sharp icicles covered the rigging, waves swept over the decks. The ships became separated and d'Urville began to fear a 'ghastly shipwreck'.

L'Astrolabe crossing the Arctic Circle, 19 Jan. 1840, painting by Adolphe Bayot, pic-an20826696 NLA

Soon after, they had a brief encounter with the *Porpoise*, an American brig from Wilkes' Expedition. Colours were hoisted, but the French and Americans went off in different directions. Dumont d'Urville announced his discoveries before the Americans. Wilkes' reputation was later, perhaps unfairly, sullied by court martial.

With winter closing in, the French Expedition returned to Hobart on 17 February 1840, laden with trophies and discoveries. They had been in Antarctic waters for some eighty-five days in two small wooden sailing ships.[20]

Charles Wilkes (1798–1877) was appointed in March 1838 to lead the initial American expedition to Antarctica

---

20 Hunt, Terry & Thomas, *Lure of the Southern Seas*, pp.48-51; McGonigal, *Antarctica*, pp.280-1.

with six ships that set off on 18 August that year, but only two survived to return to the United States. None reached Antarctica – the last continent – although lookouts on three of the ships reported sightings.

The principal ships of the American expedition were the *Vincennes* 780 tons, *Peacock* 650 tons, *Porpoise* 230 tons, *Sea Gull* 110 tons and the *Flying Fish* 96 tons. Wilkes reported on a considerable stretch of the Antarctic coast between Victoria and Enderby Lands and named it Wilkes Land.

When Wilkes had arrived with his fleet off Tierra del Fuego in March 1839, he at once dispatched the *Porpoise* and

Sea Gull to the South Shetland Islands and the *Peacock* and the *Flying Fish* to the coast of Marie Bird Land. It was a decision made too close to the winter season: the *Porpoise* and *Sea Gull* were placed in a most difficult situation as the ice was especially thick and far to the north in that season. Both ships were defective; *Sea Gull* was an old pilot ship that lea- ked like a sieve. For six weeks

Charles Wilkes

the two vessels beat to and fro off the tip of the Antarctic peninsula and their crews became progressively weaker from exposure, malnutrition and exhaustion. Then came a serious outbreak of scurvy. In much distress, the *Porpoise* limped back to Tierra del Fuego having achieved little to speak of.

In the meantime, *Peacock* and *Flying Fish* explored some thousands of miles further west. The two vessels were ill-suited to polar voyaging. *Flying Fish*, however, came close to achieving the impossible. Against all odds, the tiny, unstrengthened vessel of under 100 tons managed to force her way through near-solid ice as far as 70º S, almost in sight of Marie Bird Land of the last continent – a truly heroic feat of endurance and the only real achievement of Wilkes' first summer season in the Antarctic Circle.

At the end of April, Wilkes' squadron stood north – all six vessels were in bad shape, their canvas in shreds and parts of their decks stove in. Soon after, the *Sea Gull* foundered a couple of days from Valparaiso with the loss of her entire company. When the rest of the squadron staggered into Sydney Harbour, a full quarter of the crews deserted. They had been half-starved, half-frozen and were wholly exhausted.

Wilkes used the southern winter to patch up his battered fleet. Nevertheless, they still had basic deficiencies: there was no heating and compartments were not watertight. Wilkes, however, was determined. By December, he was heading south for the little-known sea lanes that d'Urville was entering.

Wilkes achieved something on this second voyage of discovery. Between mid-January and mid-February 1840, he sighted and closely followed a large section of the continent previously unknown. For more than a month, 'Wilkes' cockleshell armada' followed the coastline west, seldom out of sight of land. Snow, fog, high winds and heavy seas were constant companions. Crew suffered terribly from exposure, cold and malnutrition – they became completely exhausted.

The root cause of all of Wilkes' troubles was the failure of the United States administration to provide him with adequate tools for the job he was expected to do. Nevertheless, there is no denying that he was a great explorer, a man of rare if flawed heroism, tenacity and resourcefulness. He discovered a large section of Antarctica.

Together, d'Urville and Wilkes had set the scene. Wilkes had been a troubled loner. James Clark Ross, the man who followed him into the Antarctic, was the exact opposite: the chosen child of the establishment, already a great northern polar explorer of vast experience, an intrepid voyager who required to be backed to the hilt by the resources of the greatest seafaring nation of the day.

Ross had been at sea in the Royal Navy since the age of twelve. He served three gods: his homeland, the Royal Navy and polar exploration. He had spent seventeen years in the Arctic. What he didn't know about handling wooden sailing vessels in the ice was not worth knowing.[21]

Starting Out

With a distinguished versatile team of voyagers and two well-equipped and strongly built ships, Captain James Clark Ross sailed down the Thames from Chatham to commence his great enterprise on 30 September 1839. On the deck, First Mate Alexander John Smith would have gazed nostalgically at his place of birth, Greenwich, which he would not see again for several years.

By this time, his family had left for Yorkshire over ten years before. Still, it was a place of fond memories and where he had spent his entire childhood. As they passed further down the river, the handsome buildings of the Greenwich Hospital soon faded away.

At the time that the vessels of the expedition left the Thames and proceeded with a little difficulty down the Channel, practically nothing was known about Antarctica – as it turned out, a continent of six million square miles which carried a

---

21 Ian Cameron, *Antarctica: The Last Continent*, Little, Brown & Company, Boston, 1974, pp.94–107; McGonigal, *Antarctica*, pp.282–4; R.V. Tooley, *The Mapping of Australia and Antarctica*, Holland Press, London, 1979, p. xxiii.

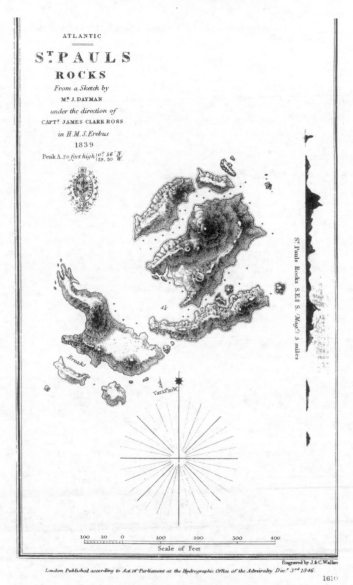

St Paul's Rocks, Atlantic Ocean,
sketch by Joseph Dayman, 3rd Mate of the *Erebus*

massive over burden of ice that if melted would raise the ocean levels of the world some 180 to 200 feet.[22]

---

22 R.E. Priestly, 'Foreword' in Ross, *A Voyage of Discovery*, unpaginated.

in the wake of the *Erebus*

Sketches during the voyage by Alexander Smith, 1st Mate, *Erebus*

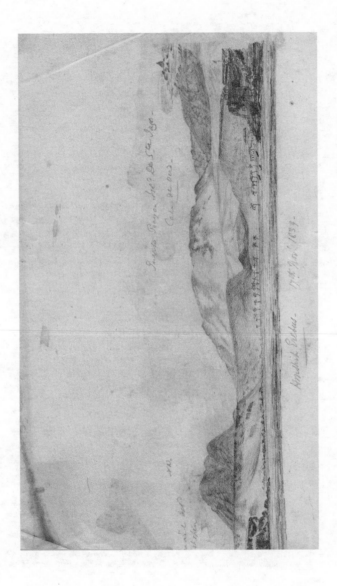

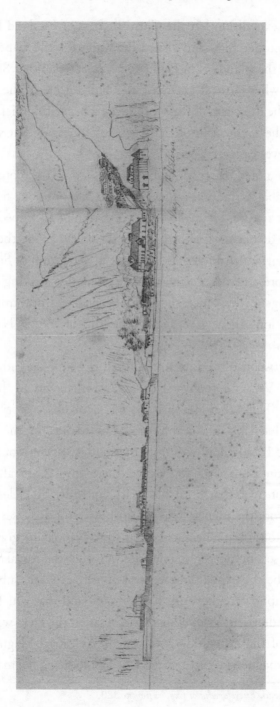

The expedition left the Cornish coast of England behind on 5 October 1839 and visited the Canaries, the Cape Verde islands, the islands of St Paul (Rocas de Sâo Paulo or St Paul's Rocks) where Joseph Dayman, the Third Mate of the *Erebus* under the direction of Ross, produced a beautiful relief sketch map. The main peak of the Rocks was measured at seventy feet above sea level.

Ross noted that while the Rocks could be considered remarkable formations, they were, in his opinion, not of a volcanic nature. He made a full collection of rock specimens. He noted that no lava or igneous rocks had made their way to the surface. And yet, as Ross put it, the group of St Paul's Rocks presented at a single glance the 'most striking effects of the agency by which they have been forced upwards'. The observations there gave a magnetic dip of 27° 8' N and a variation 13° 20' W.

They soon moved on to Trinidad in the West Indies and Martin Vaz and then arrived at St Helena on 31 January 1840.[23] There they established a magnetic observatory.

St Helena is a volcanic group of islands in the South Atlantic 1,920 kilometres from the south west coast of Africa. Napoleon Bonaparte was exiled there from 1815 after the Battle of Waterloo until his death in 1821. St Helena was taken from the French by the British in 1762. Ross set up his observatory on the heights not far from Napoleon's grave.

The setting up of observatories was what the Royal Society saw to be the expedition's central objective: 'The subject of most importance, beyond all question – and that which must be considered as, in an empathetic manner, the great scientific object of the expedition – is that of Terrestrial Magnetism'. Ross, a magnetism expert famed for first locating the magnetic

23 Howgego, *Encyclopedia of Exploration*, p. 180.

North Pole in 1831, carried out meticulous magnetic observations throughout the course of the expedition. Such careful work made the journey through the Atlantic to the Cape of Good Hope a slow, meandering one.

After the research on St Helena was completed, the expedition eventually moved on to the Cape of Good Hope where they were welcomed by the British colonial community while taking on fresh supplies and water.

*   *   *   *   *

Throughout the winter season of 1839-1840, the *Erebus* and *Terror* had pursued a rather leisurely course south through the Atlantic. Where possible, Ross had replenished the ships' diets with fresh meat, fish, eggs, fruit and vegetables, building up constitutions and morale for the more perilous cold and windy journey ahead through the ice. He, more than anyone else on the expedition, was well aware of what dangers and privations they were about to face. They had busied themselves with routine but pleasant observations on temperature, humidity and magnetic dip. In the meanwhile, the French under Jules-Sébastien César Dumont d'Urville and the Americans under Charles Wilkes were making their 'first groping contact with the new continent [Antarctica]'[24] unknown at this stage to James Clark Ross.

The journey to the Cape of Good Hope from England in itself gave no hint of the momentous events ahead for the expedition. And yet James Clark Ross, with his 'tumultuous past' in the Arctic Region, part of which he had shared closely with his First Mate Alexander Smith, had glorious 'visions of a

---

24 Cameron, *Antarctica: The Last Continent*, p. 108.

The Arched Rock, Christmas Harbour, Kerguelen Island

full success'.[25] At the Cape, Ross took on fresh stores to replace those that had been expended.

The expedition departed south-east from the Cape on 6 April 1840. By May, they had received a foretaste of Antarctica when the *Erebus* and *Terror* hove-to with difficulty off Kerguelen Island, sometimes appropriately called Desolation Island, in thick fog, squalls of snow and heavy dangerous seas.

They were eventually anchored with strenuous efforts in Kerguelen's purse-like Christmas Harbour on 15 May 1840. During the sixty-eight days spent on Kerguelen Island, the expedition suffered gale force winds nearly every day. The weather was relentless.

Kerguelen Island had been first discovered in 1772 by a French expedition led by Lieutenant Yves-Joseph de Kerguelen-Tremarec of the French Navy who was in search of the Southern Continent. His expedition, made up of the *Fortune* and the *Gros Ventre*, had sailed south from Mauritius and had encountered terrible weather, just like Ross. With his ships separated during a furious storm and continuous bad weather, Kerguelen-Tremarec sensibly decided to return to France and safety.

Captain James Cook had heard of the French discovery when he was in Cape Town in October 1772 at the start of his second voyage of circumnavigation. On 24 December 1776 on his third voyage, he anchored in and named Christmas Harbour. He stayed a week and referred to it as the Island of Desolation,[26] foretelling the experience of the Ross Expedition in 1840.

Despite the desolation and continuous gale force winds while in Christmas Harbour, the determined Ross fitted up

---

25 The poet Robert Browning, as cited in Mill, *The Siege of the South*, p. 249.

26 Ross, *Ross in the Antarctic*, pp. 51-2.

a magnetic and astronomical observatory on shore at the head of Christmas Harbour. Systematic observations were made on 29 and 30 May 1840, two of the days set aside for simultaneous observations at all the European and British stations. They happened to be days of great magnetic disturbance and it was subsequently proven that every movement of the needle at Kerguelen was simultaneous with a similar movement of the needle in Toronto and in almost all of the antipodes outposts.

While scientific research was being painstakingly conducted, the ships remained at their anchorage for more than two months, mostly being bombarded by gale force winds. There were only two days when neither rain nor snow fell.

Kerguelen Island watercolours, John Webber 1777, ML

Nevertheless, magnetic observations were kept up hourly day and night without a break for sixty-eight days.[27] Ross'

27 Mill, *The Siege of the South*, pp. 264-6.

magisterial persona as a leader and as a relentless taskmaster dominated the situation while maintaining a reasonably good morale in difficult circumstances.

To keep the spirits of the crew up, Ross like Cook before him experimented in the cooking of unusual wild seabirds to supplement the usual somewhat boring diet on board. Duck was obtained in abundance and 'formed a delicious addition to our table'. He found it close in flavour to English teal. On Kerguelen Island, the wild ducks lived chiefly on the seeds of the wild cabbage which was profusely scattered over all parts of the island. The species of wild cabbage that grew on the island was regularly served up to the crew with salt beef or pork. During their whole stay on the island, no sickness was reported on either ship. The men were in the pink of condition because of Ross' earlier meticulous preparation.

The penguins, despite the 'disagreeable dark colour of its flesh' and fatness, were found to make excellent soup which from its colour and flavour Ross claimed resembled English hare soup. Probably for that reason, the crew called it hare soup anyway. It is not sure whether Alexander Smith enjoyed it or not.

Ross went on to describe the place of his anchorage demonstrating the sharpness of his observations and work ethic:

> The level beach at the head of the harbour afforded us convenient sites for our observations, which were immediately erected; that for magnetic purposes being placed at the north extreme, under the protection of the hill to the north, which effectually prevented the sun's rays deranging the temperature, and within a few feet of high-water mark; that for the astronomical and pendulum observations on nearly the same level, at more than a hundred yards distant from it towards

the centre of the beach; and close by this two small huts were erected for the convenience of the officers and men employed at the observatories.[28]

This shows Ross, as always, to be nothing if not meticulous down to the finest detail.

The members of the expedition found the birds on the island, unused to man, unusually tame. They greatly enjoyed the penguins:

> At first we had about a dozen on board, running wild over the decks following a leader, they cannot climb over any obstacle two or three inches high so we thought them safe until one day, the leader finding the hawse hole empty immediately made his exit, and was followed by the rest, each giving a valedictory croak as he made his escape.[29]

The penguin 'of the Jack Ass species' was a very majestic-looking fellow who stood 'bolt upright like a soldier'. Nevertheless, the crew killed, cooked and ate them as a 're-markably good supper'.[30]

The expedition got their ships ready for sea by the middle of July, but adverse weather delayed them a few days longer. As James Clark Ross commented, they were not able to leave 'this most dreary and disagreeable harbour until the 20th July'.[31] Two days out of Kerguelen, the ships were separated in a violent gale and were not able to regroup until reaching Hobart. They were anxious days and nights for James Clark Ross. The furious gales that were experienced required skilled

---

28 Ross, *A Voyage of Discovery*, p. 90.

29 Cited in Ross, *Ross in the Antarctic*, p. 58.

30 Ross, *Ross in the Antarctic*, p. 59.

31 Ross, *A Voyage of Discovery*, p. 94.

seamanship of an exceptional kind. Both Ross and Crozier were up to the task.

*   *   *   *   *

Bad weather followed them as the two ships headed for Hobart in Van Diemen's Land. On 28 June not far from the fiftieth parallel, they ran into a fearsome hurricane. The *Erebus* and *Terror* were reduced to close-reefed topsails. Seas broke green over their quarters. The decks were continually awash with two feet of water. Ross later wrote in a matter-of-fact manner: 'it was indeed an unusual sight to see the crest of the great waves driven completely over us in solid sheets of water'.

In such exceedingly tempestuous weather, the *Erebus* boatswain was blown from the rigging and drowned. Four men who tried to rescue him almost shared the same fate,[32] but survived.

As a result of the hurricane, *Erebus* and *Terror* became separated, but they survived and, a fortnight later on 16 August 1840, the *Terror* was the first to creep a little battered into the Derwent River heading upstream to the port of

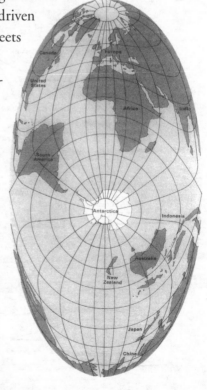

Antarctica in relation to other continents

32   Mill, *The Siege of the South*, p. 266.

Hobart Town and safety.

Storms in the roaring fifties are considered the worst in the world with their enormous seas as the westerly-wind drift revolved clean around the globe in a 13,000 mile circle unchecked by any land mass.[33]

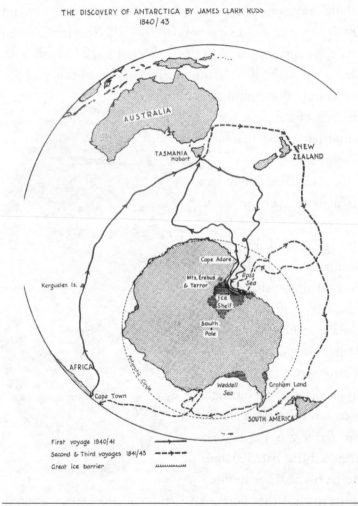

THE DISCOVERY OF ANTARCTICA BY JAMES CLARK ROSS
1840/43

---

33 Ian Cameron, *Lodestone and Evening Star*, Hodder & Stoughton, London, 1965, pp. 222-3.

5

South to the Antarctic
August 1840 – February 1841

While the *Terror* was the first to arrive in Hobart, the *Erebus* reached there the following day. Their voyage from England to Van Diemen's Land had taken nearly eleven months.

Ross and Crozier were made most welcome by Lieutenant Governor Sir John Franklin and his charming vivacious wife Jane. Franklin had already been given written instructions to assist the expedition in setting up an observatory. A labour force of two hundred convicts was promptly assigned to the construction. They completed it in nine days and the observatory was fully operational by 27 August. Franklin had personally selected the site and named it Rossbank after his old friend. Lieutenant Joseph W. Kay RN of the *Terror* was first placed in charge with two mates – Joseph Dayman, Third Mate of the *Erebus*, and Peter R. Scott, First Mate of the *Terror* – as assistants.[1]

On his arrival in Hobart, however, James Clark Ross found to his dismay and expressed disgust that he had been forestalled by both the French and Americans so far as the direct approach to the South Magnetic Pole along the 146th meridian was concerned. He was disappointed and expressed his feelings in a nationalistic competitive manner.

He was forced to change his own plans, to take another line, and later, to his great good fortune, chose the 170th to 180th meridian, where, as it turned out retrospectively, the Antarctic pack was most penetrable and where a great indentation occurred in what seemed, at the time in the collective imagination, to be the main symmetrical Antarctic land-mass.[2]

In the meantime, however, his ships and their crews were in desperate need of a break from the dangers and sometimes the seemingly relentless monotony of the deep. Members of the whole expedition were fêted abundantly while their ships were in Hobart Town. With great enthusiasm, a spirit of British patriotism was heightened. Patriotic celebrations involving the intrepid voyagers were many and varied.

Both officers and men enjoyed much hospitality from an enthusiastic local community. Mail from home that was awaiting them was in the main an intense and longed-for pleasure for most of the two ships' companies. During their stay, the ships were refitted with great thoroughness and fully stored.

Replenishing the ships' stores in Hobart Town was expeditiously carried out; the officers and crew were in the best of health and the highest of spirits after all the attention they had received from the local colonial community. They were

---

1   Markham, *Lands of Silence*, p. 414.

2   Priestly, 'Foreword to the 1969 Edition' in Ross, *A Voyage of Discovery*, unpaginated.

considerably buoyed up by their celebrity status. Walking the streets and pathways in uniform, they had even been cheered and enthusiastically waved to; in the pubs, the sailors had received toasts and complimentary drinks from mine host. Given such opportunities, heavy drinkers amongst the crew moved from pub to pub on a regular basis. The three hundred or so Blue Jackets were to be found everywhere in the streets of Hobart Town strolling to find their land legs and enjoying life free from the restrictions of their wooden world in the dangers of the high seas. They were indeed the heroes of the hour: their gallant exploits brought liveliness and vitality to the sedate port at the extremity of the Western World. For the Blue Jackets of the *Erebus* and *Terror*, popular recognition in the streets as well as hospitality in the pubs and in homes of the denizens of the town were a suitable and gratifying reward for their seafaring gallantry.

Ross and Crozier stayed at Government House. The officers were invited in pairs to dine there every second night by the hospitable Sir John and Lady Jane Franklin. They had received almost overwhelming welcome into the homes of other prominent local citizens. Sir John Franklin went out of his way to give the expedition all possible help and regard. There were kangaroo hunts and opossum shoots and daily trips into the interior in search of fossils for the scientifically-minded like Joseph Hooker. There were elaborate dinners of many courses at Government House; there were tea-parties and picnics. Lady Franklin recorded many of these comings and goings in her diary.[3]

Joseph Hooker was not so responsive to all this attention. In November 1840, he wrote:

---

3   Cameron, *Lodestone & Evening Star*, pp. 222-3.

Lady Franklin ... would like to show me every kindness, but does not understand how, and I hate dancing attendance at Government House. I have dined there five or six times ... She very kindly invited me to go to Port Arthur in their yacht, to botanise; we were three days away, – two of them at sea, and the third, a Sunday, it rained furiously. I got 500 specimens on Monday and a few after service on Sunday, though Lady F. did not like it, and very properly, but I thought it excusable as being my only chance of gathering *Anopterus glandulosus.* Do not think this is my habit. Captain Ross is too strict, were there no other reasons.[4]

Joseph Dalton Hooker, Assistant Surgeon of the *Erebus*

Hooker's disinclination to spend his time in what he saw as meaningless amusements can be gathered from several of his letters of the period. This first stay in Hobart Town lasted from 16 August to 12 November 1840. Ross was anxious, however, to get going south to the mysterious uncharted continent.

It seems as though at some point during his first sojourn of nearly four months in Hobart Town that Alexander Smith, First Mate on the *Erebus*, met twenty-year-old Sarah Aubrey

---

4   Leonard Huxley, *Life and Letters of Sir Joseph Dalton Hooker*, Vol. 1, John Murray, London, 1918, p. 106. (Huxley's book was substantially based on material collected and arranged by Lady Hooker.)

Read at one of the many social comings and goings. They were clearly attracted to each other from their first encounters. Alexander had found his future wife and his future prospects changed radically towards Australia after he had completed his full term-of-duty with the expedition.

Sarah was always called Aubrey by her close family and friends. She had been born on 25 February 1820 in Hobart Town, Van Diemen's Land, to Captain George Frederick Read and Elizabeth (née Driver). She was their second daughter. Elizabeth Driver was the daughter of transported convicts John and Elizabeth Driver who were enterprising enough to set up a general store in Old Castlereagh Street in Sydney Town at the beginning of the nineteenth century which they styled the 'Universal Warehouse'. It was the first retail business of any consequence in the Colony. The land on which it stood was granted to Driver in 1810. He and his wife had five children including Elizabeth. John Driver died on 28 February 1910. His widow married Henry Marr, an innkeeper of Pitt Street, on June 1911. Together they acquired several businesses and properties. Mrs Marr died without further issue.[5]

Captain Read had met Elizabeth Driver in Sydney. After they married, he brought her back to Hobart Town. Sarah Aubrey Read, therefore, had a convict ancestry, but was brought up as a well-educated genteel lady.

George Read was prosperous and well established in Van Diemen's Land and had at one time seen service with the East India Company. He was one of the founders and Governor of the Bank of Van Diemen's Land by the time Alexander met Aubrey. She lived with her father and stepmother in a large two-storey stone house in New Town, Hobart – the upper

---

5   Charles H. Bertie, 'Old Castlereagh Street', *Journal of the Royal Historical Society*, Vol.22, Pt 1, 1936, pp. 44-5.

windows commanded views of Mt Wellington, which was snow-capped in winter, as well as the lovely deep water estuary of the Derwent.[6] This was where the *Erebus* and *Terror* found anchorage. Alexander Smith was a frequent visitor at Captain Read's residence between the expedition's arrival and his first meeting with Aubrey and the expedition's departure in November for Antarctica.

Departure for the South

The *Erebus* and *Terror* weighed anchor and left Hobart Town on the morning of 12 November 1840 for what was to be an epic adventure. It was overcast with low cloud and a gentle breeze. Sir John Franklin and other friends came on board the *Erebus* at 7.30am and accompanied the ships to the mouth of the estuary, where Franklin said goodbye to Ross and returned to Hobart on his yacht which was standing by. The crews manned the rigging to salute Franklin with three cheers as they passed out on what was to become their greatest voyage. Franklin would have desired to go with them and leave behind the troubles of his administration in the prosperous colony.

That night Robert McCormick, surgeon of the *Erebus*, made an entry in his diary that was full of eager expectation: 'Our future promises to be full of interest, for we may soon make great discoveries in a region of our globe fresh and new as at creation's first dawn'.[7]

Alexander Smith as *Erebus*' First Mate must have felt very much the same emotions, but one mingled with regret for having left behind in Hobart Town his new-found love,

---

6   Modified Register for Bishop John Smith. Entry 47M on Alexander John Smith (Merilyn Pedrick Collection) p. 12.

7   Cited in Cameron, *Lodestone and Evening Star*, p. 224.

the twenty-year-old Sarah Aubrey Read, so 'very pretty, petite and vivacious'.[8]

*   *   *   *   *

At the time, there was a tri-national contest to explore Antarctica. During his second voyage, on 17 January 1773, Captain James Cook was the first to cross the Antarctic Circle north of Enderby Land. Two months later, he reached 71° 10'. No explorer had yet gone further apart from Weddell. With his small sailing ship, Cook could not penetrate further into the icepack. Nevertheless, he conjectured that a large continent, an unknown continent, lay within it.

Around sixty-seven years later, d'Urville, Wilkes and Ross carried out their expeditions in the early 1840s on behalf of France, the United States and Britain respectively. They explored the coasts immediately south of Australia, the two former voyagers delineating a coastline which was later extended by Mawson in the early twentieth century, while Ross sailed into the sea since named after him and discovered the regions that the names of Scott, Shackleton and Amundsen will always be associated with. Dumont d'Urville and James Clark Ross also mapped the extension of Antarctica towards South America where it stretches northwards to 63°S – about as far from the equator as the Faroe Isles are in the Arctic.

*   *   *   *   *

Be that as it may, soon after noon on 12 November 1840, the Ross expedition passed the lighthouses on each point of

8   As Alexander John Smith described her later in a letter to his family in England.

in the wake of the *Erebus*

Sketches during the voyage by Alexander Smith, 1st Mate, *Erebus*

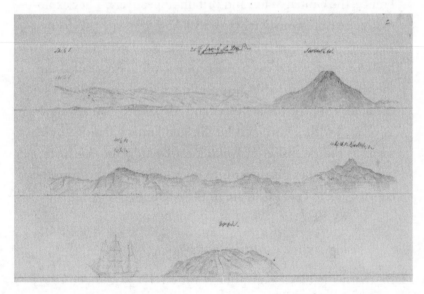

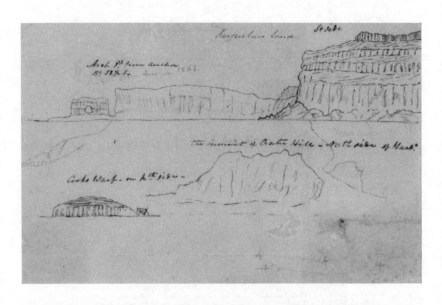

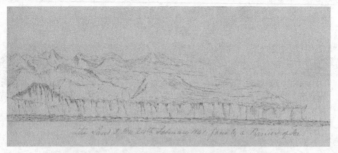

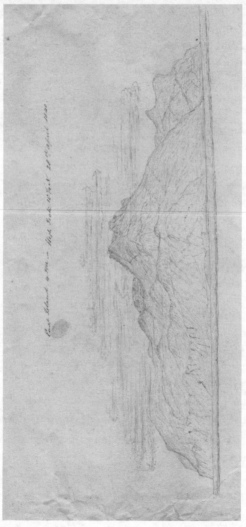

the Derwent, stood out of Storm Bay and were a fair way out to sea by 1.30pm. Both crews were expectant, in excellent spirits and health. Their spirits had been even further lifted by the three cheers in parting from their new-found friends in Hobart. The evening was squally with rain, but the wind still favoured them. They cleared the land on the horizon before dark. Their course was shaped by Ross for the Auckland Islands, a distance of 800 to 900 miles from Hobart.

The next day, the favourable breeze continued and both ships carried all sails with the smaller *Terror* keeping up with some difficulty. Several beds of sea-weed were encountered and albatrosses and petrels of various kinds followed the two vessels in numbers. By 9am the next day, they were nearly becalmed and soundings were taken revealing the great depth of the ocean.

The First Landfall
Just after 3.30am on 20 November 1840, the north-western cape of Auckland Island was seen directly ahead. Almost immediately, a thick fog enveloped it. They had only been a week at sea. No landfall could be seen through the fog for the rest of the day and the wind increased to a strong gale. They were still in the midst of a thick fog that made the crew anxious. The cape reappeared later through a thick haze less than a mile from the *Erebus* and the prospect of a shipwreck was suddenly averted. They were able to run along the northern side of the island under its protection.

The sight of the north-western cape for Alexander Smith and the rest of the ship's company aboard the *Erebus* was remarkable with its rocky islet with a curious conical rock off it. Just to the eastward of it was a dark-looking promontory known as Black Head which had a deep cavernous indentation at its base. This may have brought back memories of the wreck of the *Thetis* to the First Mate on the *Erebus*. Later they found it was but a short distance from the westernmost part of Laurie Harbour. For Alexander Smith and his shipmates, it was the first of many remarkable sights in the vicinity of the relatively unexplored Antarctic Circle.

Robert McCormick and a small party of officers later reached the cape by land by following the course of a stream that emptied into the head of the harbour and whose source was found in the steep hills above Black Head which was some eight hundred to nine hundred feet high.[9] Smith's friend Hooker enjoyed collecting botanical specimens. The Auckland and Campbell Islands, where they landed for a while, also provided the keen botanist with an abundance of specimens. On some occasions, Alexander Smith was able to assist Hooker in his botanical excursions. The yield of land plants diminished dramatically after this short stop.[10] Eventually on 1 January 1841, the Antarctic Circle was crossed.

As Alexander Smith regretfully put it in his account written in April 1841 on their return to Hobart Town, they left Campbell Island on their Antarctic voyage of discovery 'with but poor hope of effecting much after the two preceding Years had been forestalled by French and American Voyagers who penetrated to 66° and 66°2 S Lat. & between 150° & 130° East Long. & discovered several patches of land and a Barrier of ice of many hundred Miles extent lying off it'.[11] Smith was

9 Ross, *A Voyage of Discovery*, pp. 129-32.

10 Joseph Dalton Hooker, 'Summary of the Voyage' in Sir John Richardson & John Edward Gray (eds), *The Zoology of the Voyage of HMS Erebus and Terror under the command of Sir J.C. Ross during 1839-1843*, Reeves Bros, London,1844-5, p. vii.

11 'Alexander Smith's Account of the Voyage of the Erebus & Terror From VDL [Van Diemen's Land] to the Antarctic Sea & Back Between Novem [*sic*] 1840 & April 1841', quoted in R.S. Boumphrey 'Alexander Smith's Account of the Discovery of East Antarctica, 1841', *The Geographical Journal*, Vol. 130, No 1, March 1964, p. 114.

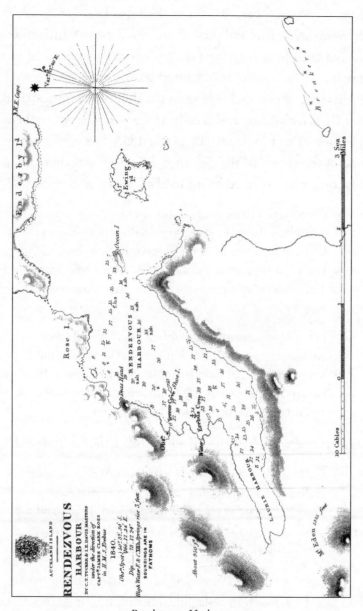

Rendezvous Harbour

echoing Ross' feelings of disappointment – it seemed at the time – at having been beaten in the race. They soon were to recover their spirits and pressed on with great determination.

On one of the Auckland Islands where they anchored in a small cove for a time, two painted boards placed in a conspicuous spot caught their eye from the ships. Ross immediately despatched an officer and crew in a long boat to examine them. He found them to be records of the d'Urville expedition and one of the vessels of the disjoined American expedition. The first on a white painted board in black letters read:

> Les corvettes Francoises L'Astrolabe et la Zélée, parties de Hobart Town le 25 Fevrier 1840, mouillées ici le Mars, et reparties le 20 du dit pour la New Zealand. Du 19 Janvier au 1 Fevrier 1840, découverte de la Terre Adélie et détermination du pôle magnetique Austral!

> [The French corvettes, Astrolabe and Zelee, left Hobart on 25 February 1840, stuck [in the ice] in March, and left on 20th of that month for New Zealand. From 19 January to 1 February 1840, discovered Terre Adelie and determined the southern magnetic pole!]

The second was a blackboard with white lettering and read:

> US brig Porpoise, 73 days out from Sydney, New Holland, on her return from an exploring cruize along the antarctic circle, all well; arrived the 7th, and sailed again on the 10th March, for the Bay of Islands, New Zealand.[12]

A paper was found enclosed in a bottle, but the writing had faded too much to be legible. Due to these messages from the other two expeditions, Ross decided to name the location Rendezvous Harbour.

---

12 Ross, *Ross in the Antarctic*, p.75.

Members of the Expedition seal hunting
to supplement their diet, sketch by J. D. Hooker

Continuing South

The messages Ross received at Rendezvous Harbour drove him and his two crews more urgently on and with greater determination despite the commander's disappointment that the French and the Americans had been there first.

After departure from Campbell Island, mid-summer day and Christmas Day came and went. The latter was uncomfortably celebrated in a strong gale. Many whales were sighted – the sea swarmed with the seemingly tame creatures – as well as the first iceberg on 28 December in 63°S & 175°E. For several days, they encountered difficult adverse winds. They found themselves in the 'most trying Situations amongst loose ice & enormous icebergs which required our utmost Vigilance to avoid',[13] Alexander Smith later recorded.

On 1 January 1841, the Antarctic Circle had been crossed and the stock of warm clothing provided by the Admiralty was served out to both crews and their officers. All of the Arctic veterans like Alexander Smith were, nevertheless, astonished at the stupendous masses of Antarctic ice. Both the bergs and

13 Alexander Smith's Account of the Voyage.

whales increased in numbers and the heavy swells created a certain amount of grave anxiety with several of the more experienced crew of each vessel.

New Year's Day had brought extra food and grog and Scottish conviviality as well as the issue of complete suits of warm clothing. Spirits were lifted. Robert McCormick, as already noted, had prophesised that they would soon make great discoveries in a part of the globe so untouched by human kind it would seem like 'creation's first dawn'. He was not exaggerating. The less poetic Ross confined his observations to the state of the wind and the sea and the sighting of 'much weed and many albatross'. And as Joseph Hooker put it, 'the ships finally sailed for an entirely unexplored region of discovery'.[14]

Good fortune was with them as they approached the Antarctic Circle, the weather could have hardly been better, the sun shone brightly out of a cloudless sky; winds were relatively light and visibility was outstanding. The iceberg, the first they sighted on Boxing Day, was flat-topped, white-crested, sapphire-based and over a hundred feet in length – an astonishing and mesmerising sight. It had drifted past them streaming water and surrounded by whales and petrels. By the evening, the temperature had rapidly dropped and five other bergs were in sight.

In the next couple of days, the bergs increased in number and size. From the crow's nest, as many as thirty could be sighted at the one time. But due to superb seamanship, the *Erebus* and *Terror* picked their way through them without too much difficulty. The experience in this context of Arctic veterans like Alexander Smith and the others proved invaluable.

---

14 Hooker, 'Summary of the Voyage', p. vii.

Challenging the Ice Pack

In a moment, however, the weather chose to worsen. A northerly gale brought both snow and high seas forcing the two ships to shorten sail and haul away to a safe distance from the ice. During the night, visibility was terrible. The many icebergs presented an ever-present danger and lookouts had to be constantly vigilant. The roar of waves dashing against the sides of the ships was frequently the first warning the crew had of their imminent approach. The watch had to be doubled. The night, full of anxiety for everyone, finally passed. By dawn, the wind had shifted, the weather cleared and the ships were able to stand and carefully consider the ice pack that was before them.

In a 'shimmering damask of white', the ice pack stretched away to the south as far as the eye could see or the mind conceive. But much to Ross' satisfaction, leads to the open water inside were to be noticed. He ran the ship parallel to the ice floe for several miles, always searching for a break, a place to enter. At first, there seemed no flaw in the solid ice floe.

Ross soon had to apply his judgement and his vast experience and make a firm decision whether to proceed or not. At that moment, the wind was in the right quarter, but the weather was, nevertheless, unsettled. If he delayed, it could easily shift. He decided that fortune was with him. He took his chance and, ordering the *Terror* to follow, he charged full-tilt at the ice floe that seemed impenetrable.

The bows of the *Erebus* and *Terror* smashed into the ice again and again, but they held together despite the shocks to their hulls. Ordinary vessels would have staved in quickly. The *Erebus* and *Terror* with their double skin and strengthened bows were relatively undamaged. The great avalanches of dislodged ice did no damage to their hulls – there were no protuberances against which the shattered floes could lodge, they had been so smoothed down while in dry dock. Strength alone would not have got the vessels through – they needed fine seamanship and they received it in kind. Ross' own account takes up the story:

> After about an hour's hard thumping, we forced our way into some small holes of water, connected by narrow lanes, for which we had steered. We found the ice lighter and more scattered than it had appeared, and by no means of so formidable a character as we had been led to suspect ... At noon we were in latitude 65° 55'S; and the clear sea was no longer discernible from the masthead as we pursued our way through the pack, choosing the clearest 'leads' and forcing the interposing barriers as they occurred, at times sustaining violent shocks which nothing but ships so strengthened could have sustained.[15]

By nightfall, they had penetrated fifty miles through the pack ice and the omens were more auspicious than Ross could have dared hope for. Progress was equally encouraging over the next few days. Hour after hour, they forced their way south, twisting, tacking, running and occasionally cutting a path through floes and sea lanes by calculated brute force. They were frequently accompanied by friendly whales. Penguins on ice floes watched them silently. Seals appeared more infrequently. Petrels circled overhead. Snow fell. The great silence of the unknown on occasions mesmerised them into long periods of contemplative silence.

By the night of 5 January 1841, nature decided to put up a harder fight. Progress became increasingly slow and difficult. By the dawn, Ross and Crozier, the two captains, were twisting

---

15 Cameron, *Lodestone and Evening Star*, p. 225.

their ships this way and that to avoid being frozen and locked into the ice floe. A little before midday, they had to heave-to in a small circle of water from where they could find no way out. They seemed to be stranded. Silence closed in.

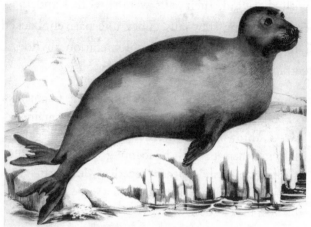

Female Sea Elephant

The heavy swell was continually shifting and breaking the ice. Ross was optimistic and knew a break would eventually occur. Persistence was necessary. But by evening, the weather worsened. Storm clouds rolled out from the north; the barometer dropped.

About that same day, Alexander Smith later recalled: 'We all had become heartily tired of what had become most monotonous & begun to fear progress further S° was debarred'.[16]

By dawn, it was snowing hard and a full hurricane was blowing. The swell steepened ominously. To Ross and the crews' horror, the pack ice began to break up dangerously. Great columns of waves alive with solid blocks of ice continuously swept down on the still-imprisoned vessels.

The situation became life-threatening. With frenzied violence, the storm raged hour after hour. For a while, there

16 Alexander Smith's Account of the Voyage.

seemed little hope of survival. They tried to moor to the lee of a floe but, like rotten strings, their stoutest and strongest hawsers parted. Again and again, great blocks of ice weighing hundreds of tons crashed into the vessels. When they tried to run with the wind, their sails were shredded and they were reduced to rigging stay sails. They alternatively backed and filled to avoid the heaviest 'conglomeration of floes'. Ross wrote graphically of the situation:

> Our ships rolled and groaned amidst the fragments of bergs, over which the ocean rolled its mountainous waves, throwing huge masses one upon another then burying them beneath its foaming waters, the while dashing and grinding them together with fearful violence. The awful grandeur of such a scene can neither be imagined or described.[17]

It was a surreal, unbelievable experience for Alexander Smith as First Mate on the *Erebus*, but his earlier experience of shipwreck on HMS *Thetis* and his polar voyage aboard HMS *Cove* with Ross stood him in good stead. His steady calmness in such a fearful situation provided a steadfast role model for his crew who he was able to keep on the job.

Clearing the Ice Pack
The storm was too violent for too long. But during the night, the wind dropped and the waves became less malevolent. The ships limped to shelter behind a line of mammoth bergs. As Alexander Smith put it, 'Seals and Penguins were our only companions' and they had had 'many and many a severe shake'. But they were able to congratulate themselves 'on our strong built Ships'.[18]

The phlegmatic Ross had held his nerve magnificently and

17 James Clark Ross cited in Cameron, *Lodestone and Evening Star*, p. 226.
18 Alexander Smith's Account of the Voyage.

this had inspired his crews to work like maniacs. Thankfully, they cleaved the Antarctic ice pack on the 8th at 69° 15'S, 176° 15'E and were able to proceed south on open sea, later to be called the Ross Sea. It was a great relief after what they had experienced. The open water felt by the crews as most unexpected and even magically because of the continuous danger they had suffered for more than five days.

On 6 January in anticipation of their success, the officers including Alexander Smith celebrated with a cake prepared for Captain Ross which was cut into portions. Through several toasts, they recalled 'our Friends in Old England & Children' and the dead King and new Queen. Many good humoured jokes went around the group during the long evening.[19] They finally retired and fell into a deep and satisfying sleep.

They had been six dangerous days amongst bergs and whales when, on 10 January in the middle watch, Lieutenant James Wood reported land distinctly visible ahead. What he saw were lofty peaks, but still at a great distance at 71° 15'S.

Watering the *Terror* in the pack ice 1842,
painting during the voyage by John E. Davis, 2nd Master, *Terror*

19 Alexander Smith's Account of the Voyage.

Catching penguins

The next day, they were fairly close to the northern point of what was named Cape Adare. Soundings were obtained at 60 fathoms. The mountains were crowned with snowy peaks and were about 7,000 to 10,000 feet. Ross named them the Admiralty Range after the Lords of the Admiralty. The principal peak of about 10,000 feet was named after Sir Edward Sabine who had been with Ross on two Arctic voyages and who had stimulated his interest in a scientific approach to magnetic observations.

In 1818, Sabine, who became a general in the Royal Artillery, had been the astronomer to the Arctic expedition in search of the North-West Passage under John Ross, James Ross' uncle. Sabine was a member of the committee to consider the establishment of magnetic stations throughout the British Empire. He made a scientific study of magnetism over the globe and was the intellectual spirit behind the James Clark Ross British Expedition to the Antarctic.

At the time, James Clark Ross, with a reading variation of 44° and the dip 86°, calculated that the magnetic south pole would have been 76°S and 145° 26'E, or about 500 miles inland.

'Cape Davis Lat.70° 32'S., long. 166° 6'E',
watercolour by J.E. Davis during the voyage

With difficulty Ross, Crozier and several officers (we don't know whether Alexander Smith was with them) landed briefly on a small island near the coast covered with penguins in 71° 56' S and 171° 7' E and named it Possession Island as they claimed it for the Crown.

In stormy weather, they sighted a further range of lofty mountains whose peaks were named after members of the Royal Society and the British Association, while one island received the name of Coulman (after Ross' future father-in-law Thomas Coulman) and its northern point Cape Anne, the name of Ross' fiancée as it was her birthday the day they reached it. By this time, a few whales, penguins, cape-pigeons and stormy petrel were their companions. They were moving in a procession of wild life in what was to them a strange and haunting experience – an experience as fresh and new as 'creation's first dawn', as expressed by McCormick.

On 27 January, the ships were in sight of another island that was promptly named after Sir John Franklin. They were

THE BOTANY

THE ANTARCTIC VOYAGE

OF

H.M. DISCOVERY SHIPS *EREBUS* AND *TERROR*,

IN THE YEARS 1839—1843.

UNDER THE COMMAND OF

CAPTAIN SIR JAMES CLARK ROSS, Kt., R.N., F.R.S., &c.

BY

JOSEPH DALTON HOOKER, M.D., R.N., F.L.S.,

ASSISTANT SURGEON OF THE "EREBUS" AND BOTANIST TO THE EXPEDITION.

Victoria Barrier and Land. Lat. 78 deg. S. Mount Erebus (active Volcano), and Mount Terror

Published under the Authority of the Lords Commissioners of the Admiralty.

LONDON:

REEVE, BROTHERS, KING WILLIAM STREET, STRAND.

1847.

entirely free of bergs and loose ice and had been sailing into completely unexplored space. The two captains and several officers rowed to shore in two boats. A heavy surf was beating on the rocks as Ross and a few officers stepped on land. Joseph Hooker slipped and fell overboard from one of the boats and nearly drowned. He was half frozen from the intense cold when they pulled him out and they had to return to the ships, but Ross had had time to collect several rock specimens. Franklin Island was 76° 8' S and was about twelve miles long and six miles wide.

Smoke and Flame

Later the same day, the ships sighted a mountain 12,400 feet high emitting flame and smoke in great profusion. Ross named it Mount Erebus. Alexander Smith described it as 'a most Magnificent Volcano... bursting forth Volumes of fire & Smoke'.[20] And an extinct volcano to the eastward 10,900 feet high was duly named Mount Terror. A small rounded island that was in sight all morning was named Beaufort Island.

Ross and his two crews were then astonished at the sight of a mighty ice cliff one hundred feet high with a remarkable even summit that stretched as far as their eyes could see, even assisted with telescopes, in an easterly direction. This barrier was a bitter disappointment to James Clark Ross as he had desired to go much further south. And yet to Smith and others it was 'One of the most wonderful Scenes ever beheld an undeviating line rising full 200 ft high without the least break'.[21]

After naming two capes Crozier and Bird, after expedition members, and the bay formed on the island of the two volca-

---

20 Alexander Smith's Account of the Voyage, p.115.

21 Alexander Smith's Account of the Voyage.

noes (Mt Erebus and Mt Terror) McMurdo Sound after the first lieutenant of the *Terror*, the expedition followed the ice cliffs as far as they could to the south. They towered over the mastheads of the two ships. Behind them could just be seen mountains which Ross named the Parry Mountains after his old commander. (These peaks were in fact the peaks of islands at the back of the volcanoes).

The Mighty Wall of Ice

As they headed eastwards running parallel to the tall ice cliffs, they could still see smoke and flames in great volume emitting from Mount Erebus, 'affording a grand spectacle' to the intrepid voyagers on the two ships.[22]

While they made good progress beside the giant ice wall, no rent or fissure could be discovered. After sailing for a hundred miles (Alexander Smith claims 300 miles and so it seemed), they could still see it stretching further and further eastwards, ever eastwards. Bad weather came with more snow and Ross reluctantly turned back at 78° 5'S. At the time, this position was a record-penetration south – an amazing accomplishment with wooden sailing ships. It was 13 February 1841 and they headed back to Franklin Island, sighting Mt Erebus again three days later. By this time, the winter was rapidly closing in and new ice was forming. They did not want to face the 'horrors' and dangers to human life of a winter stuck in the ice.[23]

Soon the return course was northward along the coast and, after more life-threatening adventures on 6 April 1841, the *Erebus* and *Terror* arrived safely in the Derwent River in southern Tasmania. Battered, but safe and not a single life had been lost.

---

22 Alexander Smith's Account of the Voyage

23 Alexander Smith's Account of the Voyage.

Mt Erebus with the *Erebus* & *Terror* in foreground,
28 January 1841, by John E. Davis

In 1844, Alexander Smith's friend Joseph Hooker had the final say about that great voyage. During the epic voyage, the vast extent of the continent, since called Victoria Land, had been discovered together with the active volcano Mount Erebus, the extinct one Mount Terror and 'that icy barrier, which, running east and west in the parallel of 78° S, prevents all farther progress towards the pole. Two small islets were landed upon ... but neither of these spots presented the slightest trace of vegetation.'[24]

Reflecting on an Astonishing Achievement

They had returned, astonished at their own achievement, after five months at sea in the most stirring of adventures. They had penetrated south further than any other voyagers and had discovered the Ross Sea and Victoria Land of Antarctica. They had located and discovered the volcanoes of Mount Erebus and Mount Terror. They had reached Britannia's Barrier: 'How many thousands Years the Barrier has stood ...

24 Hooker, 'Summary of the Voyage', p. vii.

probably from the Creation of the World'.[25] Their discoveries would revolutionise geography and science. At times as the night became dark, they had witnessed the Aurora – most brilliant and most varied in appearance.

All sailors rejoice, however, in returning safely. As Alexander Smith put it: 'on the Evening of the 7 April to our great Joy we once again dropped [anchor] in the Derwent having been 146 days out. Not a man had been lost & not a Man on the list & in as good health & Spirits as when we left'. When they got ashore the celebrations were wild: 'last night about 25 of them had comfortable lodgings in Jail having nearly taken the Town owing to the Hospitality of the Inhabitants'.[26]

* * * * *

The unexpected arrival of *Fram* in the Derwent in March 1912 caused similar enormous interest amongst the denizens of Hobart. It carried the Norwegian Roald Amundsen who had been on an expedition to the South Pole. Like James Clark Ross, he had brought all his men back alive and fit. For days, Hobart residents and the wider world wondered whether he had beaten Britain's Captain Robert Falcon Scott to the Pole. After the manager of Telegrams at the Hobart Post Office transmitted Amundsen's dispatch to the King of Norway, the news was finally out: the Norwegian had won the race.[27]

Back in early 1841 before the winter had set in, James Clark Ross had won the race for Great Britain against both

---

25 Alexander Smith's Account of the Voyage, p.115.

26 Alexander Smith's Account of the Voyage.

27 Tim Bowden, 'Antarctic Links with Tasmania' in Alison Alexander (ed.), *The Companion to Tasmanian History*, University of Tasmania, Hobart, 2005, pp. 18-19.

the French and the American expeditions by penetrating the furthest south and showing the way for Amundsen, Scott, Mawson and other intrepid Antarctic explorers of the early twentieth century to follow.

Left: King penguin. *Right*: Emperor penguin

James Clark Ross' 1847 account of the Expedition

6

The Second Antarctic Voyage
November 1841 – April 1842

Few people of the present day are capable of rightly
appreciating this heroic deed, this brilliant proof of
human courage and energy. With two ponderous
craft – regular tubs according to our ideas – these men
sailed into the heart of the pack, which all previous
explorers had regarded as certain death.

Roald Amundsen (seventy years later)

The great explorer Roald Amundsen felt that it was not merely
difficult to grasp the achievements of the James Clark Ross
Antarctic Expedition, it was simply impossible to do so. To
the twentieth-century Norwegian explorer, every member of
the mid-nineteenth century British expedition under brilliant
command was a hero in the highest sense. He gave its commander full credit. Ross' experience, daring and good luck
combined to provide the first detailed and prolonged examination of Antarctica. Scott, Shackleton, Amundsen and Byrd
much later, all followed in his giant footsteps.

Respite in Hobart Town and Sydney
Sir John Franklin was the last to take leave of the voyagers to
Antarctica from the head of the Derwent and the first to greet

the returning heroes when the *Erebus* and *Terror* dropped anchor again in the Derwent on the morning of 7 April 1841. They had been absent in the Antarctic for one hundred and forty-five days. Every man was in perfect health, in spite of the hazards they had faced.

The First Mate of the *Erebus* was overjoyed to be once again with his lady love. As for Ross as commander, rarely if ever had an explorer returned from uncharted seas with so great a wealth of geographic and scientific discovery and so complete an absence of misfortune in terms of loss in human life.[1]

Three months were to elapse before the news reached London. In those times, communication with the motherland was slow. With such splendid results when the word got around, pride vibrated through the scientific and naval communities. The Royal Geographical Society, although it had taken no part in the promotion of the expedition, was prompt with lavish praise at its next annual awards. The Founder's Medal of the Royal Geographical Society was enthusiastically awarded to Captain James Clark Ross of the Royal Navy.[2]

Back in Hobart Town, great celebrations were almost a daily occurrence. As Alexander Smith had pointed out, some of the crew were so enthusiastic about finding their land legs once again that they ended up in gaol as a result of their unbridled celebratory efforts. For the wearied Antarctic voyagers, a stay in Hobart was paradise enough. Both the Governor and the local citizens fêted them. And they had many months of double pay to spend on liquor and women and other perhaps more civilised things.

Even a special play 'The Antarctic Expedition' was staged in their honour. It was sincerely meant but, as one more critical

---

1   Cameron, *Lodestone and Evening Star*, p. 231.

2   Mill, *The Siege of the South*, p. 289.

spectator remarked, 'it was but rather indifferently got up and not much better acted'. Nevertheless, it gained an enthusiastic reception by a packed audience. The crews of the *Erebus* and *Terror* bathed in the glory of the dramatic recounting of their heroic deeds.[3] Unfortunately, there is no extant copy of the play's script.

While the crews worked hard to refit the ships under the supervision of the junior officers like Alexander Smith and the other Mates, the senior officers seemed to enjoy frequent and elaborate parties and picnics put on by the wealthier classes.

Three months of pleasant respite from the dangers of the deep were experienced in Hobart and then in Sydney and in New Zealand's Bay of Islands. But they were by no means spent in idleness for the ships had to be refitted and resourced and magnetic observations inspired by Sabine had to be kept up to the mark.

Dr Joseph Hooker and others took opportunities to conduct serious scientific research and gather valuable collections. Hooker tried to avoid parties and other social occasions as much as possible by going outside of Hobart Town on nature rambles that both fascinated and absorbed him. He was to throw much light on the geology and botany of Tasmania. Alexander Smith accompanied his friend when he was not otherwise engaged in courting Aubrey Read. Together they collected many specimens.

Ross and his investigations in Tasmania

James Clark Ross threw himself into frenetic activity during the daytime. He studied the fossil trees of the Derwent Valley and remarked on its geology. He visited the Tasmanian peninsula commenting on Eagle Hawk Neck and the tessellated

3   Mill, *The Siege of the South*, p. 290.

pavement, the Entrecasteaux Channel, the timber on the banks of the Huon River, the advantages of the silent system of reform for transported convicts at Port Arthur, the Point Puer institution for delinquent boys, and so on.

He examined the mean level of the ocean, visited Launceston and constantly prepared for his next voyage.[4] His intellectual energy was unbounded. He was certainly a man with the keen mind of the scientific enlightenment that had flickered brightly for several years in the Royal Navy.

Ross' particular interest, apart from exploring and magnetic observation, was in geology. He found his excursion to the Tasmanian peninsula fascinating. He described it in scientific terms as a 'kind of argillaceous deposit, situated a little to the northward of the neck, or low sandy isthmus, connecting Forrester's with Tasman's Peninsula; having an inlet of Norfolk Bay on the west, and Pirate's Bay on the east'.

He described Pirate's Bay as being bound by steep argillaceous cliffs with their base forming a kind of platform on which the wash of the sea breaks at high water (or high tide). These platforms consisted of siliceous clay and were remarkably divided into symmetrical slabs making a strong relief pattern like ceramic tiles that Ross illustrated in his published account.[5]

He also examined the argillaceous cliffs at Point Puer beside Port Arthur and found they contained the same species of shells as those surrounding Pirate's Bay. He found the same at Eagle Hawk Neck and made a pen and ink diagram of it. He also examined the old coal mines on the Tasman's Peninsula and descended bravely into one 'twenty-six fathoms deep'. He was nothing if not intrepid and did not mind risking himself

---

4   Ross, *Voyage of Discovery*, Vol. 2, Chapter 1.

5   Ross, *A Voyage of Discovery*, pp. 400-01.

to expand his scientific knowledge.

Ross had been clearly impressed with the Juvenile Establishment at Point Puer for transported convict boys when he first visited it on 24 October 1840 before leaving on his first voyage. He noted that the boys ranged in age from ten years to eighteen. He was surprised to find an establishment of 555: 207 of them from London, others from Liverpool, Manchester, Birmingham, Bristol and Dublin and from various other places in England, Ireland and Scotland. Their sentences ranged from seven years to life. 239 had both parents still living. He was impressed with the provision made for them in general education and trade training. He went back to visit the place on his second stay in Hobart Town.[6]

Ross was a seeker after truth, an absorbed man of the scientific enlightenment, full too of patriotic fervour and an overwhelming powerful work ethic.

McCormick, Hooker and Kay publish their findings

Robert McCormick, Joseph Hooker and Joseph Kay were also hard-working in their scholarship and scientific research. While in Hobart the second time, they wrote scholarly scientific papers that were later to appear in the first issue of *The Tasmanian Journal of Natural Science, Agricultural Statistics &c.* For this worthy pioneering scholarly journal, Robert McCormick, surgeon of HMS *Erebus*, produced two major articles: 'Geological Remarks on Kerguelen Land' and 'A Sketch of the Antarctic Region, embracing a few passing remarks'.

Not to be outdone, Lieutenant Joseph Kay RN of HMS *Terror*, who Ross had put in first charge of the Magnetic Observatory in Hobart, also produced two articles for the

---

6   Ross, *A Voyage of Discovery*, pp. 402-03.

same first issue: 'Terrestrial Magnetism' and 'Description of the Instruments employed in Magnetical Observatory, Tasmania'. (When he returned to Hobart to get married in 1844, Alexander John Smith worked at the observatory in a senior position under Joseph Kay as Director. It was an entirely land-based position in the Royal Navy, maintaining his officer rank of lieutenant.)

Joseph Hooker's paper was entitled 'On the Examination of some Fossil Wood from Macquarie Plains, Tasmania', work he conducted during his second sojourn in Hobart.[7]

All three men, through these publications, sought to establish their credentials in the scientific and scholarly world of the new Queen Victoria's reign. They rushed to get themselves into print before the expedition was even complete. Joseph Hooker went on to fame as the Director of Kew Gardens and a close associate of Charles Darwin and stalwart defender of his origin of the species theories.

Thus, three months of the southern winter were spent in well-earned rest and refreshment before voyaging south again, but by no means in idleness.

The Ball Aboard: Reciprocating Hospitality

During their stay in Hobart, the celebrated voyagers reciprocated the hospitality shown to them. In the middle of the Hobart winter, they gave an elaborate party and ball on 1 June 1841. The *Terror* and the *Erebus* were lashed together and temporarily roofed in with canvas to keep out the winter chill on the Derwent. A covered way ran to shore over a bridge of boats lashed together and even a direct road for three hundred yards was cut through the forest to the moorage.

---

7   *The Tasmanian Journal of Natural Science, Agricultural Statistics &c.*, Vol. 1, James Barnard, Govt. Printer, Hobart, 1842, McCormick: pp. 24 & 241; Kay: pp. 124 & 207; Hooker: p. 24.

Each officer was allowed to invite ten personal friends and by lottery drew tables for dining. (One can well imagine who Alexander John Smith, First Mate of the *Erebus*, might have invited!) There was an elaborate preparation of decoration, food, drink and lighting. The 51st Regimental Band stationed in the pioneering colony and the Hobart Town Quadrille Band provided lively music for the festive evening. The party lasted till the following morning's sunrise.

One young local girl wrote excitedly to a friend the next day:

> … the ball on board the *Erebus* and *Terror* … eclipsed anything else that has taken place in Van Diemen's Land. We danced on the *Erebus,* and the *Terror* was the supper room. 350 persons were present and all sat down to supper together. You would not have fancied yourself in ships for they were so beautifully arranged with flags and flowers.

Two hundred and fifty looking-glasses lent by locals were arranged around the sides of the ship reflecting the light 'beautifully'. Chandeliers of officer's swords created 'a very pretty effect' with lighted candles. This young girl claimed that she had the honour of dancing with both Captain Ross and Captain Crozier. They were all a little tired as they didn't even leave the ball before 7 o'clock in the morning. Coffee was provided, but the guests declined breakfast when it was offered.[8]

The ball gave Alexander Smith an opportunity to consolidate his relationship with Sarah Aubrey Read. In February 1841 back in England, his older sister Jane Mary Smith had been married to John Fewson and this information may have encouraged him as well in the matrimonial stakes.

---

8 Dodge, *The Polar Rosses*, pp. 202-03.

An Affair of the Heart

From the Magnetic Observatory near Hobart on 23 April 1841 where he was stationed, Alexander Smith wrote to his father to congratulate his sister Jane on her marriage and to wish her every happiness. His other intention was to break the news of an affair of the heart. At the time of writing, Alexander was heavily employed at the Observatory carrying out the same observations as he had on a previous occasion for the sake of comparison.

He told his father about the daily parties, the dinners and the dances in honour of the polar explorers, that people were vying with each other to be hospitable. He then introduces Aubrey to his family via this letter: 'A young lady of course perfection itself and a Tasmanian, the second daughter of a large family residing a few miles from here [the Observatory].'

He related that he had first met her when she came with her father and sister to see the harbour master and to inspect the explorers' ships. They were nearly ordered out by a seaman on guard duty. They turned away to leave. Alexander, hearing of the occurrence, hastened after them and 'made all the apologies' he could. Then he showed them over everything (presumably the two ships on display, the *Erebus* and the *Terror*).

As they left after the conducted inspection, 'the old gentleman', Aubrey Read's father, gave Alexander his card and a pressing invitation to visit him. Alexander apparently threw the card 'amongst a heap' on his sea chest and forgot about it and the incident. It seemed that ships' officers had been overwhelmed with invitations from all and sundry.

After a week or so elapsed, he met the attractive young lady in question out shopping. She had just driven up in her carriage to where he was standing outside a shop. Aubrey bowed to Alexander no doubt resplendent in his blue and white naval uniform. They then exchanged some polite small talk as she was entering the shop. He recognised her face, but had totally forgotten her name and where he had previously met her. To try her out, he mentioned that she had not been at the last Governor's Ball conducted by Lady Franklin in the absence of her husband. She told him that at the time she had been indisposed with the mumps and could not attend.

Two days later, he met her at yet another ball given by the township in honour of the brave voyagers. He danced twice with her on that occasion and told her that he would like to avail himself of her father's invitation to visit.

A day or two later, Alexander turned up at the family home where 'the father, an old sailor gave me a welcome'. He spent many 'a quiet time' there from then on when he was off duty. The two-storey house (which still stands) had a beautiful garden with fragrant English flowers shadowed by oaks and elms. Alexander claimed that, at this time, he was not thinking of anything serious.

Aubrey's father took him on an excursion into the interior of Van Diemen's Land where they spent several days amongst some of Captain George Frederick Read's close friends and associates.

Not long after, Alexander, ardent with an all-consuming passion for Aubrey, proposed marriage to her. Her answer was 'tears'. Her "papa"'s consent was then sought which was to prove more difficult. Captain Read's response was that they should wait until Alexander was in a better financial situation (that is, promoted in the Royal Navy from First Mate to Lieutenant) and Aubrey was older and more mature. The old 'sensible, stirling, excellent man', as Alexander Smith described him, was concerned that his daughter would be in a financially secure position in the future. She was his much-loved daughter after all!

In reality, Captain Read demanded a stern test of their relationship: that their affection for each other would remain the same in a year's time. Alexander Smith was optimistic. He believed it was certain that he would be promoted to Lieutenant on the expedition's return to England 'from the Ice'. Aubrey would then be a year or so older to make up her mind about marriage.

Sarah Aubrey Read was born on 25 February 1820 in Hobart Town to George Frederick and Elizabeth (née Driver) Read. At the time of Alexander's first proposal, she had just turned twenty-one years of age, although some sources claim that she was barely eighteen.

After this first crucial encounter with Captain Read over the question of marriage, Alexander Smith acknowledged himself as 'her intended', but kept it secret to all but one aboard the *Erebus*. (He may have taken his close friend Joseph Hooker into his confidence.)

He eventually parted from Aubrey on the *Erebus* as it set sail for Sydney. His heart was heavy. As his mentor, Captain Ross joked with him about his 'blue young lady' as he had noticed him paying attention to a young girl dressed in blue at Lady Franklin's masked ball at Government House.

Ross obviously had encouraged the relationship with a deal of good humour. He was even prepared to approach Captain Read on Alexander's behalf, but the good Captain was away in the interior for several days. It is clear then that Alexander Smith had confided his intentions to his commanding officer.

Ross advised Alexander, in a fatherly way, on no account to rush into marriage until the expedition had ended. The passionate Alexander confessed to his father that he was of a mind to marry immediately, that otherwise he would have to eke out a 'miserable existence' 'for two years longer'. But practical sense prevailed.

In his letter to Lord Henry dated 28 April 1841, Alexander expanded on the suitability of Aubrey's family:

> I must tell you now who they are. Her father many years ago commissioned one of the [East India] Company's Ships. He made money ... Purchased a ship in the East Indies, made a most successful speculation at Sydney, came here when first the Colony [Van Diemen's Land] was established, having sold his Vessel, being taken like many others with this delightful climate, he got a grant of 4,000 acres of which now is of enormous value and by little and little is noted almost the wealthiest man in Van Diemen's Land and he is director of the Bank and I imagine the most influential man here, he lives very retired, but most universally esteemed by all who know him. I however do not expect I shall get more than £200 a year with my young Lady. He told me that was all I should give his daughter yearly as by giving more it only encouraged idleness on the part of the Husband...

Captain Read believed that there were plenty of good opportunities in the Colony for an enterprising young man, 'for any man of an active turn of mind' to make a 'fortune with the right contacts and connections'.

Alexander went on to espouse the virtues of Aubrey to his family: 'My love is nearly 18'. (If she was born in February 1820, she would have just turned 21.) She had a 'pretty figure, but too short', he joked, to please Lord Henry's tastes, who apparently liked taller women. She was not one of Alexander's mythical dark beauties, 'but very fair' and she was well brought up and could do what most girls could not do. As an example, he pointed out that she made all her own clothes. Aubrey, according to Alexander, was good tempered and had only been angry with him on one occasion when he had been flirting with another, 'an old failing' of his.

Alexander was clear in stating to his father and his mother about his intentions to marry Sarah Aubrey Read. He went into full particulars 'regarding this affair' of his 'heart'. He did not, however, think that anything would take place until the expedition was complete and he was 'paid off of a surety' (while on the expedition he was entitled to double wages). Then if he was to marry Aubrey, he would need to venture forth, 'to cross the salty seas once more in a quest of love' to Van Diemen's Land.

He was also anticipating further success in the second voyage into Antarctica. In his letter, he presented an extract from James Clark Ross' official despatch to Lord Minto, Lord of the Admiralty:

> I trust that the brilliant success which has resulted from the Zealous and persevering exertions of those under my command placed so unexpectedly as they have been in competition with two Rival Powers [the French Expedition under Dumont d'Urville and the American Expedition under Wilkes] may justify me in expressing a confident hope that your Lordship will be pleased to manifest the sense you entertain of those exertions in that manner which every officer is most desirous to receive the approbation of the Admiralty and which alone conveys to our Brother officers a due sense of that approbation by the promotion of Commander Crozier whose cordial cooperation has been of the utmost importance to the success of the enterprise. *My Senior Mate "Mr. A.J. Smith" in addition to the responsible duty of Officer of the Watch has*

devoted every other moment of his time in assisting me in making Magnetic observations and the devotedness and Zeal which he has ever manifested in addition to his long service as a Mate characterized as they are by several events of deep interest and of usually strong claims on the service, will, I humbly hope meet your Lordship's most favourable consideration and the promotion of these officers would give an impulse to the service and induce many others to continue to pursue the path of merit who have entered upon it, and whose hopes in it have alone depended upon your Lordship's administration of its rewards...[9]

Alexander Smith as a twenty-eight-year-old could not have hoped for a stronger endorsement for promotion from his Commander and mentor. His future career in the navy seemed bright as were his prospects of marriage to Aubrey. In his letter, he underlined these two factors with great vigour and clarity.[10]

Sir John Franklin, as has been related, was deeply interested in the Ross Antarctic Expedition. When the *Erebus* and *Terror* departed north for Sydney, he happened to hear through the Hobart Town gossip network that Sarah Aubrey Read had received a letter from Alexander Smith, her intended. It had been sent by means of a ship travelling south to Hobart and encountered on the way. Franklin immediately sent his aide-de-camp to the Read household in New Town, Hobart, with a request 'that Miss Read would graciously give any information of interest in regard to the expedition that she had received

---

9   Author's italics for emphasis.

10   Alexander Smith to his father Lord Henry Smith, Magnetic Observatory, Van Diemen's Land, 28 April 1841.

from Lieutenant Smith'.[11] (Alexander, while recommended, had yet to be promoted.)

A Wet Respite in Sydney

The two expeditionary ships cruised into warmer Australasian seas on 7 July 1841. After a pleasant week-long voyage north along the Australian coast, they reached Sydney Harbour and Port Jackson.

The Sydney people had recently seen something of the American and French expeditions. They were keen to examine the *Erebus* and *Terror* and their special equipment for service in the ice that had enabled them to break through the dreaded ice pack and enter for the first time into the Ross Sea, thus penetrating to the very edge of the Great Ice Barrier, a place where no human being had gone before. There was much public excitement. Sydney Australians wanted to satisfy their curiosity and welcomed the heroic voyagers with the usual elaborate colonial hospitality.[12] Their patriotic fervour was on fire as much as the Hobartians.

The expedition's officers were soon hard at work installing a magnetic observatory on Garden Island in Sydney Harbour as the more desirable site at Fort Macquarie, where Charles Wilkes had made his observations in 1839, had been rendered useless for magnetic work by the erection of fortifications containing a mass of metal in the guns and cannon balls. Such a large amount of metal would radically disturb the compass needle. Rainy weather then delayed the preparations. On one day, eight and a half inches of rainfall was measured – a huge

---

11 While Smith's promotion had been strongly recommended, technically he was still First Mate on HMS *Erebus*. Franklin's request was cited in the entry on Alexander Smith in 'Modified Register for Captain Alexander John Smith' (Merilyn Pedrick Collection).

12 Mill, *The Siege of the South*, p. 290.

deluge as Ross saw it. Storms nearly every day convinced the intrepid explorer that Sydney was a very rainy location. Bad weather persisted for much of their stay.

However, all was got ready for the annual term day of 21 July – the main purpose of the visit to Sydney. On that day simultaneous magnetic observations were made at hourly intervals in many observatories in various parts of the world, particularly in parts of the British Empire, in an important international experiment.

It was a day that Alexander Smith, with his acquired skills, had to work and concentrate upon around the clock. Although he was exhausted the following day, the instruments had to be dismounted under his supervision and brought on board the *Erebus* and *Terror*. Ross was most disappointed that they could not record at Fort Macquarie in Sydney Cove because of the storage there of military guns and cannon balls.[13]

In his account of his arrival, Ross observed that Sydney Harbour was one of the most magnificent harbours in the world. The Colonial Governor Sir George Gipps, in welcoming the intrepid voyagers, offered every assistance in his power (as he had been instructed to do from official sources in the motherland). The *Erebus* and *Terror* had been anchored between 'the government demesne and Garden Island', not in Sydney Cove.

Hospitality from Sir George and Lady Gipps was shown to the officers of the expedition during their sojourn in Sydney. While he was extremely busy with the observations on Garden Island so as to decline the hospitality of many of the prominent Sydney citizens, Ross met with his old friend Captain Phillip Parker King RN and a few others that he knew like W.S. McLeay, the Speaker of the Assembly. In their stay of

13 Dodge, *The Polar Rosses*, p. 204.

twenty-one days, it rained so frequently as to astonish Ross, although this was partially compensated by time spent in the impressive McLeay residence with its magnificent gardens on the foreshores of Sydney Harbour.

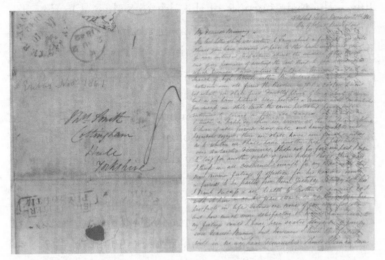

Alexander's letter to his mother from the Bay of Islands, New Zealand, *Erebus* 31 Nov. 1841. Note the method of saving paper by writing across the text. (Paper was an expensive item.)

The officers dined and spent their last evening with the Governor and a number of invited friends. When they returned to the ships, the *Erebus* and *Terror*, they found they had been unmoored in the afternoon and were ready to sail at daylight on the morning of 5 August 1841. At noon, they were well out at sea again.[14] The vessels were heavily laden, having taken on board provisions, stores and fuel for three years. Their progress across the Tasman Sea was sluggish and the weather proved difficult. Eventually they reached the Bay of Islands on the northeast coast of the north island of New Zealand. There they laid up for three pleasant months to wait for the Antarctic summer.

---

14 Ross, *A Voyage of Discovery*, Vol. 2, pp. 34-48.

The Bay of Islands

Dr Joseph Hooker and others carried out much valuable collecting work on shore around the Bay of Islands. Hooker was later able to publish the results of his research that considerably enhanced his growing reputation in the scientific world as a botanist.

Ross decided not to let his officers make any extensive excursions away from the two ships on account of political discontent amongst the warlike Maori peoples. During the time spent in the Bay of Islands, the expedition met two foreign men-of-war. The French corvette *Héroine* arrived and its commander Captain l'Eveque gave Ross, as a good will gesture, a chart showing Dumont d'Urville's discoveries. It was a better chart of the Chatham Islands than Ross had available. He had not previously seen it.

The other separate occasion was the arrival of the American sloop *Yorktown*. Its commander Captain J.H. Aulick had recently left Lieutenant Wilkes' squadron and was expected to rejoin the American explorer later. Ross sent Wilkes a note telling him that he had sailed over a large space of clear water where Wilkes had placed mountains on the chart he had sent him. Unfortunately, Wilkes did not receive the letter before reading a distorted account in the newspapers that expressed angry rivalry.

Ross himself made an extensive three-day trip into the surrounding countryside despite banning his officers from doing so because of the dangers of Maori discontent. Danger was no stranger to him and he seemed to relish it. He visited the Mission Station at Waimati, the Keri Keri Falls, enjoyed a fishing party to Lake Mapere, made an ascent of Puki Nui, visited Lakes at Taiami and the Hot Springs of Tuakino. On his return, the French corvette *Héroine* had anchored nearby and the French crew were in a sickly state. Ross exchanged visits as recounted.[15]

From their anchorage in the Bay of Islands, Alexander Smith wrote a letter, apparently to one of his brothers, in which he expressed the object of the next voyage south, which was to locate the position of the Pole 'of the greatest intensity of the needle'. He hoped that their great discoveries would be appreciated in England especially because of the huge tract of Antarctic territory they had taken possession of on behalf of the Crown. They had penetrated further south, he explained to his brother, than any other Antarctic explorers before them.

He also described the most exciting events and sights of their first voyage. He spoke of the possibilities of his promotion to Lieutenant as a result of the huge 'Waste of Water' he had travelled over during his sailor's life: 'Few have had the roughs more than myself...'

In New Zealand, he had found the Maori to be 'the finest independent looking Savage I have ever seen – all more or less tattooed'. He no-ticed that the Maori women were slaves to their men and that their wars against each other were in-cessant. The chiefs in this warfare were the greatest warriors.[16]

The *Erebus* had one accident in the

Erebus & *Terror* in the ice floe

15 Ross, *A Voyage of Discovery*, Vol. II, Chapter IV; Dodge, *The Polar Rosses*, pp. 204-05; Mill, *The Siege of the South*, pp. 290-2.

16 Letter by Alexander Smith, HMS *Erebus*, Bay of Islands, September 1841.

Bay of Islands – one of the marines drowned by capsizing the dingy. He was the biggest man of the expedition and the most jovial and popular. But he could not swim.

The Second Voyage to the Antarctic

The three months in the Bay of Islands passed pleasantly and was a well-deserved rest for the entire expedition. Fresh fish were in abundance in the Bay but eventually the siren of the south beckoned as the days lengthened and became warmer. Ross was more and more anxious to embark on his second Antarctic adventure.

The approach of the southern summer made it possible to return to Antarctic waters. By the time live-stock and fresh provisions were taken on board in the last days in the Bay, the decks of the *Erebus* and *Terror* looked like farmyards.

On 23 November 1841, they sailed from the Bay of Islands at 5am and set a course for the Chatham Islands. They were accompanied for a few hours by HMS *Favourite*, whose Commander Sullivan was stationed in New Zealand. When the expedition departed from the *Favourite*, their crew manned the rigging and cheered them off. *Favourite* then made the signal 'Honour and success attend you all'. The weather was fine and good progress was made south. Ross set a south-eastern course for the Chatham Islands. They crossed the International Date Line and enjoyed November 25th twice. The crew were in perfect health and high spirits. The day before on the 24th, however, a man jumped overboard to escape punishment. He was thrown a life-buoy, got hold of it and was saved. He then received his due corporal punishment and was de-ranked for theft and lack of personal hygiene.

Due to a thick fog and heavy winds, the expedition passed the Chatham Islands without stopping as it seemed too dangerous to do so. They then bore off into the Antarctic. The object was to steer as far as 150° W and then proceed to the southward on that meridian. By about 10 December, it became much colder and both crews felt it after having experienced the delightful warm weather in the Bay of Islands. They put on their worsted socks and gloves and some of their cold weather gear. All tended to shiver while on watch whatever time of day it was.

By this time, there was some tension on board. John Edward Davis the Second Master on *Terror* records in a letter to his sister Emily, which was later privately published, that Crozier the Captain on the *Terror* was 'very much out of temper' and the gunroom officers were quarrelling hea-tedly amongst themselves. He blamed the First Lieutenant Archibald McMurdo for the conflict who, he claimed, had 'whims and fancies'. As a more junior officer, Davis was glad he did not mess with him:

> I am very content here [in the Masters mess] where there are only three of us and no superiority … We have got a very good rule, that is, if two of us quarrel and do not speak the third is not to speak to those two till they have made up. However we have not had occasion to put that into force yet, and hope we shall not.[17]

The more senior officers mess was less companionable or friendly.

When the fog lifted beyond the Chatham Islands, the members of the expedition sighted their first iceberg – a flat-topped giant ice-island rising majestically 130 feet above the

---

17   Captain J.E. Davis RN, *A Letter from the Antarctic*, William Clowes & Sons Ltd, London, 1801, p. 9.

Alexander Smith's sketches on the Expedition

water's surface, its sides caverned by the action of the waves.[18] Davis saw it as 'one of the most magnificent and stupendous in nature'.[19]

Heading due south, the expedition entered into the ice pack proper on the morning of 18 December 1841 at 4am. The weather was beautiful but cold, the temperature below freezing point. The pack was loose at first and the ships sailed through it steadily for about thirty miles, then it grew much heavier and compelled a change of course to the south west. The lookout from the crow's nest at the masthead guided the ships gingerly from one pool of open water to another, between the huge ice floes, thus making slow progress.

The natural sea life swarmed about the ships, intensely curious but not alarmed or frightened. Numerous whales seemed to perceive the two vessels as fellow creatures and scarcely moved aside. On one occasion, the *Erebus* passed right over a whale and experienced a shock to its timbers.

Opportunity was taken to land the magnetic instrument on a large floe to conduct the inevitable magnetic research away from the iron fittings on the ships to gain more accurate results.

The Antarctic Circle itself was approached on Christmas Day, the ships working to and fro in the heavy pack ice wherever a lead seemed to open here and there. They were shrouded in fog most of the time.

Christmas Day was spent beset in the pack: 'we, nevertheless, managed to do justice to a good old English fare, which we had taken care to preserve for the occasion'.[20] The seemingly impenetrable mass of ice in which they were caught stretched as far as the eyes could see, even from the crow's nest.

---

18 Mill, *The Siege of the South*, p. 293.

19 Davis, *A Letter from the Antarctic*.

20 Cited in Dodge, *The Polar Rosses*, p. 205.

Erebus & *Terror* caught in a gale, 20 January 1842, watercolour by J.E. Davis

By New Year's Day, they had advanced 250 miles through the pack. The crews of the ships had the opportunity to visit each other across the ice. The *Erebus* and *Terror* fifty yards apart were attached to either side of a massive iceberg. The ice between acted as a playground of enjoyable social activity and sport which greatly improved morale. People were able to let their hair down. Davis takes up the story:

> … we made fast to the same piece of ice, and of course being only about 50 yards apart there was a great deal of visiting, for we had but to walk across the ice to get to the *Erebus*. So we proposed to see the Old Year out and the New Year in in style on the 31st. I dined on board the *Erebus*, and after dinner Hooker… and myself went on the ice and cut out in hard snow the figure of a woman, which we called our "Venus de Medici".

The statue, some described as a beautiful Grecian girl, was seated about eight feet long and was frozen so hard it remained in perfect condition until after they left the floe. In hardness and whiteness, it almost rivalled the finest Carrara marble. Soon other ice sculptures made their appearance around the site.

A quadrangular space was carefully excavated in the ice for a dance floor – a novel kind of ballroom with a crystal appearance in its floor. A table of ice on which to drink the Old Year out and the New Year in was built in the middle of a refreshment room adjacent to the ballroom and cut out of the ice. An elevated chair was constructed of ice for both captains. On the refreshment table, bottles of wine and grog were placed for the use of dancers. The dancing was most enthusiastic and wild in the Scottish manner. The only thing lacking were women and they were sorely missed after all the balls in Hobart, but this made the ball unique; the men danced with each other.

New Year's Day Celebrations 1842, watercolour by J.E. Davis

At a few minutes before midnight, the noise across the silent ice floes was stunning and no doubt a shock to the natural life of the region. Each ship was trying to defeat the other with the blowing of horns, the beating of gongs, the squealing of pigs (the men took these like bagpipes under their arms to make them make a noise). Pandemonium broke loose. There were all kinds of diabolic music. At the magic hour of twelve, it was increased by each ship ringing forty-two bells so as to bring the 'New Year In'. It was an event never to be forgotten by those present.

Both captains joined the officers in the refreshment room built in the ice. Ross, in high spirits, shook hands with everyone wishing them a happy New Year. He then drank the health of all crew members. They cheered their commander and Crozier then did the same. Crozier and Ross highlighted the ball with a nicely executed quadrille to loud applause and cheers of everyone.[21]

A good time was had by all. The surviving boatswain had played the part of 'mine host' of the 'Antarctic Hotel' under a highly symbolic sign depicting Bacchus Britannia. Other figures had proud signs such as 'Pilgrims of the Ocean' and 'Pioneers of Science'. Both captains entered very heartily into the entertainment that ended in a great snow-ball battle between the two crews. It was something to talk about for many a dreary day to come.[22]

After the ball was over, the two ships drifted south and more and warmer polar clothing was issued, but the morale amongst the men was high and they were at the peak of physical fitness and prowess. By a curious coincidence, they had crossed into the Antarctic Circle on the same day in the previous year of their first great voyage, now some 1,400 miles to the west of them.

Alexander Smith had realised that, during this second voyage, they would find 'plenty of Ice and plenty of dangers' and they knew from experience what they expected to find

---

21 Davis, *A Letter from the Antarctic*, pp. 12-13; Mill, *The Siege of the South*, pp. 294-5; Dodge, *The Polar Rosses*, pp. 205-6.

22 Mill, *The Siege of the South*, p. 295.

between their 'old friend the Barrier in 78° & 200° E'.[23] He hoped that the 'same protecting power' would guard them against 'all dangers' and that they would arrive at the Falkland Islands having successfully completed their 'hazardous voyage'. And there to find their final orders on whether they should prosecute another, a third voyage, of 'Antarctic discoveries'.[24] He was not looking forward to yet another voyage south having already spent three years on the expedition as well as many other dangerous cruises earlier with the Royal Navy. He was beginning to tire of life at sea now that he had good marriage prospects.

Progress after New Year's Day on the second voyage was painfully slow and most difficult and exhausting. On 4 January 1842, the ships and pack ice with them were driven twenty miles to the north. Tacking and twisting were ceaseless; scarcely a quarter of an hour without having to go about. It was tiring, relentless work. On the 10th, a gale from the south drove them back to 65° 59'S.

Nothing could be done, but to hope for a favourable change. Ross stoically interested himself in scientific work to fill out the dreary days. Several gigantic penguins were killed. The weight of one specimen was at least 75 pounds. The expedition's commander 'skinned some of them and preserved others in pickle with his own hands'. Capturing these huge birds was 'a constant delight to the sailors'. Two stalwart tars were sometimes seen marching a 'solemn penguin in custody toward the ship, each grasping a flipper'.[25]

Birds of many varieties as well as seals were secured for

---

23 Alexander Smith to his mother, 31 November 1841, HMS *Erebus*, Bay of Islands, New Zealand.

24 Alexander Smith to his mother.

25 Mill *The Siege of the South*, pp. 295-6.

scientific research. Nevertheless, Alexander Smith and others must have had anxious thoughts about the future as week after week of the short Antarctic summer went by and yet the ships still drifted with the pack. When a gale blew the ships amongst the masses of floating ice, they were in extreme peril.

On 20 January, the ships were caught in a gale in the middle of large masses of ice with an extremely heavy see-sawing swell. No ordinary ships would have withstood the hammering that both ships received. The *Terror's* rudder snapped and was rendered useless. When the weather moderated, it took a whole day to ship the spare rudder as the gudgeons had been badly bent. Both ships had survived imminent dangers but, for the first time, Ross had looked anxious and care-worn although still exhibiting fortitude.

They had taken forty days to go a hundred miles with many setbacks. On 20 February, they encountered a fearful gale, the spray dashing over the ships and becoming ice as soon as it touched the deck. Ross, however, was determined to go on. He showed an indifference to danger. And on the 28th, they reached latitude 78° 10'S and the Great Ice Barrier was at last in sight for a second time – the first and last being on that first great voyage.

As the summer season was advanced and had begun to close in rapidly, Ross found it necessary to abandon further exploration and turn the ships in a northerly direction. The crew breathed a sigh of relief, but not for long. On 1 March 1842, 'a magnificent range of icebergs was in sight, extending in an unbroken chain as far as the eye could discern from the masthead'.[26]

Again on 4 March 1842, a furious gale was suddenly

26 Markham, *Lands of Silence*, p. 419.

encountered and on the 12th several bergs were seen during thick weather with constant squalls of snow frequently concealing the view.

Suddenly a large berg was ahead. It was to be a close encounter of a most perilous kind. *Erebus* was hauled to the wind on a port tack with the expectation of avoiding it. At that moment, the *Terror* came in sight running down upon her consort. As an eye-witness on the *Terror*, Davis takes up the story:

> … as we were both suddenly hauling to the wind on opposite tacks, we came in contact; the *Erebus* striking this ship [the *Terror*] heavily on the starboard cat-head, breaking our anchor right in two and taking the cat-head and a part of the anchor away, carrying away flying jibboom and jibboom, the former of which broke in three places and snapped close off at the cap, and carried away the lower studding-sail boom. Her [*Erebus'*] damage was much greater, losing her bowsprit close off at the bows, fore-top-mast and main-top-gallant-mast, and the whole of the cat-head and anchor. After striking several times very hard she worked further aft, our anchors being cleared. She next struck us near the gangway, she then splintered the immense strengthening pieces outside which prevented our being cut down.

The *Terror's* yard-arms were striking at every roll and broke all the booms and boom-irons which came down, luckily without hurting a soul. Amazingly, no one on either ship was badly injured. The *Erebus* then struck the *Terror* abreast of the mizzen-mast several times, smashed the quarter boat, broke the ice-plank and again shattered the strengthening piece outside and tore off all the iron work. As the ships separated, the *Erebus* carried away the *Terror's* spanker-boom.[27]

---

27 Davis, *A Letter from the Antarctic*, pp. 27-8.

The Collision, 13 March 1842, watercolour by J.E. Davis

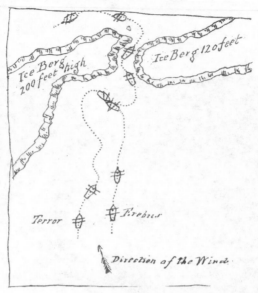

John Davis' sketch map of the collision

The collision had been severe and the danger was not yet over, but Ross was up to the task in the emergency that followed. Dangerous icebergs were in front and all around. Ross picked a narrow chance between two bergs – two perpendicular walls of ice – and thankfully found smooth water beyond. They had had no time to reflect on their imminent danger as they

John Edward Davis RN

had been caught up in 'the necessity of constant and energetic action to meet the momentarily varying circumstances of our situation...'[28] As Senior Mate, Alexander Smith had worked frantically with the other officers directing the crew.

---

28 James Ross, cited in Markham, *Lands of Silence*, p. 420.

The *Erebus* breaking through the gap, sketch by John Davis

James Clark Ross, still very much in charge, then shaped a direct course around Cape Horn to the Falkland Islands before strong westerly gales. On 6 April 1842, the *Erebus* and *Terror* limped thankfully up the Berkeley Sound and anchored in Port Louis.

Good news from Ross was awaiting Alexander Smith, the Senior Mate of the *Erebus*. He had received his Lieutenancy. Commander Crozier and Lieutenant Bird were also promoted. Lieutenant McMurdo was invalided and repatriated to England and Lieutenant Sibbald took his place aboard the *Terror*. The refitting of the *Erebus* and *Terror* proceeded as rapidly as possible and by July's end both ships were in good order and ready for sea again.[29]

*   *   *   *   *

Naturally, Alexander Smith was anxious to write to Aubrey, but not one vessel had arrived in Port Louis suitable for sending mail. On 6 April 1842, Captain Ross used his rank and

29 Markham, *Lands of Silence*.

seniority to order the Man-of-War Ketch HMS *Arrow* to wait for the expedition's dispatches and letters for conveyance to Rio de Janeiro. It was understood that many vessels bound for Sydney put in to Rio on the way. Alexander got his letter away to Aubrey in Hobart Town by that conveyance. He trusted, therefore, that she would eventually receive his communication joyfully on a ship bound from Sydney to Hobart.

While the Navy List had not yet been issued at the time of writing, Captain Ross had taken it upon himself to officially appoint Alexander as Lieutenant on board the *Erebus*, as it was in his power to do so.

This was the good news Alexander conveyed to his beloved; the bad news was there was every chance of a third voyage to the Antarctic before they returned to England. At the time, however, official dispatches had not yet arrived to authorise such an expedition, but it was confidently predicted and Ross was determined to once more enter the Antarctic Circle. He was almost obsessed with the future prospect of yet another voyage.

At the same time, Alexander Smith was hoping that a brother or someone in Aubrey's family would accompany her on an excursion to England where she would receive 'an affectionate and warm welcome from' his 'dear Mother and Father'.[30]

Alexander recounted to Aubrey with a great deal of pride and gusto his adventures of the second voyage including:

> The most wonderful escape upon record was one that
> the two ships had on the 13th March [1842] in Lat.
> 60. 11½ and 147 West. It was my middle watch i.e.
> from midnight to 4 a.m. I came on deck and found

---

30 Alexander Smith to Sarah Aubrey Read, 2 May 1842, HMS *Erebus*, Falkland Islands.

Captain Ross up there and [a] strong gale of wind blowing, before which we were running and the weather densely thick. We could just make out the Terror's light, and she was no more than a cable's length from us. The Captain ordered me to close reef the main top sail. While in the act of clearing it up a large ice berg was seen upon our Starboard bow, and steering the ship to clear it, we saw the Terror coming right down on top of us. In less than two minutes the two ships came in violent collision, The Terror striking us on the starboard bow and carried away our Bowsprit fore top mast,

and so on.

Each moment the heavy seas drove the ships together, every soul expecting each crash to be the last and the ships to sink. After hanging together for more than ten minutes the ships cleared each other …

And soon after, there appeared close to them:

… a stupendous Berg towering more than 150 feet above us and of so great a length that no one could make out its extremes. We braced the fragments of the Courses up to endeavour to weather it but soon saw it was useless …

But they were able to avoid by a hair's breadth further disaster:

Daylight which had seldom been more anxiously looked for dawned and showed us a line of 7 very large Bergs, that we had driven past, and incredible as it may appear, our Bower anchor driven with its two Palms firmly into the ship's bottom. In that way it remained for upwards of 700 miles, before it tore itself away … However thank God we are safe again and snugly moored in a very comfortable harbour and waiting anxiously for letters from England and your dear self which I fully expect by the first arrival at this place. Many and many a time my dear Aubrey I have thought of you in this last our worst and most dangerous cruise.[31]

Love and good fortune thus conquered all!

Petrels in the Ross Sea by Edward Wilson

31 Alexander Smith to Sarah Aubrey Read.

7

The Final Antarctic Voyage
December 1842 – March 1843

... we are of the opinion that the Erebus and Terror
should be moored henceforth on either side of the
Victory, floating monuments of what the Nelsons of
discovery can dare and do at the call of their country
in the service of the world.

Earl of Ellesmere, 1858

This is praise indeed! The identity of one of 'the Nelsons of
discovery' was Sir James Clark Ross, the greatest Antarctic
voyager of the nineteenth century. He was portrayed as having
lived to see many of his expectations as an explorer justified
and fulfilled. The ships under his command were personified
as gallant and 'rough with many a scar' from the bloodless
conflict with floe and iceberg. Their log was 'one continuous
record of danger and difficulty vanquished by courage and
intelligence'. Their triumph 'unpurchased by other human
suffering than voluntary endurance of the wise and brave in
pursuit of noble ends'.[1] Had Alexander Smith read this glowing
passage by the Earl of Ellesmere in 1858, it would have made

---

1   Earl of Ellesmere [Francis Egerton], 'Voyage to the Antarctic Regions', *Essays
on History, Biography, Geography, Engineering &c.*, John Murray, London, 1858,
pp. 324-5.

him feel proud to have been part of it. And he may have, but now we cannot confirm it!

Unlike Ross, however, he was not keen to embark on the third expedition into Antarctica. Without a doubt, many of the officers and crew had similar views and some expressed them privately to one another. Nevertheless, they remained faithful to the 'pursuit of noble ends'.

Apart from an officer who had been invalided home, Lieutenant Archibald McMurdo, they were all fit enough physically, though mentally burnt out because of their long tense sojourn in southern seas facing immense dangers. Moreover, the Falkland Islands did not provide as pleasant and fulfilling a respite as they had found in Hobart, Sydney and the Bay of Islands. On top of everything else, Alexander Smith was anxious to be reunited with Aubrey, his new-found beloved, and to visit his family in England after a long absence in the Royal Navy. Duty, however, had to be placed first before personal considerations. Such was the culture of the Royal Navy in early Victorian times.

Antarctica was a silent, cold windy battlefield – a lonely continent. Earlier, George Forster, sailing with James Cook in 1773, thought of the icebergs as 'the wrecks of a shattered world'. Cook himself believed it was 'a country doomed by nature never once to feel the warmth of the sun's rays, but to lie buried in everlasting snow and ice'.[2] And yet there was a magnificence and a mystery about the place that, like a powerful magnet, drew explorers like Ross back again and again.

While waiting in the Falklands for the next Antarctic summer to take them on their final voyage of discovery,

2   Cited by Peter Pierce, 'White Warfare' (Reviews of three books on Antarctica), *Australian Book Review*, February/March 1997, p. 20.

the expedition was beginning to fracture psychologically although the crews of both ships were generally in good health. Arguments broke out among the officers, especially on the *Terror*. Social life on the Falklands was depressing in the extreme for the crews – there were few pubs and apparently no brothels. There was no lively township with a variety of activities for them. And no one seemed interested in celebrating their recent triumphs.

To keep themselves busy in a positive way, Crozier and Ross had carried out a systematic survey of the Falkland Islands. As a result, they suggested to authorities that Port William (later Port Stanley) was a much better harbour port than Port Louis for the use of shipping.[3] Their recommendation was later acted on.

Sailors depended emotionally on news from home and an absence of news always lowered morale. Communication by letter from the Falklands was dreadfully slow and erratic which made everyone seem particularly isolated, especially Alexander Smith. He was, however, delighted to receive a letter from Aubrey in response to his own first letter. He was immediately reassured as to the future of his love life. The same ship that brought her letter also brought the dispatches to Ross from the Lords of the Admiralty endorsing Smith's promotion to lieutenant. Alexander felt his prospects could not be brighter – he was now potentially second-in-command under Ross on the *Erebus* as Sibbald was transferred to the *Terror* as a replacement for McMurdo.[4]

The crews' first impressions of their home port in the Falklands were not at all favourable and remained so during their entire time there. Hooker even described the gale-swept

---

3   Howgego, *Encyclopedia of Exploration*, p.515.

4   Alexander Smith to Sarah Aubrey Read, HMS *Erebus*, 26 November 1842.

Kerguelen Island as paradise compared to it – an exaggeration perhaps, but the point was made. When talking about the Falklands, he exclaimed: 'Desolation stares in our face'. There were a few houses and only sixty souls including the governor resident on the islands. They were mostly army personnel and some miners or sappers. They did not seem that interested in marine achievements or polar exploration. Britain had annexed the place from the Spanish Empire only in 1833. The sole recreational activity available was hunting wild or feral cattle[5] – a dangerous sport at the best of times. Heavy consumption of alcohol from boredom was another danger.

Ross completed his term-day observations at the Falklands on 4 September 1842 and was anxious to be off for a similar experiment in the vicinity of Cape Horn now that both ships had been sufficiently repaired and refitted. The men had worked hard to fill in the time. The Falklands stay had not been pleasant in a number of respects. The expedition leaders' relations with the Governor had been troubled when compared with those that had prevailed both in Hobart and in Sydney, especially the excellent relationship they had had with Sir John Franklin as lieutenant governor of Van Diemen's Land.

A rumour had spread among the crew that the Falklands had been chosen to prevent seamen from jumping ship. Such rumours were a sign of worsening morale.

Hooker had also remarked that when word had come that James Ross had been awarded the Founder's Gold Medal by the Royal Geographical Society some officers, especially those aboard the *Terror*, had become jealous and believed they should have received similar recognition.

Before sailing, Ross was compelled to reassure his officers. The prospects of promotions for all helped. The charismatic

5   Ross, *Ross in the Antarctic*, pp.169-76.

commander was a master at restoring ship morale. Spirits lifted as soon as they left the Falklands and were once more in the open sea.[6] It seemed that all preferred being at sea rather than at anchor in such a dismal place.

The ships sailed on 8 September with a fresh westerly wind. Lieutenant Archibald McMurdo, the first lieutenant of the *Terror*, was left behind as he was declared by the entire medical team too ill to travel on the third voyage. He was to await passage home as invalided as recounted. They left him depressed about his future and perhaps about losing contact with shipmates who had become close friends. He had been suffering from a stomach complaint for some time. After the expedition arrived back home, he was promoted to Commander along with John Sibbald and James Wood.

Despite his continued ill-health, McMurdo reached the rank of Rear Admiral before he died in 1875. Ross had honoured him by naming a bay after him. His name will never be forgotten since McMurdo Sound became the entry point to Antarctica for the historical expeditions of Scott and Shackleton in the early twentieth century. Today it is the principal American base on the continent and carries the same name.[7]

The season for another Antarctic intrusion had not quite arrived for the James Clark Ross expedition and the journey to Cape Horn was to visit Tierra del Fuego to make magnetic observations and comparisons with readings on the Falklands where Ross had set up yet another observatory. Hooker was in his element collecting exotic plants including 120 flowering ones. Alexander Smith assisted. They had had a very rough and stormy passage to Cape Horn.

---

6 Dodge, *The Polar Rosses*, pp. 212-3.

7 Ross, *Ross in the Antarctic*, p. 218.

They then headed for the wildness and beauty of St Martin's Cove, Hermit Island. There they met indigenous natives who lived in what were described as wigwams on the beach in large communes or extended families. The people were naked except for skin cloaks and used canoes extensively to fish and hunt for seals. Again, Hooker made an extensive collection of plants and compared the place in geographic features to the windswept islands in the north of Scotland (which Alexander Smith had once visited and surveyed). Perhaps refreshed, the expedition returned to the Falklands for a little while to await the Antarctic summer season.

The ships were made ready by early December. Ross' plan was to sail south on the meridian 55° W in the expectation of reaching Louis Phillippe's Land, the French territory in Antarctica which had been discovered by Dumont d'Urville five years earlier, and then to follow the coastline between the land and the pack ice as far south as could be penetrated. If baulked in this endeavour, his second plan was to sail east to the meridian on which Captain James Weddell in 1823 had reached latitude 74° 15'S in the hope of finding a clear sea in which they could penetrate further south.

Ross was full of confidence and optimistic about success – or at least projecting it to the men under his leadership. Some members of the expedition were not so optimistic about success. They privately mumbled their doubts. Some were immensely weary of exploration on the high and difficult seas, a voyage that would be compounded by dangerous icebergs.

Be that as it may, the expedition left Port Louis on the morning of 17 December 1842 and bravely headed south. As far as leaving the Falklands was concerned, there was no reluctance on anyone's part. A miserable time had been spent there. Several, however, would have preferred to head north

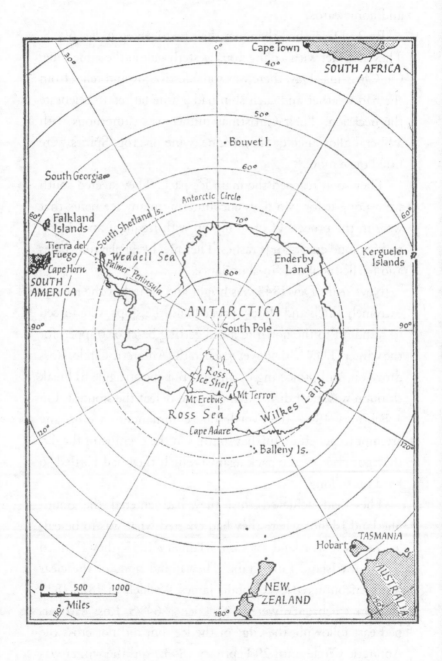

and homewards.

By 24 December, they met their first iceberg in lat. 60° S. They also met with a dangerous westerly gale at the same time. On Christmas Day, there was some festive joy and relief from the bad weather and each ship had a 'fine fat ox' to celebrate the occasion. Their Christmas dinner was sumptuous with a liberal allowance of champagne, wine or grog. Spirits were lifted once more.

They soon reached the main ice pack. They steered south west along it for two days encountering many ice bergs that were in the process of breaking up with frequent and nerve-racking loud cracks and crashes. They met lively playful whales and livelier penguins in abundance.

New Year's Day 1843 was bright and clear, but the ice was extremely thick and closely packed and the ships were forced to stand off to the north to avoid getting beset or trapped for the winter. They had not yet reached the Antarctic Circle. Ross drove on, still projecting optimism. But the struggle to break through was most difficult and would defeat the stoutest. On 1 February 1843, the expedition's commander gave up any attempt to penetrate further south. On the evening of the 4th, they got clear of the pack against which they had battled so hard for so long.[8]

They had achieved this: they had entered the South Shetland Islands where they had charted what was to be cal-led James Ross Island and, on 5 January 1843, they claimed Cockburn Island for Britain. They found none of the clear water encountered by Captain James Weddell in 1822-1823 and, on 4 February, were in pack ice at 64° S. Ross had tur-ned east following the edge of the ice, but did not cross the Antarctic Circle until 29 February 1843. And the winter was

8   Ross, *Ross in the Antarctic*, pp. 168-201.

not long off closing in.

Ross, being no fool, realised that the season was fast closing down and that the ships, therefore, should start on the homeward journey.[9] Members of the expedition were mightily relieved, but kept quiet about it. Their commander had been stopped by a great wall barrier of thick ice in the most dangerous of the Antarctic seas.

* * * * *

In sum, Ross' Antarctic adventure over three dangerous voyages was a great achievement if not a total success. Nothing ever is. The first voyage was the most important and successful. Not only had he found on that voyage an open sea leading deep into the Antarctic continent's fringe of ice cliffs, he had accurately charted hundreds of miles of sea along the Antarctic coast. The results were impressive for Ross combined the qualities of a first-class naval officer with those of a first-class scientist. He was truly one of the great men of the British scientific enlightenment of the early days of Queen Victoria's reign. Many years were to pass before Antarctica was explored again. When it was, his charts and findings proved invaluable to Scott, Shackleton and Amundsen, amongst others.

The Voyage Home

The third attempt to reach the south magnetic pole had to be given up as the way was barred, much to the private disappointment of James Clark Ross. The colours were hoisted symbolically in a last salute and farewell to the southern ice – a salute that recognised the overwhelming power of nature. At the same time as a mute gesture to history, a barrel was

---

9   Howgego, *Encyclopedia of Exploration.*

Alexander Smith's sketches on the final voyage

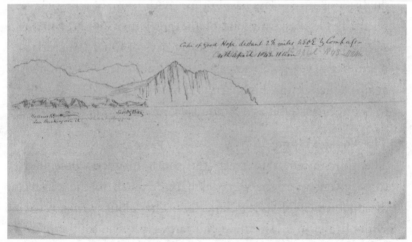

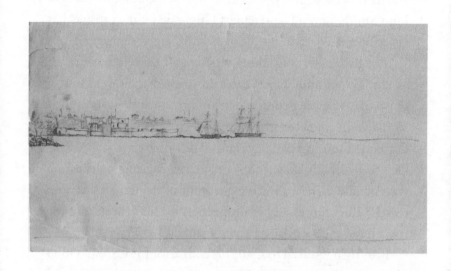

thrown overboard. It contained a statement of the position and date (71° 31' S, longitude 14° 51' W; 4 March 1843) signed by all the officers of the *Erebus* and *Terror*, including Alexander John Smith, now a Lieutenant. (This sealed 'time capsule' has never been recovered, but bears Smith's faded signature).

The barometer was falling rapidly and the wind was rising as the *Erebus* and *Terror* carefully picked their way out of the pack. They feared a collision with an iceberg but good seamanship got them through. As they emerged, a fierce gale descended causing two days and nights of great anxiety. Ross had turned back none too soon. A roaring line of crashing waves could be heard hitting the front of the ice pack behind them.[10] Ross expressed his admiration for his officers and the two crews, their vigilance, energy and cool courage.

Ross then resolved to shape his course for the Cape of Good Hope. On 4 April 1843, the two ships of the expedition anchored in Simon's Bay close to HMS *Winchester*, the flagship of Admiral Percy. There was not a single person on the *Erebus* and *Terror* in sick bay, a singular achievement of the care that Ross had taken of the health, morale and diet of the two ships' companies. Few other commanders of large-scale exploration had brought home such a result which, at the turn into the twentieth century, profoundly influenced the values of the great Norwegian polar explorer Roald Amundsen.

With Ross' final exploration, a century of feverish activity in the Antarctic Circle ceased. It was the end of an epoch and the continent of Antarctica was to lay quiet and undisturbed until the end of the nineteenth century. The Jules-Sébastien César Dumont d'Urville, Charles Wilkes and James Clark Ross expeditions were the last of a series of expeditions to the Antarctic for close on seventy years. The siege of the South

10 Mill, *The Siege of the South*, pp. 322-3.

Pole had ended at least until the beginning of the twentieth century.

It cannot be said that the third season in Antarctica had added much to the success of the British expedition under Ross. The chief glory was achieved in the first. The terrible strain of the final two years had told heavily on the officers including Alexander Smith, despite his promotion.

Ross, while not necessarily by any means a broken man, was not the man he had been. But no commander could not have been jaded at the end of such a long and dangerous epic sea journey. The third voyage south had been the worst of the three in terms of weather and impenetrable ice. Ross' quick perception and sound intuition, however, had not entirely left him. He was prepared to turn back when he saw the writing was finally on the wall.

As a personality, James Clark Ross for some reason does not come through to us as vividly as James Cook. This in itself is a shame. As the Antarctic historian Ian Cameron put it, he remains something of an enigma.[11] He was most certainly a God-fearing intensely patriotic man who cared for his ship's company and took determined initiative in promoting their career interests in the Royal Navy as clearly demonstrated in his mentorship of Alexander John Smith. Ross was clearly like Cook a supremely competent seaman, a man of courage and the most fearless and determined ice navigator of the whole of the nineteenth century (and maybe the twentieth century), whose achievements were based on most careful planning and astute judgement. He was a product of his age, environment and strict naval training as a youth – a naval officer of the days of *Pax Britannica*, a real hero of the Kipling mould. He served his country with great distinction.

---

11 Cameron, *Lodestone and Evening Star*, p. 232.

After repairs and refitting at Simon's Bay, South Africa, the Ross expedition proceeded to St Helena arriving there on 13 May 1843, staying for a week and then going on to the Ascension Islands (briefly for three days) on 25 May and to Rio de Janeiro on 18 June where more magnetic observations were conducted. They finally sighted English shores early in the morning of 2 September 1843. On 5 September, the *Erebus* and *Terror* were to be found anchored off Folkestone having arrived there at midnight on the previous night from where Ross immediately went ashore and travelled by coach to London, leaving Alexander Smith and other senior officers in charge of the *Erebus* and *Terror*. Ross was most anxious to report his findings personally and as soon as possible to the Lords of the Admiralty. He knew without a shadow of a doubt that he had reached the apex of his naval career.

The crews of the *Erebus* and *Terror* were paid off at Woolwich on 23 September 1843 having been away from England for about four and a half years.

On that day, Alexander Smith left the *Erebus* which had been his home for four years and five months. He had been a part of a thrilling discovery and an extraordinary set of circumstances that were to dwell within him for the rest of his life. The expedition, however, may have had a permanent impact on his health.

On his return, despite the immediate response being strangely muted, James Clark Ross was eventually showered with accolades. As well as receiving the Founder's Medal of the Royal Geographical Society that he had already heard about while still in the Falklands after his second Antarctic voyage, he was awarded the Gold Medal of the Royal Geographical Society of Paris. The following year after his return, he was given a knighthood and later was awarded an honorary Doctorate of Common Law at Oxford University. The Gold Medal of Paris, however, pleased Ross the most as it was recognition from his nation's rival.

Soon after his return on 18 October 1843, James Ross married Anne Coulman under the condition that he would participate in no more polar voyages. Francis Crozier was best man and Edward Bird was amongst those that signed the register.

In 1847, Ross published *A Voyage of Discovery and Research in the Southern and Antarctic Seas* in two volumes. He wrote this while settled quietly as a country gentleman of Buckinghamshire in Aston Abbotts, Aylesbury, but he had worn himself out to a degree both physically and mentally in the service of his country. He also found writing a difficult and laborious task. He was more a man of action than anything else, but he wrote the books with typical determination.

In the first instance, Ross was offered the command of the great new and elaborate expedition to discover the North West Passage for the British Government. He quietly refused on the basis of his promise to his wife Anne and the fact that he was still too drained from his Antarctic expedition of 1839-1843. The command was then offered and accepted by his friend Sir John Franklin. Captain Francis Crozier, also a close friend, was chosen as Franklin's second-in-command.

In 1845, Captain Sir John Franklin RN with Crozier led a large well-equipped expedition to complete the conquest of the Canadian Arctic and to find the fabled mystical North West Passage connecting the North Atlantic to the North Pacific. Franklin had returned to England from Van Diemen's Land in June 1844. They sailed on Ross' two famous ships, the *Erebus* and *Terror* which had been fitted out with steam engines. But the elaborate expedition was fated never to return. One hundred and twenty-nine men of the Royal Navy disappeared into the icy snowy wastes.

In the summer of 1848, James Ross was strongly urged by the determined Lady Franklin to take command of the third and most costly of the Admiralty's search missions to find the *Erebus* and *Terror*. He reluctantly agreed and in doing so broke his vow to his wife Anne. HMS *Enterprise* and HMS *Investigator* were placed under his command. Both ships had been reinforced and fitted with iron-plated bows and removable winter roofs. Ross would not hear of using steamships. He believed that sailing ships handled the polar regions better. Ross' orders were issued on 9 May 1848 and he departed on 12 May. His search was arduous, but fruitless and he had exhausted himself and his rescue crews by 1849.[12]

James Clark Ross took part in no further active service though he continued to be consulted as the highest authority in Britain on polar navigation. He was made a Rear Admiral in 1856. He died in his home at Aston Abbotts, Aylesbury[13] on 3 April 1862. His wife Anne had predeceased him in 1857, leaving issue of three sons and a daughter.

Ross' oil portrait by Stephen Pierce formerly hung in the Painted Hall at Greenwich, but was transferred to the National Portrait Gallery in London, which also possesses the plaster medallion by Bernhard Smith,[14] Alexander John Smith's

---

12 Andrew Lambert, *Franklin: Tragic Hero of Polar Navigation*, Faber and Faber, London, 2009, pp. 184-92.

13 Aylesbury is the picturesque county town of Buckinghamshire about 27 km (17 miles) north-east of Oxford. It lies in the valley of Aylesbury north of the Chiltern Hills. It has architectural fragments of its medieval and Tudor past (the medieval gateway and the King's Head Inn). The murder-mystery television series (Midsommer Murders (1997-) is filmed in the town and its environs.

14 'Ross, Sir James Clark (1800-1862)' in Sidney Lee (ed.), *Dictionary of National Biography*, Smith, Elder and Co., London, 1897, pp. 265-6.

younger sculptor brother who also migrated to Australia in the gold rushes of the early 1850s. During his retirement, Ross kept in contact with Alexander Smith as much as possible.

James Clark Ross and his wife are buried in the churchyard at Aston Abbots. The story of his Antarctic adventures leaves no doubt about his fearlessness, resolution and ability as an ice navigator. His approach to scientific investigation was painstaking. He was on a parallel with James Cook in regard to his concern about the health and welfare of his officers and his men. He was a faithful mentor to Alexander John Smith who repaid him in absolute loyalty. His geographical discoveries were of tremendous significance in opening the road to Antarctica and preparing the way for the discoveries of Scott, Shackleton and Amundsen in the twentieth century.

Sir James Clark Ross RN in later life, portrait by Stephen Pierce

*   *   *   *   *

Alexander Smith was full of joy when the *Erebus* left Rio as it was the last foreign port they had to drop anchor in before heading for home. He was clearly sick and tired by this time of the drudgery involved in the tasks for so long, 'for we have all had sufficient of that work and hope not to see the Instruments again until they go over the side at Chatham' (which he believed at the time was their destination).

When he reached England, his plan was to go on to half-pay as a reserve for perhaps twelve months (or less) and then endeavour to seek an appointment with the Australia Station of the Royal Navy and thus get back to Sarah Aubrey Read. In this plan, he was well aware of unreserved support and patronage by Sir James Clark Ross, his mentor and friend.

While Alexander Smith was uncertain at the time about the exact future of the Royal Navy's Australia Station, it functioned until 1913. When he returned to Tasmania, he became a part of the Australia Station's history, part of the Imperial presence in Australia. And until his death in 1872, he played a significant role in Australian political, cultural, social and economic life.

As he never went to sea again with the Royal Navy after he arrived in Hobart, Alexander Smith was destined to play a peripheral role in the Australia Station as such, as he was posted to look after the magnetic observatory that had been set up by Ross near Hobart before his first venture into the Antarctic. The major Royal Navy work in Australia was done by the Hydrographic Department in meticulously surveying the coastline making it safer for commercial coastal shipping.[15]

Alexander thought, at the time he arrived back from the epic voyage, that an appointment in the Australia Station was likely because of the growing interest by the French in the Polynesian Islands and the recent political squabbles with them. He viewed the colonies in Australasia as being too valuable to be neglected by the British Empire. And he was right!

*   *   *   *   *

Alexander's personal journey from Rio to England was not, however, a particularly happy one as he was beset with serious

15 John Bach, 'The Royal Navy in the South West Pacific: the Australia Station 1859-1913' *The Great Circle*, Vol. 5, No 2, 1983, pp. 116-32.

illness. He suffered from severe headaches, an ulcer just above his right knee that needed continuous dressing and he felt sick generally most of the time. He was eventually confined to his cabin bed as his condition deteriorated rapidly with a fever and uncomfortable eruptions all over his body which seemed to be something like Scarlet Fever. He became so ill that he was eventually moved by the surgeon to the open quarterdeck in a cot hung under a tent foxed on to the larboard side.

His strength was fast failing; he had fainting fits, palpitations of the heart and 'horrid nervous fits'. Captain Ross was extremely worried about his health. Hooker and McCormick as the ships' surgeons believed that nothing more could be done for him than what had already been done except to place him out on the deck in the fresh salty air. There was a strong belief at the time in the curative powers of fresh air. Alexander Smith was indeed at death's door. But the crisis fortunately passed. Alexander's fever abated and he began to recover.

The severe illness that Smith had suffered in the last lap of the voyage indeed may have weakened his heart and could have been the root cause of his final illness when he was fifty-eight years of age in rural Victoria, Australia.

His complaint had deeply puzzled the surgeons on both ships, especially as he had changed suddenly from being in a robust healthy condition that he had maintained for over four years of the epic expedition. Nevertheless, he was eventually able to walk to dinner in the mess and hold down the normal heavy meals. He began again to look forward to seeing his family. He was pleased that they were going to dock and pay off at Woolwich rather than the original destination of Chatham.

He was entirely off the sick list only a day or two before they docked at Woolwich, but he looked forward to being with his father and mother and family and friends, to walking around their beautiful garden at Cottingham in the enjoyable weather of England 'after all our horrid, horrid days cruising in the most Horrible South'.[16]

Thus he saw himself as returning from a relentless battle against the ice, a battle against the forces of nature itself. At the time he was writing this last of the many letters he had written during the epic expedition, the pilot was just coming up alongside them to guide them through the English Channel and direct the *Erebus* and *Terror* up the Thames River to Woolwich.

---

16 Alexander Smith to his father, HMS *Erebus*, 21 June 1843, Rio Harbour; Alexander to Emma, HMS *Erebus*, Entrance of the English Channel, August 29th & 4th September, 1843.

8

Aftermath
The Tasmanian Years

... for many still felt the psychological scars of previous polar expeditions and showed little enthusiasm
for another tilt at a frozen snow-covered windmill
... [James Clark] Ross and [Francis] Crozier, both of
whom, two years after returning from the Antarctic,
still found their hands shaking when holding a
glass.[1]

On a polar expedition that took nearly four and a half years
to complete, every action was part and parcel of survival and
automatically geared to that end. Life experience had been
for Alexander Smith and the rest of the officers and crews a
war against the forces of nature – the dangerous ice floes and
gales that stalked the southern seas. Day-to-day life followed
a terribly narrow line restricted to doing what was absolutely
necessary. Almost everything else was a dull nightmare-
filled sleep in bunks struggling against the perpetual cold.
Nothing much else was permissible as it used up too much
energy. Ordinary existence was in icy suspended animation.

---

1   Cited in Michael Durey, 'Exploration At The Edge: Reassessing The Fate
of Sir John Franklin's Last Arctic Expedition', *The Great Circle*, Vol. 30, No 2,
2008, pp. 15-16.

The voyagers were constantly on guard against the threat of death. Sensitivities had to be blunted so that one didn't go to pieces in unexpected emergencies that had the potential to destroy the fragile fabric of the *Erebus* and the *Terror* despite their reinforcements. Vigilance was a twenty-four-hour-a-day awareness full of stress.

The closeness of companionship aboard such confining vessel spaces was absolutely necessary. The continued re-awakening of comradeship, of friendship between Alexander Smith, his fellow officers and the ships' crews helped each man escape the abyss of loneliness away from loved ones. Everyone realised that interpersonal conflicts would cause things to fall apart.

The dreams that Smith had of Sarah Aubrey Read and the prospects of a loving married future helped him to draw out the best essence from every moment. He stored up his romantic attachment as a protection against the onslaught of depression and even oblivion. On board the *Erebus*, Alexander Smith eked out a closed, hard and at times exhausting exis-tence in which, every now and then (and quite unexpectedly), a flame of heavy and terrible longing burst through. For nearly four and a half years, he had had a desperate psychological struggle to maintain calmness. In the Antarctic, the silent war against the ice had always been with him.

In contrast with the perpetual freezing white, the vitality, culture and colour of Hobart Town and the times of respite and recreation seemed like a heavenly existence – a memory of enchantment that embraced him through thick and thin, through the most dangerous moments and hours. The very idea of dropping anchor in the Derwent remained in Alexander Smith's mind a most joyful expectation to hold on to in dangerous circumstances.

In August 1843, Alexander Smith was pleased and relieved to reach Woolwich on the Thames – the final destination of the epic Antarctic expedition. At last the days and nights of cruising 'in the most Horrible South' were over. When the *Erebus* was paid off, he was free at last to go on leave and visit his family at Cottingham. They already knew of his engagement to Aubrey and his intention to return to Hobart Town to marry her as soon as he was able to acquire a new posting with the Royal Navy in the Australia Station. But first, he needed to get over his psychological scars and physical fatigue.

During his shore leave with his family, Alexander, no doubt, frequently reflected on his experiences at sea and indeed on his whole career in the Royal Navy while quietly recreating himself and convalescing. Because of his close-to-death experience of an unknown but sustained fever between Rio and Woolwich, the last leg of the mammoth journey, he worked hard to prepare for his marriage and to restore himself to full health through rest and other healthy means such as fresh food, pleasant sociability and relaxing exercise. Cottingham was the ideal place for him to be after the dangerous expedition into the ice – in beautiful rural surroundings and with his family of loved ones and friends. There were tranquil lanes for strolling by the river and in the woods and walkways among the gardens. Cottingham boasted of affording pleasant walks in different directions. And all the while, Alexander meditated and gradually relaxed and, step by step, regained his old vigour. Time heals, and he looked forward eagerly to his reunion with Aubrey. And yet memories of his exciting experiences at sea sometimes came flooding back to him as he recovered his health wandering the lanes of the small village during the sunnier days.

He had been, by that time, in the service in the Navy for

some seventeen years in all climates and conditions. The first four were as a Volunteer First Class Midshipman, from the tender age of fourteen. He was one of the survivors of the fearful night of 5 December 1830 when HMS *Thetis*, a frigate, was wrecked on the cliff-face of the Island of Cape Frio in South America. Afterwards he spent three and a half years service in the remote East Indian Station aboard HM Sloop *Harrier* captained by Sir Spencer Vassall. During that time, he was engaged in at least two dangerous but successful military engagements against Malay pirates in the Straits of Malacca.

He later volunteered in even more arduous service under Sir James Clark Ross in a search expedition for missing whaling vessels with the ultimate but thwarted hope of pursuing the fabled North-West Passage. His conduct and service during that voyage won him the praise, friendship, patronage and mentorship of Sir James Clark Ross. He then spent a few months service on the north coast of Spain in the Bay of Biscay after which he joined HM Surveying vessel *Mastiff* on a major survey of the windswept bleak Orkney Islands in the extreme north of Scotland.

Gaining an outstanding reputation, he was especially selected by Ross in a pivotal role as Senior Mate of HMS *Erebus* for the great but highly dangerous expedition of Antarctica between 1839 and 1843. In August 1841 after nearly fifteen years of dedicated service as a Mate, he was promoted to Second Lieutenant aboard the *Erebus* in the isolated Falkland Islands. The expedition was not completed until September 1843.[2]

All these thoughts of past experience continued to roll around in Smith's mind. A major chapter in his life was beginning to close and another to open.

---

2   Copy of an undated letter signed by Alexander John Smith, circa 1845.

In the course of his seventeen years of service at sea between 18 December 1826 and 23 September 1843, Alexander Smith had been keenly aware of the diversity among the sea officers he was serving with. He had sailed with men of great families and with others promoted from the lower deck; with companions who had never opened a book and with men of poetic and literary or scientific disposition; with captains who could scarcely write a coherent dispatch without help.

Although most sea officers came from the middle rank of British society, this species had such a bewildering series of sub-species that only an erudite observer like Alexander, brought up among the complexities of the English caste system, could find his way among them. He did so astutely by assessing their origin and present status.

There was a great difference in wealth. Those like Alexander who had to live on their naval pay led a meagre anxious life as promotion in peacetime was an extraordinary slow process. Nevertheless, they were all marked with 'the stamp of their profession' as sea officers: 'rich or poor, loutish or polite', they had been battered by the elements and many of them by the monarch's imperial enemies.[3]

Even a most recently promoted lieutenant like Alexander Smith had served all his youth at sea from the age of fourteen (or even twelve like James Clark Ross). There had been endless vigilant waiting in the wastes of the sea together with irregular bursts of furious activity. For Alexander and his shipmates on the three dangerous voyages into the Antarctic, the bursts of furious activity had been not so occasional, but rather daily, regular and frequent leading to a sea fatigue that took time to overcome, to heal even in the best of surroundings.

Eventually, Alexander was offered and accepted a senior

---

3   Patrick O'Brian, *The Surgeon's Mate*, Folio Society, London, 2010, p.32.

position at the Rossbank Magnetic Observatory near Hobart, Van Diemen's Land. But would this be as dull as dishwater after his adventurous seafaring life climaxed with a Homeric Odyssey and heroic voyages full of tensions and adventures into the unknown in search of the Golden Fleece – the South Magnetic Pole? Geographically, they had ranged over the world: the Atlantic, Indian, Pacific and the Antarctic Oceans and in diverse climates and cultures.

By the age of thirty-three in 1845, Alexander Smith may have been worn out by his chosen vocation as far as active service was concerned. Most men would have been. Such a seafaring life was an abrupt journey from one stressful episode to another, of involvement in one exotic culture after another in vastly different parts of the world. His whole existence from the age of fourteen had had more than just the mere atmosphere of a Homeric epic. All such experience built up to a climax of historical dimension and, then suddenly, a reduction in the tension of life took place. His next more sedate and peaceful destination was to be Hobart and joyful marriage to Aubrey.

*   *   *   *   *

On 8 May 1844, Alexander's mother Jane Mary wrote Sarah Aubrey Read an anxious letter welcoming her into the Smith family. By this time, Jane Mary Smith's health was declining. She had been ailing for some time and she was to die the following year on Saturday, 13 December 1845 at the age of sixty-two.

In her letter to her prospective daughter-in-law, she felt she could not let Alexander depart for Tasmania without wishing her the best for their future together, that their marriage

would be one of 'proliferation' like her own. That is, to produce metaphorically 'flower buds', or many children. She then
continued:

> … we all feel in the prospect of happiness in his union
> with yourself of whom he speaks in the most grati-
> fying & affectionate terms he is of course we feel most
> anxious for future prospects his marriage with you will
> be one of the most important events in his life, there-
> fore we cannot but feel deeply interested in his welfare
> combined with your own. We sincerely congratulate
> you on his appointment to the Observatory as it gives
> you the opportunity of remaining some length of
> time with your relatives and friends after your union.

Jane Mary expressed a hope that they would all meet Aubrey
as she was expected soon to make a visit to England. They
were keen to meet her 'as a much loved daughter and the Wife
of our own dear and very affectionate Alexander'.[4]

Four of Alexander John Smith's brothers and sisters had
married before him: Jane aged thirty-three to John Fewson
aged thirty-one on 11 February 1841; John aged twenty-six
to Emma Juliana Gray, his cousin aged thirty-three, on 4
November 1841; Edward aged twenty-nine to Mary Thetis
Partridge on 17 August 1842; and Henry aged thirty-four,
Alexander's elder brother, to Jane Hardy on 22 February
1844.[5]

Alexander was then to be the fifth of Lord Henry and Jane
Mary's children to take the vows of matrimony.

*   *   *   *   *

4   Mrs. Jane Mary Smith to Miss Sarah Aubrey Read, 8 May 1844,
Cottingham.

5   Note by Alexander John Smith, 'List of Birthdays' 1844; Attwood, *The
Wilsons of*, pp. 29-30.

Lieutenant Alexander John Smith of the Royal Navy, the second son of Lord Henry and Jane Mary Smith of Cottingham, Yorkshire, England, was married to Sarah Aubrey Read, the second daughter of Captain George Frederick Read Esquire of New Town, Hobart, by the Reverend T.J. Ewing in St John's Church of England, New Town, Hobart, on 12 October 1844.[6]

Sarah Aubrey Read was the daughter of George Read's first wife Elizabeth Driver who he married in St Phillip's Church in Sydney, New South Wales, on 13 March 1816. They had one son and two daughters, the youngest being Sarah Aubrey, who was born on 25 February 1820. Elizabeth, the daughter of transported convicts,[7] died on 19 August 1821 at the age of twenty-four. She was buried in the Old St David's Church Yard, Hobart. Aubrey was not even two years of age.

The immediate ancestors of Sarah Aubrey Smith (née Read) provide some fascinating connections that are found occasionally in early Australian family histories. Her grandmother on her mother's side, Elizabeth Needham (née Gore), was tried at the Old Bailey in London on 19 July 1786, a couple of years before the Colony of New South Wales was founded. She was guilty of stealing clothing to the value of thirty shillings. Her occupation was listed as servant or needle worker. At about the age of twenty-five years, she was sentenced to transportation for seven years and left England on the *Lady Penrhyn* in May 1787 as part of the First Fleet under Governor Arthur Phillip. (Henry Needham and Elizabeth had a son that she left behind in England.) It was intended that the overcrowded *Lady Penrhyn* would transport the whole of the women prisoners in the Fleet amounting to 104 as well

---

6   *Launceston Examiner*, 19 October 1844.

7   John & Elizabeth Driver of Sydney Town.

as five children.

Elizabeth had a child to a marine of the First Fleet. Soon after arriving in Sydney Cove of Port Jackson on 9 February 1788, she was assaulted by a soldier 'for refusing to go into the woods' with him – to provide sexual favours. On 17 February 1788, she married William Snailham, also a First Fleet convict.

William Snailham (a.k.a. Snaleham, Snailam, Strachan) was tried at the Old Bailey in London on 21 April 1784 on two separate charges of stealing clothing to the value of thirty-nine shillings. He was transported for seven years at the age of about twenty-one years. Snailham left England on the *Scarborough* on May 1787. He seems to have died in 1796, after which Elizabeth Snailham married John Driver. She bore John Driver three children in Sydney Town, one being Elizabeth Driver – Aubrey Smith's mother. When John Driver died in 1810, Elizabeth married Henry Marr, but bore no more children. She died in 1825 as Elizabeth Marr.

Aubrey Smith's grandfather, John Driver, had come out to Australia on the Second Fleet (*Neptune*, *Scarborough* and *Surprize*) as one of the 1,063 convicts transported from England in December 1789. He was under sentence for seven years transportation. Some time after his arrival, then, he married the widow Elizabeth Snailham. Together they made an enterprising couple and by 1803 were known as storekeepers in Old Castlereagh Street, Sydney Town. Their retail store was styled the Universal Warehouse and was the first general retail business of any consequence in the Colony. An early advertisement claimed that salt butter might be purchased from their shop for three shillings a pound. They stocked a wide range of goods.

Their daughter, also Elizabeth Driver, was probably born

in 1797. Aged about nineteen, she was to marry Captain George Frederick Read, Aubrey's father, at St Phillip's Church of England in Sydney on 13 March 1816. By this time, her father John Driver had been dead for six years and had been replaced by Henry Marr. After their wedding, George and Elizabeth Read headed for Tasmania and Hobart Town where Sarah Aubrey Read was born at New Town.

In the meantime, Henry Marr clearly took over the Universal Store in Old Castlereagh Street from his wife Elizabeth when they married on 29 June 1811. On the property left to her by John Driver, Mrs Marr erected two new houses and the business continued in these under Marr's name, with the address of No 15 Castlereagh Street. The premises became well known in Sydney as Marr's Rooms.

Marr, originally an innkeeper in Pitt Street, added sheep and wool to the Castlereagh Street business. He raised sheep on his farm at South Creek and sold merino rams on the Castlereagh Street premises. When his wife died without further issue, he took on a second wife, Ann Wood.

Henry Marr was listed in the November 1828 Census of New South Wales as having arrived on the *Royal Admiral* in 1799 as a transported convict, but by 1828 he was free from servitude, that is having completed his sentence. Significantly, he was also listed as a merchant of Castlereagh Street, Sydney (page 261). He died at No 15 Castlereagh Street in 1835 and his widow Ann Wood in 1848. The building then passed into the hands of his son to Ann Wood, Henry James Marr, but that's another story.[8]

8   Malcolm Sainty & Keith A. Johnson, *Census of New South Wales November 1828*, Library of Australian History, Sydney, 1980 , p.261; <firstfleet.uow.edu.au/details.aspx?surname>, accessed 24/6/2011; Charles H. Bertie, 'Old Castlereagh Street', p.44.

On 24 November 1824 at St. David's, Hobart, Read, a widower, married Margaret Terry who became Aubrey's step-mother. Margaret, whose family were flour millers, brought her up. She had six sons and four daughters to George Read. He died at his residence 'Leyburne', New Town, on 23 July 1860. In all, George had thirteen children to his two successive wives.[9]

Captain George Frederick Read, Sarah Aubrey's redoubtable father, was born on 29 September 1788 in London and went to sea in the merchant navy at the age of eleven. Apparently, he was engaged in the East India Company's maritime service until 1808. He visited the Derwent settlement of Hobart Town that year and again in 1812, but he was annoyed and disappointed by having his cargo commandeered and his ship's crew placed on rations in the port.

Despite this setback, it is believed that he was the first to bring a merchant vessel through the Torres Strait to Hobart Town, apparently from Batavia. Read continued a lucrative trade between the emerging settlement of Hobart Town, Sydney, Batavia, Calcutta and some southern Chinese ports.

In May 1814, as master and part-owner of the *Amelia*, a brig built in Calcutta, he shipped tea, sugar, rum and tobacco – all valuable cargo – from Calcutta to Sydney and then returned with a cargo of whale oil and wine. In 1816-18, he made several commercial voyages in his brig *Lynx*. In 1816, he married Elizabeth Driver and was granted a town allotment in Sydney as well as 500 acres in the countryside, but he began to suffer badly in the Sydney climate from asthma. By this time, he was a wealthy man. Under doctor's advice, he moved to the colder climate of Hobart Town on the *Sophia*, arriving there on 11 July 1816. His wife joined him with their child

9   Ahnentafel Chart for Sarah Aubrey Read (Merilyn Pedrick Collection).

on 11 October that year and they made their home on the Derwent.

Read eventually transferred his growing merchant business to Hobart Town. There, he formed partnerships with W.A. Bethune and Charles McLachlan to form a larger company that brought further wealth. In 1819, he was granted 800 acres at Redlands and four government servants (that is, transported convicts). Read built a stone warehouse in 1822, the first of others, and was appointed a magistrate. He helped found the Bank of Van Diemen's Land and was its managing director between 1827 and 1849. He took a considerable part in the colony's development – reputed to be the richest colony in the British Empire at the time, especially its lucrative maritime and mercantile industries. Read obtained other properties and grew wheat, made bricks and established commercial salmon ponds. His ships also took part in sealing and whaling activities.

A strongly-held family legend has it that George Frederick Read was actually the eldest son of George, the Prince of Wales (later George IV) and Mrs Maria Fitzherbert, but no direct evidence, link or proof has ever been uncovered. The connection is tenuous, even though Prince George and Mrs Maria Anne Fitzherbert (whose second husband had died in 1781) were privately married at her house in 1785 in what was probably a Roman Catholic ritual. Three years later, George Frederick Read was born in London.

Prince George denied the marriage in order to conciliate a hostile parliament. He broke with Fitzherbert when he was installed a prince regent when the king was permanently disabled by insanity. (He married Caroline of Brunswick in 1795, but soon separated from her and returned to Fitzherbert.) The whole matter of this vaguely possible but improbable royal connection is shrouded in mystery. Despite the research efforts undertaken by Lillie Muriel and Amy Maud Smith, the twin daughters of Alexander Henry Smith, son of Alexander and Aubrey Smith, it is unlikely ever to be established. The twins found pages were missing from every document they examined.[10] The given name of George and the date of his birth are only minor unconvincing points to confirm the family legend.

For Sarah Aubrey Read to have both convict and royal connections is the stuff of historical romance. Nevertheless, the convict connections have been proven.

On his marriage to Aubrey, Alexander Smith took up a senior position, as a naval officer on the naval payroll, at the Rossbank Magnetic Observatory under Lieutenant Joseph Kay as Director. In effect, he directly managed the day-to-day work there, continuing the painstaking scientific observations commenced during the Ross Antarctic Expedition. He held the appointment until 1852 when he resigned and, after a visit home to England, proceeded with Aubrey and their three children to Victoria.

Three daughters were born in Hobart: Aubrey Emma Elizabeth on 27 August 1845 (d. 26 October 1914), Georgina Jane on 8 June 1847 (d. 31 May 1899) and Frances Maria on 8 July 1849 (d. 7 April 1921).

Alexander and Aubrey subsequently had four other children: Alexander Henry was born in Blackheath, England, on 21 April 1852 (d. 6 July 1935); Edith Margaret was born in Castlemaine, Victoria, on 15 August 1854 (d. 14 April 1906); Edward Bernhard was born 21 August 1857 in Castlemaine (d.

---

10 Ahnentafel Chart of Sarah Aubrey Read; *The Concise Dictionary of National Biography*, Vol.1, Oxford University Press, 1992, p.1016 (entry on Fitzherbert, Maria Anne, 1756-1837); Vol.2, pp.1125-6 (entry on George IV, 1762-1830).

Rossbank Magnetic Observatory, Hobart Town

19 April 1861) and Maud Margaret was born in Castlemaine on 15 September 1859 (d. 3 June 1946).[11]

Aubrey and Alexander, therefore, had seven children, but only one son survived into adulthood.

*   *   *   *   *

But back to Tasmania in the mid-1840s when Aubrey and Alexander were first married!

With the cessation of transportation to New South Wales in 1840, convicts were poured into Tasmania, where Aubrey and Alexander settled into marriage, at the rate of 4,000 a year, previously a matter of concern to Sir John Franklin when the Ross Antarctic Expedition was taking place. Alexander Smith would have had first-hand knowledge of this during his early sojourns in Hobart Town.

---

11 Modified Register for Captain Alexander John Smith.

Lieutenant Joseph Kay as a
fourteen-year-old midshipman

A marked feature of the Franklin term of office from 1837 was his support as lieutenant-governor to science, education and art, especially with the founding of The Royal Society of Tasmania which was also a passionate interest of the ebullient Lady Jane Franklin. Together, husband and wife forged a cultural and religious renaissance in the colony. Hobart Town became, for a time under the Franklins, the intellectual and educational centre of the Australian colonies.

The establishment of the Rossbank Magnetic Observatory had put Tasmania on the imperial scientific map. As we already know, Alexander Smith was later appointed there as a naval officer.

With the use of convict labour, Lady Jane Franklin built a beautiful little museum near Hobart. It was later used for storing apples. By 1853 when transportation to Tasmania ceased, the total number of convicts sent there had risen to 67,655 or more than half as many as were sent to the mainland between 1788 and 1868. The country was simply flooded with unemployed prisoners and bushranging was revived. By this time, Alexander Smith had married Sarah Aubrey Read and was working steadily each day at the Rossbank Observatory. Such work was demanding and had to be scientifically precise.

Before Ross and his expedition had even arrived on 17 August 1840, Sir John Franklin had surveyed several possible sites for the observatory that was to make Ross' task much easier. The design for the building that had to be erected without any use of metal had been sent to Franklin earlier from the Admiralty together with an authority to spend up to £208. He had all the materials at the ready when the *Terror* and *Erebus* arrived. Even the timber for the building had been cut to size.

In the afternoon of 18 August 1840, the day after the Ross Expedition arrived in Hobart Town to spend the three months of winter refitting, Ross and Franklin selected a site for the observatory where Alexander Smith was eventually to work and conduct observations close to the proposed Government House. The local sandstone had been quarried by convict labour to a sufficient depth to ascertain the geological character, a critical issue for a magnetic station which needed to be built on a deep layer of sandstone. Soon a forty-eight by sixteen foot wood and stone building held together without a single piece of iron (so that magnetic readings would not be distorted) was taking shape. After their first anchorage, Ross warped his ships to a nearby cove called Yacht Cove (later Ross Cove) to be refitted while he personally supervised the erection of the observatory. Franklin's preparations and ample convict labour ensured that the observatory was ready for term-day observations on 27 August 1840, only nine days after the Ross Expedition had arrived.[12] Later at Rossbank on his return to Hobart, Alexander Smith continued to conduct term-day observations from October 1844 to the end of the decade.

The site of the observatory was just on the northern side of

---

12 Andrew Lambert, *Franklin. Tragic Hero of Polar Navigation*, Faber and Faber, London, 2009, p. 130.

Rossbank Residence, Allport Library & Museum of Fine Arts

the present Government House. Apparently, convicts had excavated down about ten metres and formed a foundation from the cut blocks of sandstone. After the building was erected, the instruments had been installed on their sandstone pillars. The portable magnetometers from the *Terror* and *Erebus* had been set up nearby to calibrate the initial readings. Franklin organised a group of scientifically-inclined gentlemen volunteers to assist in taking the early readings. During the three months the *Terror* and *Erebus* stayed in Hobart, Ross and Lieutenant Joseph Kay worked hard to set up the observatory. (Lady Franklin had persuaded her husband to name it after Ross.)

When the two ships and their crews left for the Antarctic, Joseph Kay remained behind in Hobart in the position and title of Director of HM Magnetic Observatory at Hobart. Two mates from the ships were appointed by Ross to stay with him – Peter Scott and Joseph Dayman. Kay was reunited with his other shipmates when the Antarctic voyagers returned in considerable triumph and that second stay culminated in a much talked about ball held on board the ships. By this time, a building to accommodate the staff at Rossbank had been constructed. Soon the Rossbank site took on the appearance of a small pretty village.

The portable instruments were again brought ashore and further cross-readings were taken. Kay and his staff took readings of the earth's magnetic field hourly each day, apart from Sunday, and once a month every two and a half minutes for a whole day. This onerous work, which Alexander Smith was soon to face, became a concern for Kay in November 1842. He sought more people to lessen the strain. He complained that ceaseless work combined with its sedentary nature was affecting the health of the staff for they had no time for relaxation of any kind, nor exercise to preserve their health. While Kay remained Director, Alexander Smith took complete charge of the day-to-day running of the observatory.

In 1844 when Lieutenant Alexander Smith and Francis Simpson replaced Scott and Dayman, Hobart Town was still a small place with a population of twenty thousand, many of them convicts.

In Franklin's time, social and intellectual activities were centred on Government House. Kay, Franklin's nephew, was popular there; he sang and played the flute competently. He was one of a gifted circle of artists that included John Skinner Prout and Simpson de Wesselow, a nephew of Lady Jane Franklin. Meanwhile, Alexander Smith worked his heart out at the observatory every day except Sunday.

Simpson de Wesselow, a talented artist, produced several scenes around Rossbank Observatory during his few years in Hobart Town. Convict engraver and social portraitist Thomas Bock executed an oil painting of the observatory with Ross and Crozier portrayed in the foreground and Joseph Kay off to the side.

Kay became linked to one of Tasmania's foremost colonial families by marrying Maria Meredith, the fourth daughter of George Meredith of Cambria, Great Swan Port.

Lieutenant Alexander John Smith worked under Kay as Director from when he was appointed to Rossbank, but increasingly took on many of Kay's responsibilities. Kay turned up only occasionally at the observatory. His interest in the work had waned. By 1847, he was tired and bored and fretting about the effect his stay in Hobart was having on his prospects for promotion in the Royal Navy. He felt that Ross could have done more to progress his naval career. He was sick of 'the continuous and unvarying routine day and night without cessation'. He had now completed seven and a half years of observing work of hourly observation. Despite these claims, it was Alexander Smith who was conducting the majority of the work and providing staff with clear direction.

Kay was promoted to Commander at the time, but remained at Rossbank although the hourly observations were halted while his cottage was extended and made more comfortable. He seemed to have sought another better-paid local position, without success.

Because of the Crimean War, the Admiralty could not afford to spend so much on scientific pursuits. By 1851, Kay and Samuel Jeffrey, a volunteer, were the only ones left on the payroll at Rossbank Observatory. Alexander and Aubrey Smith and their three children had left for England. Alexander was considering his position with the Royal Navy after working so hard and well for many hours a day at the Rossbank Observatory in Hobart town.

Finally in 1853, the Admiralty ordered that the Rossbank Observatory be handed over to the Tasmanian Government. Jeffrey took over from Kay for a short period. Governor Denison, a practical-oriented engineer, saw the cost of the observatory as an indulgence and closed it down.

Kay became the private secretary to the eminent naval officer Sir Charles Hotham when he was appointed to replace La Trobe as Governor of Victoria. When Hotham died after the Eureka debacle, Kay was appointed Secretary to the Executive Council of Victoria in 1855 and held the post till his death from diabetes on 17 July 1875,[13] a few years after Alexander Smith's death in 1872.

While Alexander Smith was second-in-command at Rossbank in the 1840s carrying out and directing most of the relentless work, Joseph Kay had remained in charge as the years rolled by, but only in the form of a sinecure. Kay became most anxious about his chances of promotion with the passing years. In October 1848 when his patrons Franklin, Crozier and Ross were in the Arctic, he had written to Lord Beaufort in the Admiralty claiming: 'I was ordered here by Sir James Ross against my inclinations, who had no choice in the matter further than in the selection of the individual whom he thought most fitted for the charge'. It appears he was white-anting his own mentor.

On February 1851, the anxious Kay wrote again to Beaufort telling him he had been placed on half pay from 1 January 1850 and asked to be included on a list of candidates for full employment on a survey so he could get back to his profession and his native land. He did not receive a favourable response. It was not until 1853 that he was relieved when the Admiralty handed the Rossbank Observatory over to the Colony.[14] While Kay was not an Antarctic exploring hero, Alexander Smith had developed a fine reputation assisting Joseph Hooker in collecting important specimens that enhanced his great botanical work.

---

13 'Physics in Australia to 1945', <www.asap.unimelb.edu.au/bsparcs/physics/P000530p.htm>, accessed 10 June 2011.

14 Ross, *Ross in the Antarctic*, pp.221-2.

The 1840s was a turbulent time for Hobart Town. Land sales fell off and the cost of the police establishment increased. When the lieutenant governor, Sir John Eardley-Wilmot, took over from Sir John Franklin on 21 August 1843 and tried to increase taxation, he came into conflict with the Legislative Council. There was, nevertheless, an accumulating debt due to widespread economic depression in the Australian colonies.

Sir William Denison inherited these troubles when he was appointed in January 1847. In the late 1840s in Tasmania, the movement against transportation continued to gain political momentum and strength. By the time transportation ceased in 1853, the rush to the fabled Victorian gold-diggings had drawn a large proportion of Tasmania's adult male population across the strait to the mainland including a great number of convicts and ex-convicts. However, the diggings brought about a great demand at boom prices for Tasmanian timber, grain, potatoes and other products. With the cessation of transportation, the old name of Van Diemen's Land was officially changed to Tasmania.

Tasmania's first parliament under responsible government was called together on 2 December 1856.[15] Alexander and Aubrey had already departed earlier for a visit to England where their fourth child, a son, was born, as related. They then returned to Australia – not to Tasmania, but to the Victorian goldfields.

*   *   *   *   *

Alexander wrote to his mother a few months before her death in December 1845 describing his words as a few hurried lines

---

15 T.D., 'Tasmania' in A.W. Jose & H.J. Carter (eds), *The Australian Encyclopaedia*, Angus & Robertson, Sydney 1926, pp. 535-8.

so that his letter could be placed aboard a small vessel that was ready to leave the port at Hobart for Sydney carrying a bundle of mail. His comment captures the sense of isolation he may have felt living so far from the mother country. He took delight in informing her that at 11pm and 29 minutes on the day before, the 27 August, their first daughter Aubrey Emma was 'brought into the troubles of this world'. He reported that both mother and daughter were as well and comfortable as could be expected under the circumstances, although there was on one occasion some trouble – a crisis – and Aubrey's stepmother and the local doctor from New Town had to be called in. Aubrey had become almost delirious. 'Poor girl, she could not speak, only just gave me a smile. I am sure I could not for my tears and feelings half suffocated me'. There was great tension for some hours, but Aubrey finally began to recover. He then went on to say as a proud father that the baby 'is a very fine one', a handsome child with a 'pair of very large and very black eyes, a very high forehead, a nose like mine, and you know that's a handsome one, dark hair and a pretty smiling mouth…' He already found in his opinion his first daughter quite ladylike and well behaved 'like my own dear Aubrey'.

After more understandable gushing about his newly-born, he proudly described his garden to his mother and the rest of his family in England:

> Our garden is beautiful. We have all your spring flowers now blooming more luxuriantly, all the English trees are just putting forth their leaves and the Almond in full bloom & the bright green of the corn fields & the young grass makes this Country I think the most beautiful I ever saw out of old England – on the Evening of the 25th A [Aubrey] & I walked

a few hundred yards from our Cottage upon the Government Domain & it was one of the sweetest Evenings I ever enjoyed … The day had been most lovely & the sun was just sinking across the beautiful river Derwent, which where we were was about 2 miles broad. Most beautifully broken ground with beautiful clumps of trees all round us & below about 50 feet was the River as calm and silvery as ever I remember to have seen water.

There were a few rural sounds of 'lowing cattle' and a few boats 'puttering about just breaking the stillness of the water'. On the opposite bank of the Derwent, he could see a few houses 'with the many tints of the setting sun falling upon the land and sea'. To finish his landscape painting in words to his mother, the view of the town to their right was softened by the evening fog and smoke from the houses. Mt Wellington looked over the scene with its surface of 'pure white snow' and a 'fantastic column' of basalt just below the snow line.

The busy qualities of the port and town and the multitude of houses contrasted with the bright corn fields and the 'most lovely quietude of Country'. He quickly closed his letter with fondest regards as Aubrey called out at that moment for him to help her on some domestic matter.[16]

In his next extant letter to his family in England, he wrote about a trip – an almost land voyage – he and Aubrey took into the interior, leaving behind Aubrey Emma, now an infant, with her grandparents at New Town. For obvious reasons, Aubrey Emma was usually simply referred to as Emma in his letters.

The trip was in part an opportunity to visit old friends he had met during the time he spent in Hobart while on the

---

16 Alexander Smith to his mother, 28 August 1845, Van Diemen's Land .

Ross expedition some seven or so years earlier. They travelled by coach and various horse-drawn vehicles and enjoyed the countryside and the hospitality of various prominent home-steaders on various large properties. Clearly, it was a grand holiday for the couple – a brief respite for Alexander from the relentless demanding work at the observatory.

Their first visit was made to the prominent Kermode family who were considered by Alexander to be the wealthiest in Tasmania. William Kermode was a friend of Alexander's father-in-law and lived almost in the centre of Tasmania about seventy miles inland from Hobart Town. At Blackman River, Kermode met his two guests on the mail coach in his 'very handsome Phaeton and pair' and conveyed them up a 'pretty drive' of seven miles to his homestead. (Alexander had previously stayed there with Sir John Franklin, the lieutenant governor, and his captain Sir James Clark Ross). Kermode's place was:

A large majestic building of 3 stories with very ex-tensive outbuildings. Artificially he [Kermode] had brought the Blackman river round the House formed a superb lake from which many hundreds of acres of land are irrigated & at that time when all else is burnt up and parched for want of water, fine rich green grass & Clover form great relief to the Eye. Beautiful fountains and waterfalls constantly playing upon the sheet of water close to the House are 27 Black Swans & innumerable wild Duck, Pigeon, Teal &c. The former now become very rare in this Country are here perfectly tame a splendid Emu about 8 feet in front [of the house] is a fine open park like view for 5 or 6 miles ...[17]

17 Alexander Smith to E[mma] & M[aria], 7 April 1847, Hobarton [Hobart town].

William Kermode had been one of the 'patriotic six' along with Dry, Gregson, Fenton, Kerr and Swanston who resigned from the legislative council when Sir John Eardley-Wilmot as lieutenant-governor came in conflict with them over increased taxation measures. They questioned his right to exercise both a deliberative and casting vote.

When Sir William Denison replaced Eardley-Wilmot after he was dismissed by the British Parliament, he reinstated the 'patriotic six' on the legislative council. Thus Kermode was a powerful mover and shaker in Tasmanian politics.[18]

The stay at Kermode's mansion was a most pleasant respite for Aubrey and Alexander. To the right of the front of the building was 'a perfect garden' with a 'pretty creek' winding round behind the River South Esk with Craig Ellichie, a hill 'frowning dark and rocky over the House'. The drawing room windows provided an extensive view of the river. Beyond was the Lomond Mountain Range, the highest in Tasmania (5,000 feet high) and generally covered in snow. Plenty of recreational riding or driving was available for Kermode's guests and family. Aubrey and the other young ladies took their sketch books on these rides and made drawings of the scenery, no doubt on picnics.

Alexander claims in his vividly descriptive letter that 'the drawing mania' as he called it became so strong that during the last couple of evenings of their stay, the ladies drew each other's portrait. Wittily, Alexander described some of these efforts as 'most grotesque'. His artistic sensibilities were like those of the rest of his family.

Nevertheless, he preserved one of Aubrey done by a Miss Hammond which was a most striking likeness. He enclosed a tracing of it in his letter home to his family: 'Rough as it

---

18 T.D., 'Tasmania', p. 538.

is done you must be most careful of it and keep it until I return with the original'. Thus, he implies that his stay in Van Diemen's Land with his young family was only a sojourn; that one day he would return with them to England as his mother had earlier hoped.

After leaving Kermode's homestead mansion, Aubrey and Alexander moved on to Frederick von Stieglitz's castle-inspired homestead about eleven miles eastward. Von Stieglitz was a member of the Tasmanian Legislative Council at the time and another prominent and wealthy person.

According to Alexander, his home was the second largest on the island of Tasmania, a place called 'Killimoon' as Alexander spelt it (really 'Killymoon'), found on the Break O'Day Plains. The majestic mansion had been built about five years before the young married couple arrived for their visit. Alexander described it in rapturous terms:

> … it is the most complete place I have yet seen [in the Australian Colonies]. The Rooms are most superbly furnished, lofty & of great size, rich Marble Mantle pieces each costing in England 90 guineas, water laid on to all the bed rooms, Bathrooms either Hot or Cold as you feel inclined & Shower baths a handsome terrace on top of a high 3 storey house commands a most extensive view, everything kept up in great style.

The von Stieglitz family kept thoroughbred horses and a 'luxurious Carriage'. Nevertheless, privately to his family at home, he felt the day spent there rather vulgar. The von Steiglitz's – husband and wife – lived there alone. He found von Stieglitz 'a fine, kind, good hearted fellow', but he was not a 'shining star' of the legislative council, unlike Kermode, being of quieter and less political disposition.

The following morning, von Stieglitz drove the young couple 'in first rate tandem style' down the coast about seventeen miles where Alexander and Aubrey witnessed 'the finest scenery in the world'.[19]

Frederick von Stieglitz and William Kermode were the most significant of the 'Bunyip Aristocracy' of Van Diemen's Land and these visits demonstrate that Aubrey and Alexander Smith were mixing in most elevated circles of the wealthy colonial gentry. Alexander's involvement in the famed Ross expedition would have helped as an entrée along with the influence of his father-in-law, Captain George Frederick Read, also a prominent colonist of high distinction.

William Kermode, merchant and Tasmanian settler, was born in Port Erin, a small seaside place on the west coast of the Isle of Man in 1780. As a youth, he took up the sea as a career and made several voyages to India. In 1810, he married Anne Quayle of Castletown in the south of the Isle of Man, the island's capital.

Kermode first arrived at Hobart Town in late 1819 and then went on to Sydney with a cargo which he put in the hands of an agent. He made another voyage to Van Diemen's Land in 1821 and was granted 2,000 acres on the Salt Pan Plains near Ross, but he was declared bankrupt through mismanagement by his Sydney cargo agents. He returned to England in 1822 taking with him a Tasmanian Aboriginal boy, George Van Diemen, at Lieutenant Governor Sorrell's request. In 1823, Kermode again visited Australia with a large cargo intending to fulfil the settlement conditions of his land grant.

In Hobart Town, he was elected a director of the Sydney and Van Diemen's Land Packet Company and became, like Alexander's father-in-law George Read, a founding shareholder

19 Alexander Smith to E[mma] & M[aria].

of the Bank of Van Diemen's Land. He was granted another 1,000 acres in 1824 and bought 2,000 more, thus building up a property he called Mona Vale which Aubrey and Alexander Smith visited on their travelling holiday.

Kermode sailed for England in 1826 and returned the next year with his son and George Van Diemen. In June 1827, the land commissioners reported that he was improving and cultivating his excellent sheep walk.

After his wife and daughter joined him in May 1828, he set about turning Mona Vale into the showplace which Alexander Smith was deeply impressed with in 1847.

By 1834, his original modest timber house was replaced by a substantial brick building. Stone cottages for workers and farm buildings were added to make a complete homestead in the form of a private estate, all on English lines – the estate of a member of the well-off gentry, laid out and fenced, an expression of wealth and status.

Kermode was one of the most innovative of the early settlers. He established his own stud in 1829 and later won many prizes for his sheep, horses and produce. He was one of the first irrigators, damming both streams on his property (as Alexander Smith noted) and thus created hundreds of acres of irrigated pastures from previously useless waste land. He had a great sense of purpose in rural industry.

He conflicted with some of the lieutenant governors, including Arthur and Eardly-Wilmot, over various matters including convict labour and land taxes. He had better relations with Sir John Franklin, the friend of Sir James Clark Ross. Kermode was an outstanding member of the legislative council and was always fearless and forthright in his views as a typically independent Manxman.

By the time Aubrey and Alexander visited him in early

1847, his health had begun to fail. He had retired to Mona Vale where he died on 2 August 1852.[20]

The pastoralist Frederick von Stieglitz, the second person that Aubrey and Alexander visited on their round 'land voyage' trip of the Tasmanian interior, was equally distinguished and a very prominent member of the Tasmanian gentry. He was born in Ireland in 1803 to an aristocratic family of Bavarian origin, hence his surname. He and two other brothers migrated to Van Diemen's Land after the death of their father, Baron Heinrich Ludwig von Stieglitz. Like Kermode, Frederick von Stieglitz received from the lieutenant governor a 2,000 acre grant. He married and bought a further 3,000 acres and in the next decade built Killymoon House in stone in the style of Killymoon Castle, County Tyrone, Ireland. It was as Alexander Smith enthusiastically described it.

In 1841, von Stieglitz became Justice of the Peace and in 1846 was a nominee for the legislative council on the resignation of the 'Patriotic Six'. He was extremely wealthy. After his wife's death in 1857, he sold Killymoon, returned to Ireland and assumed the title of baron. He remarried in 1859. He died in 1866 at Killymoon Castle.[21]

Thus Aubrey and Alexander went out of their way to visit the wealthiest and most influential men in Van Diemen's Land. What Alexander in the manner of the nineteenth century may have been seeking was patronage (or local referees) for his own advancement in the colony.

Be that as it may, the earlier part of his letter to his folk

---

20 E.J. Cameron, 'Kermode, William (1780-1852)', Douglas Pike (gen. ed.) *Australian Dictionary of Biography* Vol. 2, 1788-1850, Melbourne University Press, Clayton, 1967, pp. 49-50.

21 K.R. von Stieglitz, 'Von Stieglitz, Frederick Lewis (1803-1866)', *Australian Dictionary of Biography*, Vol. 2, pp. 556-9.

describing his visit indicates some anxiety about his own career in the Royal Navy: 'When I come home I shall make a great effort of mine [about negotiating promotion] with the Navy'. But if he couldn't achieve it, after spending some months with his family, he intended to return to Australia because he believed he would be able, as a married man, 'to live upon half what I could in England'.

Such a decision and plans for the future depended on whether he achieved promotion within the Navy or not. He felt he would not like to serve again in the capacity of lieutenant as he had become accustomed in Van Diemen's Land to 'his <u>own</u> say'. He announced in the same letter that Aubrey was expecting a second child. Aubrey, he claimed, was in excellent health and the round trip into the interior had given her 'strength and spirit'.[22]

Alexander and Aubrey seem to have made another brief trip sometime later to northern Tasmania as evidenced by an extant extract. Again Alexander writes to his folk about the people and places they visit. They travel from place to place by carriage, staying at various prominent homesteads. Many of the folk met are known to Aubrey, some from her schooldays. Alexander skilfully describes the scenery. Another group of notable people were visited who showed the Smith couple much hospitality:

> The following morning [Ronald] Gunn drove us with his Daughters and Brother to Evandale some 17 miles to the SE of Launceston to spend the day with a fine old Bachelor gentleman named Jack Sinclair whose house & furniture & Grounds with the great beauty of his part of the Country are well worth the journey. Tarleton rode with us and spent the day, everything

22 Alexander Smith to G & M.

very beautiful & very pleasant.[23]

On 8 June 1847, Aubrey and Alexander's second child Georgina Jane was born.

In a sense, Alexander Smith found himself to be in a forgotten backwater as far as his career in the Royal Navy was concerned. He could not help but feel some disappointment when he noticed in the newspaper that Sir James Clark Ross was in charge of the expedition to go in search of 'poor old Sir John Franklin'. Thomas Moore who was the Second Mate aboard the *Terror* in the Ross Antarctic Expedition had been appointed on one of the ships of the rescue expedition. Alexander felt certain that he would have been chosen as First Lieutenant had he been in England at the time.

*   *   *   *   *

And so Aubrey and Alexander eventually bade farewell to Van Diemen's Land. After a holiday and respite in England as well as negotiations with the Royal Navy, they would return to the Victorian goldfields for Alexander to take up a new career as Goldfields Commissioner in Castlemaine, where a new era in their life together was to open up. He was a man who was not afraid of hard and exacting work in a new position of authority. He was soon to be respected by all and sundry in the turbulent life of the diggings.

During his time in Hobart at the Rossbank Observatory, Alexander was able to keep up a lively and frequent correspondence with his friend from the 1839-1843 Antarctic Expedition, the famed botanist Joseph Dalton Hooker. Unfortunately, only the letters from Hooker to Smith re-

23 Extract of letter by Alexander Smith, circa 1847.

main extant, but they range from family matters, to gossip about old polar shipmates to their mutual interest in botany. Occasionally, Hooker makes reference to Charles Darwin and his consistent support for his evolutionary theories. His work at Kew Gardens is also touched upon as is his majestic rise to fame in the scientific world. Unfortunately, Hooker's letters are often difficult to comprehend and interpret as they are succinct replies to question and subjects that would have been contained in Smith's letters to him. Despite this, they are lively, chatty and full of historical interest.

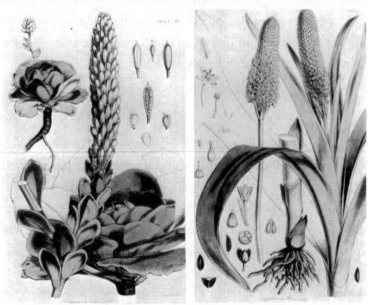

Left: *Pringlea antiscorbutica*, Kerguelen Island, drawing by Joseph Hooker
Right: *Chrysobactron rossii*, Auckland Islands, 'It is the most beautiful botanical drawing we have ever published', by Joseph Hooker

In these letters, Hooker refers at times to Alexander's younger brother Bernhard, then a promising London sculptor and a member of the Pre-Raphaelite Brotherhood. In October 1843, for example, Hooker opens a letter by mentioning that he had just returned from meeting Bernhard at his studio where a sculptured cast of 'our illustrious Jemmy' was placed in his hand.[24] "Jemmy" was their favourite term, frequently used derogatively, for Sir James Clark Ross who commanded the *Erebus* and the whole Antarctic Expedition. This relief medallion portrait by Bernhard was later donated by Hooker to the National Portrait Gallery.

Botanist Sir Joseph Dalton Hooker was born at Halesworth in Suffolk on 30 June 1817, the youngest son of Sir William Jackson Hooker (1785-1865), Professor of Botany at Glasgow University and his wife Maria Sarah (1775-1872). Hooker was only a few years younger than Alexander Smith. He became his closest friend aboard the *Erebus*. They shared the same mess.

Joseph Hooker did not so much learn botany as grow up in it. He attended his father's university lectures from the age of seven and formed a passionate interest in plant distribution. At twenty-one, he was probably the best equipped botanist of his years and he had just finished a medical course. This was why James Clark Ross chose him for his Antarctic Expedition. In October 1835, Hooker wrote to Dawson Turner:

Papa [William Hooker] has I know told you of the distant prospect there is of my going on expedition to the Antarctic Ocean: I can hardly conceive my being prepared both as a Medical Man and Naturalist; to pass the necessary examination will be a great push, while again if I do not devote a good part of this winter to Natural History, I had better not go at all. If the expedition does start and I do not go, I shall be dreadfully disappointed, though I am sure I had better not go at all than go ill prepared: this matter

24 Joseph Hooker to Alexander Smith, 6 October 1843, West Park, London (Merilyn Pedrick Collection).

will, I hope, stimulate me to exertion.[25]

As we now know, Hooker did study hard and achieved his ambition. This was indeed the making of his great career as a botanist.

On the epic voyages into the Antarctic Circle, Alexander Smith contributed much to Joseph Hooker's collection of plants. Hooker was especially grateful to him as well as to the Second Master aboard the *Erebus* John Davis and to David Lyall, the Assistant Surgeon on the *Terror*. A close, long-lasting friendship was thus forged in a wooden world on the high seas for an epic series of years between 1839 and 1843. Hooker was deeply sensible 'of the rare privilege' he enjoyed in having messmates like Smith 'who were ever ready to sacrifice their own convenience for his accommodation'.[26]

Hooker's enthusiasm, curiosity and diligence on the Antarctic voyages led to a magnificent collection of botanical specimens. These were published over sixteen years in six quarto volumes as *The Botany of Antarctic Voyages*: (1844-47), (1853-55) and (1855-60). He was supported by the Admiralty with a grant of £1,000 to help pay for the production of the first volumes and was paid at assistant surgeon's rates to complete the works. However, expenses were large and Hooker found he had to meet some of these from his own money. He began to loath what he considered to be the lack of generous support from Sir James Clark Ross.

The combined efforts of the outstanding lithographer W. H. Fitch and Hooker resulted in a classic botanical publication of great beauty and careful scholarship. It established Hooker

25 Leonard Huxley, *Life and Letters of Sir Joseph Dalton Hooker,* Vol.1, John Murray, London, 1918, p.30.

26 Hooker, 'Summary of the Voyage', p.xii.

as 'one of the world's leading botanists'[27] and Alexander Smith played an honourable role in helping establish his reputation while on the Antarctic voyages.

Throughout his life, Joseph Hooker continued to work in botany making other journeys to the world's remote places, broadening his knowledge and expanding his collections. He published many other subsequent works.

In 1865, Hooker replaced his father Sir William Jackson Hooker as Director of the Botanical Gardens, Kew. He was knighted in 1869 and remained at Kew until 1885. He then continued the administration and development of the place as 'one of the world's finest botanical institutions'.[28]

Hooker's letters to Smith in the 1840s were full of gossip about their old shipmates. In October 1843, he was moved to ask:

> What do you think of the promotions? McMurdo, Wood, Sibbald, Oakeley, Scott & Dayman all made [it] & these only, think of Kay!!! "cheer", he will cut his throat. Yule has been spooning already with that girl he once wanted to marry before, a Miss Byrnes with £4000. Sibbald dined with us, bringing his promotion in his pocket.[29]

First Lieutenant Archibald McMurdo of the *Terror*, who Captain James Ross had a high opinion of, continued to suffer ill health. Nevertheless, he attained the rank of Rear Admiral before he died in 1875 a few years after Alexander Smith. Second Mate of the *Erebus* Henry Oakeley, a courageous man,

---

27 Stephen Martin, 'Sir Joseph Dalton Hooker. The Botany of the Antarctic Voyages of HM Discovery Ships 'Erebus' and 'Terror' in the years 1839-1843', *Upfront*, November 2004, p.6.

28 Martin, 'Sir Joseph Dalton Hooker', p.7.

29 Hooker to Smith, 6 October 1843.

soon went to sea again after the expedition in HMS *Cygnet* to the coast of Africa where he served with distinction until 1847. He retired as a Commander in 1864. John Sibbald had been promoted to First Lieutenant aboard the *Terror* when McMurdo was invalided; his subsequent naval career was described as undistinguished. He eventually became Clerk of the Court in the Falkland Islands. Joseph Dayman Third Mate of the *Erebus* returned to Hobart in 1844 to work at the Rossbank Observatory like Alexander Smith. He later served under Captain Owen Stanley during the famous scientific voyage of *Rattlesnake* in the East Indies and Australasia. He continued in the surveying service and reached the rank of Captain. Henry Yule, the Second Master of the *Terror*, attained the rank of Staff Commander. Joseph Kay's career in the Royal Navy went seemingly nowhere, but he pursued scientific research.[30] As Hooker sarcastically noted, he tended metaphorically to cut his own throat as far as his navy career was concerned.[31]

Sir Joseph Dalton Hooker,
friend & correspondent of
Alexander Smith

30 Ross, *Ross in the Antarctic*, pp. 216-23.
31 Hooker to Smith, 6 October 1843.

In his letters to Smith, Hooker revealed that he considered that James Clark Ross had insufficiently supported his own subsequent career in the Royal Navy and for this reason he had remained on Assistant Surgeon's pay: 'Would you believe it! he told me that without I was made Surgeon he could not help me to get anything but Asst. Surgeons pay, but that if I were Surgeon I should have Surgeons pay and further he would do nothing'.[32] He believed that Ross had 'dropped' him 'ungraciously'. He complained bitterly about the cost of living in London. He also mentioned Ross' marriage: 'Jemmy [Ross' nickname] went down this morning to be married – Crozier & Bird in full uniform to attend the nuptials about the 18th. In his next letter dated 19 October, he implied that Ross only married for money, for £25,000. And on 31 October, he added that 'men so very fond of Jemmy are barely to be trusted'.

The same refrain continues in his next letter: 'It is very well you do not ride Capt. Ross for he is very hard in hand, vicious, by no means a free goer nor of a playful disposition...'[33] Moving away from this subject, Hooker thanked his friend for sending the dimensions of a penguin they had taken for scientific purposes and placed in the hands of a taxidermist. He also talks about plant exhibitions at the British Museum and then returned to his earlier subject:

> So Jemmy is to be knighted, & that is a great squeeze. He is promised it in January next, but Sabine wants them to give it him now at once ... Sabine wants him to go to the North on a N.W. discovery [the North West Passage] & Magnetic survey voyage, after which if ... he succeed, they probably will make him a Baronet, that is, if he should have a child to make it worth his

32 Hooker to Smith.

33 Hooker to Smith, 8 November 1843.

> while to receive it. [Such a title was hereditary.] As to
> the Knighthood he threw away that is all in my eye.

In December 1843, Hooker presents more gossip: Sibbald is to study steam engines and so on; 'Oakeley wrote me a letter the other day full of his horses & dogs & his drinking exploits'. He reports about the £1,000 grant he was promised for his botanical work and yet he was forced to go on half-pay. Fitch had just completed 'about 100 beautiful lithographic plates' and the Smith's penguin is 'nobilissimum [*sic*] & enchants every eye, it weighs, I forget how much, something enormous. It is to go in a case by itself [in the British Museum]'. Another showcase would contain a few [rare] Falkland birds and the Antarctic birds would be in a third. Hooker then claimed that the taxidermist 'stuffs beautifully' and 'one white petrel set up for the drawing room table... is so beautiful just preparing to fly'.[34] He is obviously passionate about the quality of their collection from the Antarctic expedition.

In his next letter, the same theme appears: 'My birds are all home. My big Penguin thanks to you a very splendid thing, certainly now the finest bird in Europe'. He praises Robert McCormick's work in this regard, that it could not be better. He speaks of a long letter he received from Charles Darwin: 'he is an excellent fellow' and writes 'on the philosophy of vegetation' and develops his grand extended view of Natural Science. 'Tho I have never seen him we carry on an active correspondence.'[35] After Hooker met Darwin and became his friend, he advocated his work on the origin of the species to the scientific world.

News of their old Antarctic comrades continued in Hooker's

---

34 Hooker to Smith, 5 December 1843.

35 Hooker to Smith, 10 January 1844.

next letter dated 9 March 1844. A few sarcastic comments about James Clark Ross are included. More importantly, he speaks of his close contact with Darwin and the eminent scientist's work on volcanic coral – he sent Smith a copy. Mention is made of the pending publication of Ross' account of their epic voyages.

Hooker had also developed a friendship with Alexander's brother Bernhard: 'Bernhard is here now. He tells me to say that he will do your things over again'.[36] Apparently, Bernhard was engaged in studying plant life at Kew and preparing some sketches for his brother in Australia.

The exchange of letters is frequent and testifies to their intensely personalised friendship. Another letter from Hooker, eight pages long and written two weeks later on 23 March, begins: 'this is going to be a blessed short letter'! In this letter, Hooker talks about sowing tomato seeds at Kew, about going up to London frequently and reports that John Davis

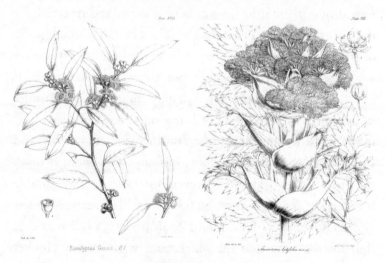

Left: *Eucalyptus gunnii*
Right: *Ansotome latifolia*, drawings by Joseph Hooker

36 Hooker to Smith, 9 March 1844.

(a former shipmate) who was originally going to Canada had abandoned such plans and 'is going to get spliced in May to a damsel of <u>excellent reputation</u>' [as well as having some money]. He believed it would be a very good match as 'Cocky [Davis' nickname] is a gentleman & would value a good wife & deserves one'.

A sentimental touch is added about 'old Jack Sibbald' who apparently Alexander was fond of: 'I hope some 6 or 8 years hence we may meet in Town [London] & go down to some seaport where Jack will be with his ship & crack some old Port [of vintage quality] ... with him'. He also reports the return to England of Sir John Franklin. Hooker hoped that his friend Alexander was happy to be living in Van Diemen's Land: 'You will however look with sorrowful eyes on the little curve in the paddock when the old Erebus & Terror were moored so long, at a time when you enjoyed V.D.L. [Van Diemen's Land] more than you ever will again. The romance of the Expedition, then at its height, is now gone [and replaced] by the girls to be fallen in love with'. Then he talks nostalgically of the celebrity they once had as part of the Ross expedition when people 'looked with awe' upon them: 'we look back with inordinate pleasure to the few happy <u>hours</u> we spent under certain instances and cannot bring ourselves to believe how many <u>days</u> of true misery the confinement of ship life and surely [the] nature of some [of] our superiors entailed upon us'. Such matters did not, however, 'interfere with pleasurable recollection' for those days: 'So now you will leave the Magnets and go down often for an hour & sit under a silver wattle & sigh for the time that the old Erebus was there...' Hooker evoked the fact that he missed the old mess aboard the *Erebus* and the close contact with his friend and boon companion Alexander John Smith.

In his next letter of 13 July the same year, Hooker is even more critical of James Clark Ross' lack of support for his work on the plant collection. (He makes a rather derogative comment on Ross' rather long nose in another letter.) Other than this, he provides news of their former shipmates of the epic voyages. He reports that he is in weekly correspondence with Charles Darwin about scientific matters.

*   *   *   *   *

The frequent letters to Alexander Smith in Van Diemen's Land continue in this vein. They contain hints that Smith, while happy in his marriage, misses the sea life and is becoming increasingly anxious about the possibilities of promotion within the Royal Navy. In his mind, Hooker has turned James Clark Ross into an enemy because of his apparent lack of support for his work on the plant collection. He keeps reminding Smith about their former colleagues and shipmates – their illnesses, behaviour and successes since the epic voyages and their activities in support of the British Empire. The scientific work of his father and that of Charles Darwin are touched upon on occasions. He implies in several places that Ross is ambitious to accept the appointment as leader on the proposed expedition to find the North-West Passage. As now known, however, Ross refused the appointment and Sir John Franklin accepted it. Subsequently, the *Erebus* and the *Terror* were lost forever in the Arctic wastes. The bodies of the companies of both ships including Commander Sir John Franklin were never found.

There are hints in the letters that Alexander Smith is sending letters of appeal to his old mentor Sir James Clark Ross via Joseph Hooker: 'Jemmy will be here on Monday when I shall give him your letter'.[37] Sometimes, Alexander is assigned the task of sending plant samples to Kew Gardens to assist the biological research of father and son, William and Joseph Hooker.

The extant letters between Alexander Smith and Hooker cease in October 1852, but correspondence between the two friends may have continued beyond that time. Those that are extant are full of the intensity that comes of a close friendship.

*   *   *   *   *

On the road to the diggings, pen & ink by W, Matherell

37 Hooker to Smith, 16 December (probably 1844).

From top: Alexander's writing desk (Private Collection)
Alexander Smith's dress sword (Private Collection)
A midshipman in uniform carrying his quadrant and folio of charts
(PW4970, NMM, Greenwich)

Clockwise from top left:

The *Erebus*, cover of Ross' account
of the Antarctic Expeditions

Lord Henry Smith

Jane Mary Smith (née Voase)

Plate from the *Erebus*

Buttons & braid from Alexander Smith's naval uniform

(Private Collections)

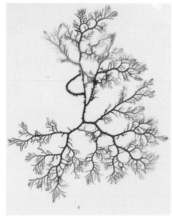

Botanical specimens collected
by Alexander Smith
(Private Collection)

Panoramic view of Hobart Town, watercolour by Sarah Aubrey Read
(Private Collection)

'Diggers licensing Forrest Creek (sic)', lithograph by S.T. Gill, (pic-an7537702, NLA)

'The Disputed Claim', hand coloured lithograph by Cyrus Mason, 1855
(Rex Nan Kivell Collection U2491, NLA)

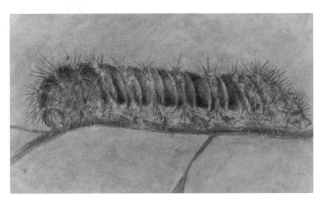

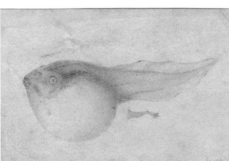

Above & left:
Drawings by Bernhard Smith
from specimens obtained at
Castlemaine, c.1858

Above: Botanical specimens collected by Alexander Smith (Private Collection)

Elizabeth Read (née Driver)

George Frederick Read

Family heirloom
& gift card
(Private Collections)

For Aubrey Read.
    born 14ᵗʰ December 1941.
on her 10ᵗʰ birthday.
Given to Aubrey Officer.
    born 11ᵗʰ December 1889.
as a christening present
by her grandmother, Mʳˢ Alex Smith
    née Aubrey Read.

Clockwise from top left:
Langley
Alexander Smith
Aubrey Smith
The Smith Family vault, Castlemaine (photo by Ian Hockley)

A Visit to the Palace &
the Leaving of England

Two important events happened to Alexander John Smith while in London in 1852: his first son and fourth child, Alexander Henry, was born on 21 April and he was presented to Queen Victoria and Prince Albert at Buckingham Palace as a fitting climax to his naval career and his retirement from active duty. Alexander had decided to return with his family to Australia. He was destined never to return to the motherland.

At the time of his sojourn in England, the Queen of the United Kingdom of Great Britain and Ireland and the granddaughter of George III was thirty-three years of age and about seven years younger than Alexander Smith. On 20 June 1837, she had succeeded to the throne. Alexander was at sea, unmarried, on the *Mastiff* surveying the chilly Orkneys off the coast of northern Scotland. The coronation took place on 28 June 1838 about a year before the James Clark Ross Antarctic Expedition left England's shores with Alexander aboard the *Erebus*. Victoria's marriage to Prince Albert of Saxe-Coburg Gotha took place on 10 February 1840 when the voyagers were penetrating the Arctic Circle. By the time of Alexander and Aubrey's visit to England in 1852, the British Empire was at its height, Queen Victoria had had several children and the Australian gold rushes were underway.

Alexander relayed his adventures at the Palace to his sister in a letter. He had come down to London to stay at the Craven Hotel with his full dress naval uniform in his bag. As soon as he was shown to his room, he unpacked his uniform and made sure it was well pressed by the hotel staff.

And with nothing else to do for the day, he stepped out to visit the Vernon Gallery and was 'never more delighted' with the collection of paintings he found there, amongst them a great many Turners and Gainsboroughs. He found the experience of seeing the originals quite different from the engravings of paintings in books like Ruskin's *Modern Painters* (1843). He relished Joseph Turner's massive *The Battle of the Nile* (1799), *Shipwreck* (1805) and his masterpiece *Ulysses deriding Polyphemus* (1829). As well, he would have viewed Thomas Gainsborough's portraits of Admiral Vernon and others and his many fine landscapes. At the gallery, he wondered how it was he had 'never heard that these beautiful things were to be seen <u>free</u> Mondays Tuesdays and Wednesdays'.

On the eve of his retirement from the navy, memories of his childhood in Greenwich and his years at sea flooded back. He made another excursion to marvel at the new Houses of Parliament where the eye of the storm of the British Empire was being played out in splendour. He had a nostalgic visit to the naval displays at the museums of Greenwich Hospital which he found disappointing and considered few paintings worth seeing apart from the beautiful ceiling in one of the rooms.

He returned to the Craven Hotel and 'rigged' himself out in his 'full dress uniform' assisted by a friend. He told Emma that he still 'cut a very respectable figure' in his uniform. And then on to the Palace by cab. In the midst of a crowd of soldiers 'and gold Lace', he passed through these ranks and entered the Palace 'without any questions being asked in passing a few sticks [attendants] in waiting' and a formidable-looking table where he deposited his invitation and admission card.

He was admitted into a splendid drawing room – 'a handsome one of course' about 80 feet by 40 feet and lushly covered with a rich dark crimson Turkish carpet. There were matching curtains and chairs and huge paintings of Liege and Tours. There were portraits of members of the 'old Royal Family & Nelson [the Naval Hero] among them'. A crowd of dignitaries gathered into the reception room. For Emma's sake, Alexander recalled how:

> … we saw the Carriages arrive with HMajesty etc & immediately afterwards the reception began. I need not tell you of the gorgeous uniforms of all Ranks & Nations, about ¼ of an hour after the reception began I had drifted with the tide to the entrance of the reception room & for about 3 or 4 minutes I was almost facing the Queen who was dressed in white Satin with a Tiara of Pearls amongst green leaves. I passed on & my card was taken … & my name loudly pronounced. I dropped at my Queen's feet on my Right Knee presenting my right arm on which she laid her hand & my

lips most devoutly kissed her dear little hand.
I rose lowly bowing first to her & then to the
Prince, backing out a few steps behind a row
of Great Nobs…

Then he was free to mingle amongst the guests and talk with anyone he felt inclined to. After about an hour, he 'walked off', got into a cab and was driven back to his hotel. He changed out of his uniform and was once again, as he informed Emma in a matter-of-fact manner, a private gentleman with the liberty to attend any levee or other drawing room in London by leaving his card at the Lord Chamberlain's Office and signifying his intention to visit. He posted his undated letter to his sister soon after and a copy of the newspaper with an account of the reception to his ageing father.*

Some time later, he departed from England forever with Aubrey, their three daughters and newly English-born son who later would establish the Smith family dynasty in Australia.

---

*Alexander John Smith to Emma Smith, Thursday, Charlton Villa 1852.

Goldfields Commissioner, Castlemaine
From Camp to Town

> On a slight elevation at a little distance was the so-
> called Camp, where the ... government officials had
> their tents, which were greatly superior to those of the
> diggers. They were lined with green baize, carpeted,
> and furnished with ... comfort, which were subse-
> quently developed into some almost akin to luxury.
> On the camp the few available police were located,
> together with the gold receivers and commissioners....
> *The function of the latter gentlemen consisted in issuing*
> *the requisite licenses to the diggers, adjusting disputed*
> *claims, and generally officiating as justices of the peace.*[1]

The eye witness author of this passage described in a nutshell
the standard of temporary accommodation provided for
government officials and their authority and function. The
author, known by the pseudonym "Resident" (J.H. Kerr), was
a well-educated and observant Scot who drew from his clear
vivid memories of the 1850s Gold Rushes some twenty years
later. While memory can play tricks on details, he is a reliable
primary source on the main and provides vivid, accurate

---

1   "Resident" (J.H. Kerr), *Glimpses of Life in Victoria*, Edmonston & Douglas,
Edinburgh, 1872, p. 120.

snapshots of events and descriptions. The official Camp (as it was called) was indeed the eye of the mortal storm, a place of calm, of straight-backed military precision and efficiency amid the struggling chaos of gold-fevered humanity that was the Victorian goldfields.

It was into this feverish environment that Captain Alexander John Smith RN was appointed in the early 1850s. It was to be a turbulent, exacting and exhausting government position to follow which was full of stress and political conflict. It was a new road that would take the quietly efficient naval officer far away from the tranquillity of the Rossbank Observatory with its pleasant riverside domestic delights.

Nevertheless, Alexander Smith was more than able to adjust and build a relationship of respect and even affection with the riotous diggers in chaotic and ever-changing public settings. This involved the protection of thousands of recently arrived men, women and children, many of whom were clamouring for attention and support in the uncertain atmosphere of an over-reacting militaristic regime created by a colonial government.

Before the great tide of immigrants had time to arrive in Australian ports by sea – from the British Isles, France, Germany, Russia, the United States, Canada, South Africa, China, Mexico, the South American nations and other countries – in crowded accommodation of a multiplicity of sailing ships of all types, a substantial population had already arrived on the goldfields from the Australian cities and countryside. They flitted and drifted from spot to spot in the early days of the 1850s. Gold fever had overheated the colonists, let alone the new arrivals.

Some were ex-convicts or 'old lags' – that is unemployed convicts whose sentences in the main had expired, particularly those from the large numbers in Tasmania. Still others were on the run from the police in the cities and townships. Many were respectable labourers who had left their original jobs to seek their fortune and gain social betterment. There were tradesmen, wharf labourers, sailors, schoolteachers, ex-soldiers, shopkeepers, office clerks and public servants. There were ship captains from Melbourne ports, doctors, lawyers, shepherds and rouseabouts from many country locations. In short, they were from all walks of life. Throughout the colonies in every place they left, they created employment shortages; some Australian cities seemed deserted. These people were hopeful, ambitious and industrious in the main, unswerving in their determination to find gold and oblivious to physical discomfort.

Emigrants landing at Queen's Wharf during the 1850s goldrushes, wood engraving by Frederick Grosse (Rex Nan Kivell Collection) S2853, NLA

As an eye-witness, J.H. Kerr put it more harshly: 'many of these men had evil faces, on which the traces of past crimes were deeply imprinted, and which were indelibly branded with the felon stamp'.[2] Colonial middle-class writers like Kerr

2   "Resident", *Glimpses of Life in Victoria.*

underlined what was seen as Australia's pervading birth stain, the negativity of the convict legacy. Faces may have actually looked more work-worn than evil and bushy beards were all the go in the environment that had few amenities or niceties.

The rush to the Victorian goldfields was like nothing else conceivable in the world at the time, apart from the Californian rushes a few years earlier. One day the lovely tranquil gully, the wild dense bushland, untouched by the hand of European man and, in less than a week, a place thronging with busy, chaotic life. The physical environment was now drastically scarred. The newcomers on arrival hastened to peg out their claims in what seemed to be the most promising spot or, if late, gratefully took any corner that happened to be left. Aborigines evaporated into hidden places in the hills and valleys.

The *Melbourne Morning Herald* of 18 October 1851 characterised the atmosphere on the Mount Alexander goldfields in a colourful way:

> Picture to yourself a space of ground covered with tents (Thousands at work! Cradles, barrows and pick-axes, all going together!) Shouting, laughing, and singing! Such a confusion and a noise that you are bewildered! And then at night, all lighted up with a thousand fires; and then old acquaintances, dressed in RED SHIRTS, and with long beards, tailors with moustachios, doctors and tinkers, all working together.

Shortly after the discovery of the great Ballarat goldfields, its attractions were rivalled by a place known then as Barker's Creek (Mount Alexander), later the site of Castlemaine township about seventy miles from Melbourne.[3]

---

3   "Resident", *Glimpses of Life in Victoria*, p. 119.

The Forest Creek diggings Mt Alexander, *Illustrated London News* 1852

The axe's echoing ring was to be heard; the great forest trees were being felled by the power of strong, sinewy arms, some that had recently learnt to wield the axe in the pine forests of California as "forty-niners". For miles around, the land was denuded of timber. Daily more of the tall old trees were levelled to the ground. Tent-poles, firewood and timber supports for the new claim shafts were an absolute necessity to the enthusiastic gold seekers. Such a scene greeted Alexander Smith.

Consequently, as if by magic in a week or less, a large canvas-and-bark town had sprung into vigorous existence – and a somewhat ramshackle and tumble-down town it was! The dwellings needed to be close to the claims. Tents sprung up like mushrooms across the landscape. Everyone was in haste to be rich and law and order was a grave problem that the Goldfields Commissioners like Alexander Smith had to face and deal with.

Ellen Clacy, dubbed the lady in the goldfields, in her 1852 account demonstrates how extensively the landscape was taken up by the Mount Alexander diggers in the Castlemaine district as she invites us to:

Alluvial gold washing, Skinner Prout, vn4496154-v, NLA

… take a stroll round Forest Creek – what a novel scene! – thousands of human beings engaged in digging, wheeling, carrying, and washing, intermingled with no little grumbling, scolding and swearing.

We approach first the old Post-office Square; next our eye glances down Adelaide Gully, and over the Montgomery and White Hills, all pretty well dug up; now we pass the Private Escort Station, and Little Bendigo. *At the junction of Forest, Barker and Campbell Creeks we find the Commissioners' quarters* – this is nearly five miles from our starting point. We must now return to Adelaide Gully, and keep alongside Adelaide Creek, till we come to a high range of rocks, which we cross, and then find ourselves near, in the head-waters of Fryer's Creek. Following that stream towards the Loddon, we pass the interesting neighbourhood of Golden Gully, Moonlight Flat, Windlass and Red Hill; this latter which covers about two acres of ground is so called from the colour of the soil, it was the first found, and is still considered as the richest auriferous spot near Mount Alexander.[4]

---

4   Ellen Clacy, 'A lady on the goldfields', *Australian Heritage*, Spring 2008, p. 31, author's italics for emphasis.

Fryer's Creek, near Castlemaine 1852, sketch by S.T. Gill, S135, NLA

Tents were most favoured as the simplest and easiest shelter to erect, but bark huts were by no means uncommon mainly built by the experienced bushmen amongst the diggers. There was no uniformity whatsoever. Each man built his accommodation to his own peculiar taste and haste. Some frail bark huts had holes and crannies through which the cold winter wind whistled. Some tents were new and white and recently purchased in Melbourne, others were a piece of tattered canvas only held together by some miracle.

Inside these huts and tents, very little furniture could be seen. The floors were trodden earth. There was a bunk but little else. Boxes and flour barrels did duty as seats and small tables. The digger's sole possessions brought with him were his mining tools, blankets, tent, a tin billy and frying pan. He was typically dressed in a blue or red work shirt, moleskin trousers tucked into high and heavy work boots and a low-crowned slouch hat while at his waist in his belt or sash, there was frequently a pistol and/or knife, both claimed to be weapons of defence – such was the violent threatening state of the human environment.[5]

---

5   Bill Scott, *Complete Book of Australian Folk Lore*, Summit Books, Sydney, 1978, pp. 60-1.

Successful diggers examine the day's yield

"Resident" described the accommodation on the goldfields as closely packed 'miserable dwellings'. While the sale of liquor on the goldfields was forbidden by government authorities like Alexander Smith, there were plenty of sly grog shops available. Some of these were actually modestly-furnished brothels which did not fail to produce the 'usual results'.[6] One of Smith's duties was to close down such establishments and to arrest their entrepreneurs.

But what of the roads and tracks from Melbourne to the diggings of Mount Alexander at Castlemaine?

A lone wayfarer was often sighted riding in a light carriage or on foot. More usually, travellers journeyed together for safety in caravans of fifty or more, women carrying young children and strong men with carts and wheelbarrows, shouldering their guns or pick-axes and followed by barking dogs of every size and breed.[7]

Many hundreds of goods and supplies carriers came with

6   "Resident", *Glimpses of Life in Victoria*, p. 121.

7   "Resident", *Glimpses of Life in Victoria*.

them with their heavy load to provide the goldfields with food, clothing, tents, work equipment and other amenities. They sometimes made huge amounts of money in the process. The new diggers somehow carried their 'houses' of new canvas, their clothes of all sorts of material, their food, their tools and their simple machinery.

There was an endless chain of humanity formed between the city and the diggings, hopeful people exiting the city's precincts on one side of the track. And on the other side, people full of deep despair returning empty-handed. As they left Melbourne or returned to the city, they were almost totally hidden by a gritty cloud of dust that resembled the smog that hung over Victorian London. A train of Chinese in single file frequently extended for some miles. They jogged at a slow trot bending under immense loads which they carried at each end of a thick and long bamboo pole.[8]

In 1862, B. Henry Brown described his arrival at the diggings in Pleasant Creek in the early 1850s:

> ... just at sunset we entered this pleasantly named gold field... I had never seen a place so disheartening as the one we were just entering; nothing was finished,

Chinese gold seekers on the road to the diggings

---

8   Charles Dickens, *Household Words*, 2 June 1855, cited in *Bound for the Goldfields: a true account of a journey from Melbourne to Castlemaine / by a carrier of supplies to the goldfields*, designed & illustrated with cuts by Mike Hudson, The Wayzgoose Press, Katoomba, 1990, unpaginated.

hardly a store was up; people were cooking around the stumps in the streets; some sheep were being killed, and the warm flesh sold, under an awning stuck upon poles; all looked wretched and poor, some few canvass [*sic*] public houses had certainly been erected, but from them came sounds that required experience to show that they were not put up for people to rest therein …

… Upon the whole I have never seen a place where, for the first three or four weeks after our arrival, a man's throat stood in such jeopardy as in Pleasant Creek. It must be remembered that there were about fifteen thousand people and that there were neither magistrate, police, priest, chapel, church, post office nor any authority whatever.[9]

The nearest place for such niceties of civilisation was at Mount Ararat, some thirty miles off. This was typical of the first stages of development of any goldfield. On all the early Victorian goldfields, however, things began to change rapidly. The government was about to intervene decisively.

Mt. Alexander gold diggings, watercolour, William Bentley, 1853, pic-an6617924, NLA

9   B. Henry Brown, *Victoria as I Found It, during Five Years of Adventure*, T. Cantley Newby, London, 1862, pp. 335, 346.

For the many parties on the road after miles of weary tramping and camping at night beside it, the wide diggings of Forest Creek suddenly appeared before them. In a few minutes, they were passing between lines of tents and rough wooden buildings in a kind of embryonic main street, most bearing the name of the trade carried on within.

The whole of the road through the Forest Creek diggings of about five miles was a succession of small hill ascents and descents, every little hill having its name: the Old Post Office Hill, the Angus Hill, the Red Hill, and so on. On the right of the road stretched an extensive flat which ran away to the celebrated Golden Point at the foot of Mount Alexander. Every inch of the ground was turned over. The hill to the left of the road was in the same condition. The whole of the country seemed to be turned inside out. It presented a broken and irregular surface of many coloured earths. In places, horse-puddling machines were at work breaking up and re-washing for a second or third time the earth from which earlier diggers had extracted gold. Some workers were breaking into old walls of old diggings; others in new holes and even the ground where tents were previously pitched but then abandoned.[10]

*   *   *   *   *

On 9 March 1853, Alexander John Smith was appointed Goldfields Commissioner of Crown Lands at Castlemaine, at first as an assistant. Related and more important appointments were soon to follow. He had resigned his naval position at the Rossbank Observatory near Hobart in 1852.

On 18 May 1853, he was appointed as a Magistrate for the territory surrounding Castlemaine. There was also a flurry of

10 Dickens, *Household Words*.

Gold licence signed by Smith, Goldfields Commissioner, Castlemaine

appointments in 1857 that increased and stretched his responsibilities to the limit; on 13 March 1857, he was appointed Chairman of the Maldon local council and, on 18 August, he was appointed Chairman of the Castlemaine local court.

With the parliamentary changes to the administration of the goldfields after the Eureka outbreak, he was appointed a Warden of the Goldfields on 5 January 1858 with similar if muted powers to those of the former Goldfields Commissioners and, on 1 March of the next year, he was appointed as Protector of the Chinese on the Goldfields. His younger brother Bernhard was appointed as Warden on the same day (after serving for a time as an Assistant Goldfields Commissioner) and as Protector of the Chinese on 7 May 1858.

Another heavy responsibility was added in 1860 to Alexander's multiple official duties. On 10 February, he was appointed as a Police Magistrate of Victoria for Castlemaine and Taradale. But on 23 April 1861, Alexander John Smith was to resign his various government-appointed positions to stand for the Victorian Parliament as a local member.

In the decade of the 1850s, Alexander Smith came upon a vast and only partly-settled territory on what was then the periphery of the western world. Before November 1850, it was not even a separate British colony and not yet called Victoria. It was the Port Phillip District and was part of the Colony of New South Wales which was under a supervisor and then, soon after, a Lieutenant Governor. With the advent of the Gold Rushes, it was a seething, restless and rapidly-expanding society shadowed by dispossession of the land of Aboriginal people and racial vilification and violence against the Chinese miners.

Chinese Joss House, Castlemaine

* * * * *

Alexander was in his early forties when he took up his first appointment at Castlemaine. He soon gained a wide feeling of respect from amongst the diggers for his fairness and impartiality in troublesome but dynamic days. He never had the 'bad odour' which was soon attached to the other less able and less effective Commissioners, government officers, magistrates and military officers and men. The diggers admired his unostentatious and polite, respectful manner. He never tried to lord it over them, but remained strict in carrying out his duties. They soon came to believe that he was a fair, firm and incorruptible man they could all respect and trust. His experience and ability to negotiate with rough-and-ready able seamen on the high seas stood him in good stead once more on the goldfields.

To take up his appointment at Castlemaine, he had to leave Aubrey and the children behind in Tasmania with her relatives for a period. His appointment had been directly made by Charles La Trobe, the Lieutenant Governor of the Colony of Victoria. His beginning salary was £400 per annum with the extra provision of a servant, rations and accommodation.

He had met the Chief Commissioner in Melbourne who offered him a position in Melbourne on a salary of £500. Alexander declined as living costs in the urban environment were too expensive, especially the cost of renting a gentleman's residence which would be on the average about £400 a year. He claimed at the time that Melbourne was a 'most horrid expensive place' that he 'had ever been in' and it was 'filthy from fleas, moschitos [*sic*] and dust and stinks of every kind'. (In a lifetime at sea, he had visited many port cities in diverse cultures. For these reasons, he believed that the Castlemaine appointment was preferable.) Besides, he loved the countryside rather than the city – a common trait amongst ex-Royal Navy men. He wanted to see the Castlemaine district as he was loo-king for a farm to purchase, partly for his eventual retirement from government service.

He was transported to Castlemaine to take up his new appointment in an open light four-horse carriage. Although more comfortable than most forms of conveyance, it proved an arduous dusty journey of two days, over bumpy dirt roads and tracks. He stayed in run-down wayside inns at night. He reached the official Camp on a Sunday 'horridly tired' having endured two nights of fleas and two days of dust in the open carriage driven by his assigned servant.

He found the resident Commissioner, another Smith but no relation, to be an old friend from Ceylon as Adjutant to the 78th Regiment as well as Captain John Bull[11] who had been brought up at Woolwich, near Greenwich, a son of Colonel Bull of the Artillery. The younger Bull had attended Wallpools School at Greenwich where Alexander had grown up. His new colleagues, Alexander found to be most congenial and they became firm friends amidst the early chaos of the goldfields.

At first, Alexander stayed temporarily in Commissioner Smith's accommodation but, after a few days, he was living under sturdy canvas with his servant in a 'very good roomy' tent of his own.

There were several officers at the Camp, so they formed 'an excellent mess' which was kept up the same as a regimental one that brought back for Smith fond memories of his naval career, especially his experiences aboard the *Erebus*. The Camp was

11 Captain John Bull was one of the few government officials who attempted, like Captain Alexander Smith, to bridge the gap between the digger community and the Camp. In 1858 four years after the report of the inquiry into the battle at Eureka was tabled, all the troopers were withdrawn from all the goldfields, but Bull like Alexander Smith remained at Castlemaine and like Smith was appointed as Warden (as well as being the first chairman of the local court).

structured as a small military establishment and the officers wore elaborate uniforms to give their appointments and public persona a high status and recognition in the vast heavily populated gold mining community of tents and shanties.

Gold Commissioners Camp, Castlemaine.
The escort leaving camp June 1853, by G. Rudston Read

The mess provided for fourteen to twenty people for dinner on a daily basis and Alexander was back in comfortable familiar territory of the male companionship of navy and army veterans. Most of the officers were old army men who had been Captains or Majors. Some had been naval officers. The formal establishment at the time of Alexander Smith's arrival was made up of five Commissioners, a Police Magistrate, two police officers in charge of the Mounted Police, some of whom were former army veterans and an old naval surgeon by the name of McRae who had known Alexander's brother, William Richard Smith, also in the naval service as Captain in the Royal Navy. William Smith had died unmarried on 11 November 1851. He had been born a couple of years later than Alexander. There was also an Assistant Surgeon and four officers of the 40th Regiment.

Gaol and Commissioners Station, *Illustrated London News* 26 February 1853

The Camp received daily visits from high ranking officials of other Camps who from time to time were invited to the officers' mess in the goldfields in accordance with their rank. Nearly all these officers had separate army tents with servants or batmen forming a strictly structured army camp line like those that Alexander remembered as a youth at Woolwich.

The officers of The Camp were in the front row of tents and the clerks and civil or administrative officers behind forming a second row. In the third row were the servants and the ten maintenance keepers and the ordinary non-commissioned policemen with military behind them in a final row.

The Camp to which Alexander Smith belonged was on a rise overlooking 'pretty country' of undulating hills. The diggings were spread out in the flats and valleys. It was a busy scene populated by thousands of men, women and children all hard at work as Alexander Smith described them, 'turning up the ground, sinking [shafts] from 10 to even I have known 112 feet deep'.

Aboriginal troopers drilling by William Strutt c. 1850,
State Parliamentary Library Collection, Victoria

Some of the miners at the time, according to Alexander, were doing well and some were making a fortune. As Alexander put it, like other trades gold mining required knowledge and skill 'not to throw away the gold without washing' as some of the more inexperienced were doing with the precious metal hidden in the soil. In a letter to his sister Emma in England soon after his arrival in Castlemaine, he pointed out that 'it is very hard work and no mistake about it'.

He then went on to define his duties as Commissioner to his sister in a simple uncomplicated form:

> My duties are to issue licenses to the diggers at 30 [shillings] for a month, receive & take charge of the money for one week, when we deposit in the Gold office, also to settle disputes amongst the diggers some of which requires a first rate Lawyer, but there is no appeal from a Commissioner's decision. Hitherto I have given satisfaction to the disputants.[12]

12 Alexander Smith to Emma Smith, The Camp, Castlemaine, Forest Creek, Mount Alexander, 13 March 1853.

He found Castlemaine in its early stages not a very healthy place to live. This was an initial worry for him in bringing Aubrey and their young family to join him there. He recounted to Emma the difficulties and tragedies besetting his Commissioner colleagues; three wives did not remain for more than six weeks and two of them died tragically of dysentery within two days of each other. They had had to rent small two-roomed cottages that were poorly built, the only accommodation available. Many of the men in 'The Camp' had suffered from a 'low fever'. He stated that they 'lost several of the finest men' – ex-soldier pensioners and police. Sandy Blight was also a common irritation that caused a 'swelling of the Eyelids which made you blind for a time'. He pointed out that many children suffered from ophthalmia at the diggings he supervised at Forest Creek, Mount Alexander. He had seen some horrid cases. He implies that the government surgeon had had an exhausting, time-consuming schedule. Alexander was obviously a man of compassion for others.

When writing to Emma, he claimed he still did not know what to do about the future. He had not made up his mind yet about his family, but the 'thought of having Aubrey and the poor little darlings [their children] here [in Castlemaine] is out of the question', at least for a while.

At the time, he had not heard from Aubrey in Hobart, but he believed that 'she will be miserable at the thought of this appointment & really nothing can compensate me for the separation'.

Alexander then was caught in somewhat of a dilemma – there was a serious and frightening health problem in Castlemaine, then a remote pioneering spot with inadequate accommodation for a family. As well, Aubrey may have been loath to leave her comfortable family situation in Hobart with her near relatives and girlhood friends.

Alexander went on to recount how he had come over from Tasmania to Victoria by himself with the idea of being absent from his beloved family for about a fortnight. By the time he wrote the letter to Emma, however, he had been absent for almost a month. He had directed his mail at first to Geelong where he had received a letter from Aubrey, but now that he was in Castlemaine the post only arrived twice a week from Melbourne. He longed 'to have a peep at them all' through an affectionate letter from his wife Aubrey, to hear all the news of his children. In other words, he felt lonely, somewhat depressed and isolated.

While he thought he might have to resign, he wanted to have a good look at the potential of the countryside from a farming viewpoint before he gave it all up and left. Although he believed he had achieved a 'first rate appointment', perhaps, he opined, it was more suited to a bachelor than a married man with young children.

He concluded this subject with Emma by writing: 'now I have told you quite enough about myself'. He then proceeds to tell her about hunting his younger brother Bernhard down at Fryer's Creek from an address he had obtained in Melbourne. (This is explored in greater detail in a later chapter that tells of Bernhard Smith's career in Australia.) Alexander was delighted to be reunited with his brother after long distances and vastly different careers had separated them: 'It was most jolly having him for a chat of the old days'.[13]

Despite Alexander's initial uncertainty about his new position at Castlemaine, on 5 March 1853, he was formally gazetted along with two other similar appointments:

---

13 Alexander Smith to Emma Smith.

Colonial Secretary's Office
Melbourne, 5th March 1853

His Excellency the Lieutenant Governor has been pleased to appoint George Macdonald Lowther, *Alexander John Smith* and George Webster, Esquires, to be Commissioners of Crown Lands for the Gold Fields of the Colony of Victoria.

By his Excellency's Command,
W. Lonsdale.[14]

Gold Escort leaving Mt Alexander

The position carried with it an elaborate, impressive military uniform to create a superiority and authority of a legal nature over the rough-and-ready gold-seekers.

Contemporary observers saw the powers of the 'Commissioners of Crown Lands for the Gold Fields in the Colony of Victoria' as of a very extensive character. As Alexander Smith settled and resolved his own personal anxieties about his family, he set to work conscientiously with his responsibilities 'of gathering in the license fee, and of general superintending the affairs' of the well-populated goldfield community.

It became well known that he detested the necessity of so

14 Colony of Victoria, *Government Gazette No 13*, author's italics for emphasis.

called 'digger hunts' by the mounted police or troopers and resorted to them as little as possible and only as a last resort. Every adult male living on a Victorian goldfield was required to pay a licence fee of thirty shillings each month whether he was mining or not.

The wording of the Act concerning the goldfields demanded that every person carrying goods into the goldfields and not staying was also required to have a miner's licence that he was required to pay on a monthly basis like the diggers themselves. This was difficult to police, but offenders caught in default were marched to the police courts and heavily fined.[15]

A tent on The Camp at Fryer's Creek was at first used as a courtroom to hear these types of cases and others of a more criminal nature. There were at the time several thousands of people at Fryer's Creek and related goldfields surrounding Mount Alexander. Unsightly mounds of earth were everywhere thrown up by the diggers making policing more difficult, especially on horseback.

Castlemaine Commissioners Camp 1852, sketch by Clarke Ismir

---

15 Brown, *Victoria as I Found It*, p. 148.

The scene as Alexander Smith first saw it was one of most lively activity; heads popped out of every hole as busy workers with pick and shovel rested a minute from their labours below and at the same time observed goings-on in the sunlight on the earth's surface. By the creek's side were motley groups of workers engaged in washing the rich, gold-impregnated soil – they extracted either much or little of the precious dust.

Women and children mingled among the crowd of diggers, some engaged in cooking over fires, others washing gold with the men. All were busy, toiling cheerfully. Their faces were eager and hopeful, scarcely showing feelings of fatigue in the joyful excitement that sustained their energies,[16] at least until they eventually lost hope.

Left: A family enterprise vn555618, NLA *Right*: Sunday washing at the diggings

At the same time, a new kind of democracy was beginning to forge itself that was to break down the old social class barriers to a large extent and create new ones.

The great tide of immigration to Australia began to change things and to create new cultural values and forces. The cry had been heard around the world. The gold rushes of the 1850s brought with them far-reaching social and economic changes. On the positive side, there was economic energy, social mobility and cultural hunger.

But what was Castlemaine, the place where Alexander John Smith was appointed as Commissioner of the Gold Fields?

---

16 "Resident", *Glimpses of Life in Victoria*, p. 119.

Prior to the European invasion, the area was occupied by the Djadjawurrung tribe of Aborigines. Major Thomas Mitchell appears to have been the first to pass through during his Australia Felix expedition of 1836. A few squatters soon followed from New South Wales and crossed the Murray.[17]

It was on the Mount Alexander pastoral run established by Dr William Barker in July 1851 that one of Barker's shepherds found gold at Specimen Gully, five kilometres north-east of Castlemaine. Soon the area's streams were being scoured by a rag-tag army of hopefuls from many other places.

Gold Commissioner Wright established a government camp on the present Castlemaine town site at the confluence of Forest and Barker Creeks. Briefly, it served as a supply centre for the local goldfields as they continued to spread out in all directions. This centre was initially known as 'Mount Alexander' or 'Forest Creek'. Either Commissioner Wright or Lieutenant Governor La Trobe (most probably the latter) named it Castlemaine. Wright's uncle was Viscount Castlemaine and La Trobe was once Inspector of Schools in Castlemaine in Ireland. The origin of the name, or else the person who named it so, is still not clear or fully proven. Nevertheless, the land just north-east of the camp was officially surveyed in 1852. Castlemaine was declared a town the following year when allotments were first auctioned to the public.

By 1852, there were about 25,000 people on the various Mount Alexander diggings living in shanty tent towns which variously housed the gold seekers, stores, the first school (started in 1852), sly grog shops, brothels and even an office of the

---

17 This included Merilyn Pedrick's great-grandfather Rev. Joseph Docker who followed Major Mitchell's tracks from Richmond in NSW to the district of the Ovens River, Wangaratta (named by Joseph), Victoria, where he built the lovely homestead mansion "Bontharambo".

Bank of New South Wales, also opened in 1852. Then a new rush began at North Castlemaine in 1855 that followed the same pattern.

The Melbourne *Argus* reported that, on 9 June 1853, Captain Alexander John Smith, Royal Navy was sworn in as a Justice of the Peace along with Captains O'Hara and White of the 40th Regiment in the Castlemaine Criminal Court by Acting Chief Justice Sir Redmond Barry. Alexander had been gazetted on the previous day as a Police Magistrate of Victoria for Taradale and Castlemaine.

The first duty Alexander Smith had as JP, together with White and O'Hara, on the day after they had been sworn in, was to hear a case of robbery with violence. Barry presided over the Castlemaine Criminal Court that morning. John Windsor and Aaron Durant pleaded not guilty to the charge that, on 24 March 1853, they violently assaulted, wounded and robbed John Wright at Bendigo. Windsor and Durant resided in a tent at a short distance from Wright's tent on the goldfields. On the night of 24 March, the two men with another unidentified man rushed into Mr and Mrs Wright's tent and pulled them out of bed demanding their money – all of their wealth. They stuffed Mrs Wright's mouth with part of a blanket and, holding her down, pulled out a pistol to reinforce the assault.

On Wright refusing to tell them where the money and gold was, one of the men struck him over the right eye, and later vigorously about the head. When the blanket was removed, Mrs Wright called out in desperation that, if they would spare their lives, she would tell them. With her admission, they located the hidden gold bars and £28 in cash.

They thrust Wright outside the tent. One kept guard over him with a pistol threatening to blow out his brains if he attempted to call out. In the meantime, the other two men inside the tent raped or, as it was put, 'ill-used' Mrs Wright.[18] This was the first case the newly-sworn in Alexander Smith presided over with his fellow magistrates.

Apart from disputes over mining claims, such violent cases were typical of the trials that Alexander Smith was required to handle in the local criminal courts during the 1850s either as a Justice of the Peace or as a Police Magistrate of Victoria at Castlemaine and adjacent districts. Difficult court cases were frequently part-and-parcel of his position.

One eye witness at the diggings at Mount Alexander claimed that 'not a tithe of the outrages' that occurred there was reported to authorities. In four or five weeks, he claimed, no less than nine people were shot there either in robberies or squabbles.[19]

Troubles at the diggings, *London Punch* 31 July 1852

18 'Castlemaine Criminal Court', *Argus*, Melbourne, Tuesday 14 June 1853.

19 'Crime at the Diggings', *Melbourne Morning Herald*, 2 February 1852.

Unlucky digger by the road,
sketch by S.T. Gill, an7537607, NLA

Alexander Smith was then faced with some awesome tasks. Armed robberies at night in tents were commonplace as well as on the road to the goldfields. According to Ellen Clacy, night was the characteristic time for a 'murder here, murder there' in the diggings themselves. She frequently heard revolvers cracking, rifles going off and balls whistling through the night air.[20]

On 11 February 1860, the *Argus* noted that Alexander Smith had been appointed Protector of the Chinese on the Goldfields. His responsibilities as Chinese Protector were also onerous.

In an article written from information provided by his two sons at the Victorian Rushes, Charles Dickens described the Chinese men as exotic others to the white Europeans; 'Their slight figures, smooth brown faces, hair carefully twisted into a huge tail, the coils of which are hidden beneath their immense hats, their short frocks and voluminous petticoat-trousers form a strange contrast to the stout forms, long beards and close-fitting dresses of the European diggers'.[21] Racial prejudice against the Chinese was rife at the Mount Alexander diggings and elsewhere – a serious matter Alexander Smith had to deal with.

20 Clacy, 'A lady on the goldfields', p. 34.

21 Dickens, *Household Words*.

Chinese at the diggings

Many Chinese were seeking gold at Guildford on the outskirts of Castlemaine. They tended to band together to protect themselves from intimidation, hostility, racism and prejudice from Europeans. In August 1857, about 1,300 Chinese gathered at Mechanics Hill in Castlemaine to protest against a parliamentary bill demanding overly-increased taxation for them to pay. There were numerous other local conflicts in which Commissioner Alexander Smith had to intervene as Protector. Some of these conflicts and disputes were of considerable proportion. The 1861 Census shows about 5,000 Chinese people in the district of Castlemaine.

Another duty Alexander Smith had to face was the closure of sly grog or illegal liquor shops. Walter G. Mason even created a wood engraving illustration entitled 'Diggers at a sly grog shop warned of the approach of a commissioner'.[22]

Sly grog shops, Castlemaine in the early 1850s

22 National Library of Australia, pic-an8003921 (see image bottom left).

The famous but ill-fated explorer Robert O'Hara Burke was Superintendent of Police between 1858 and 1860 in the Castlemaine District and thus worked closely with Alexander Smith as Magistrate. They became friendly.

By 1860, Castlemaine had become a substantial town with several fine public buildings. The 1860 Census showed about 30,000 people living in the district. The town had six banks and two newspapers – the popular press was sprouting everywhere. A gaol, market building and court house were built in 1861 and 1862 and the railway line arrived in 1862. It was believed for a while then that the town would eventually become Victoria's second largest city. But this was not to be after the end of the gold rushes.

The first slate quarry was in operation by 1859, supplying thousands of tons of flagging to Melbourne and other cities.

Over time, Castlemaine became widely recognised as one of the world's richest alluvial goldfields. The yield was remarkable with the peak achieved as early as 1852, a year before Alexander Smith was appointed there as Goldfields Commissioner.

On 20 June 1852, the *Melbourne Morning Herald* reported that the Gold Escort from Mount Alexander arrived at 3pm with 19,032 ounces of gold conveyed by pack horses. Excitement in the city increased as the extraordinary news got around like wildfire. In a six-month period in 1852, a staggering 16,000 kilograms were shipped out of the district by the Gold Escort alone and the figure was still as high as 140 kilograms a week in 1860. However, eventually, the alluvial gold began to peter out slowly and the area lacked the gold-rich quartz reefs of other centres. Thus the population began to wane, but not dramatically. The slate quarry, the flour mills, the railway foundry and the brewery continued to operate vigorously. Yeates Metallic Paints was established in Castlemaine in 1868 using iron oxide from the tailings in the goldfields. Other industries followed.[23]

* * * * *

The political background to Captain Alexander John Smith's career in the 1850s in Castlemaine was nothing less than turbulent and constantly tense for him and other government officials.

Victoria had become separated from the colonial rule of New South Wales on 11 November 1850.[24] Before that in January 1839, Charles Joseph La Trobe (1801-1875), a cultured gentleman but neither a naval or army officer nor an experienced colonial administrator, was appointed as Superintendent of the Port Phillip District. With the separation from New South Wales, La Trobe was appointed Lieutenant Governor of the new Colony of Victoria and given considerable executive powers.

In August 1851, he reported the discovery of gold at Ballarat. Almost every man in the newly

---

23 'Castlemaine (including Barker's Creek)', Castlemaine Historical Society, nd, duplicated typed notes, pp.1-9.

24 *The Australian Colonies Government Act of 1850*, British Parliament.

formed colony went to the diggings at some time or other. Several fortunes were made and some were as quickly lost. La Trobe managed to alienate all of the thousands of gold seekers by following the New South Wales example in imposing a direct tax, the monthly licence fee on search for gold. (He was ordered to do so). It was a disastrous folly for La Trobe to then raise the monthly fee from thirty shillings to £3 from January 1852.

A well-organised protest by the diggers and the popular press led to a humiliating defeat for La Trobe and his government within a fortnight of the announcement. La Trobe seemed to be setting the scene without meaning to do so for open rebellion on the Victorian goldfields. There were charges that even the 30 shillings a month demanded by the government was in itself illegal.

Following the 'Great Meeting of Diggers' held at the old Shepherd's Hut on the outskirts of Dr Barker's run near Chewton, the miners resolved to refuse to pay any licence fee at all. Delegates Captain Harrison, Dr Richmond and Mr Plaistow were sent to Melbourne to press the diggers' claims with Lieutenant Governor Charles La Trobe, but he remained stubborn and aloof. His response was to send a further 130 troops to Forest Creek, Castlemaine. There the troopers found themselves outnumbered 200 to 1. They were met with derision. La Trobe was thus forced to capitulate and the miner's fee was not increased beyond 30 shillings.

In December 1852, La Trobe submitted his resignation, but was not relieved until 1854. A broken man, he sailed for England on 6 May of that year.[25] He was replaced by Lieutenant Governor Sir Charles Hotham (1806-1855), an ambitious

25 Jill Eastwood, 'La Trobe, Charles Joseph (1801-1874)', *Australian Dictionary of Biography* Vol. 2, pp. 89-93.

naval officer. He accepted the most difficult colonial post on 6 December 1853 and arrived in Melbourne on 22 June of the following year. At first he gained some popularity with the diggers, but he was an authoritarian figure who thoroughly misread the tense political situation. He soon isolated himself from government officials and politicians, as well as the diggers.

He saw the crisis on the goldfields as a rebellion not as a protest against what had become an unfair tax. He could only see a military solution. The diggers at Ballarat on 3 December precipitated armed action which Hotham in Melbourne wrongly interpreted. The diggers' rebellion was defeated famously behind the sharpened logs of the Eureka Stockade on Sunday 3 December 1854. Troopers and police attacked before dawn taking the diggers by complete surprise. After less than thirty minutes fighting, one hundred and fourteen diggers were taken as prisoners and fifteen diggers and one soldier lay dead. Others died of their wounds later on. News of the defeat soon reached Castlemaine and the other diggings throughout the Victorian goldfields.

Hotham kept troops at the ready and refused an amnesty for the Eureka prisoners. By mid-January 1855, his popularity had completely collapsed. In March when the royal commission recommended reform of the licence, he foolishly maintained publicly that the fee was right in principle. Such utterances enflamed the political situation for a while.

Six months of relative political quiet followed Eureka. Hotham's post was raised to a full governorship on 3 February 1855 and he was commended by the Imperial Government for suppressing the so-called outbreak. He remained wildly unpopular with the Victorian Legislative Council. After he sent his resignation to London, his health began to fail. On 17

December 1855, he caught a chill while on official duty and died on 31 December.[26] He was replaced by Sir Henry Barkly on 22 September 1856.

Although the Commission of Inquiry which followed the Eureka outburst had recommended that Commissioners be removed from the goldfields, it took some time for this and all the other recommendations to be fully carried out. Commissioners (who were replaced by Wardens) and their staff were gradually withdrawn from the camps, and the 40th Regiment finally departed Castlemaine in January 1858.

*　　*　　*　　*　　*

During most of the 1850s, Alexander Smith was an integral part of the history of the Gold Rushes that had become the crucible of democracy. As Manning Clark put it, even by the middle of 1852, the presence of gold was 'subverting' the old social Imperial 'order of rank and degree. At the diggings, it was already being said by many that "Jack is as good as his master"'. Socially, there was much confusion. Wealth became a significant criterion of the new social standing in the community. It was one of those periods of history when there was a time of chaos before the significance of what had happened had become clear to everyone and a sense of direction began to take place.[27]

Charles Thatcher's song of triumph for the diggers published in the *Melbourne Morning Herald* in 1853 seemed to say it all:

---

26 B.A. Knox, 'Hotham, Sir Charles (1806-1855)', Douglas Pike (gen. ed.), *Australian Dictionary of Biography*, Vol. 4, Melbourne University Press, Carlton, 1972, pp. 429-30.

27 C.M.H. Clark *A History of Australia*, Vol. IV, Melbourne University Press, Carlton, 1978, p. 45.

Hurrah for Australia

Hurrah for Australia the golden,
Where men of all nations now toil,
To none will we e'er be beholden
Whilst we've strength to turn up the soil;
There's no poverty here to distress us,
'Tis a country of true liberty,
No proud lords can ever oppress us,
But here we're untrammelled and free.[28]

Diggers relaxing on a Saturday afternoon

Matters, however, were much more complex than the composer in the popular press had expounded. A new colonial bourgeoisie was to emerge and Alexander Smith was to be part of it.

---

28 *Herald* (Melbourne), 29 November 1853; also cited by Clark, *A History of Australia*, p. 65.

10

A Member of Parliament
Commander Alexander Smith RN, MLA

Alexander John Smith, MLA

By the early 1860s, Alexander Smith's name in Castlemaine was as familiar as *Household Words*, a popular book of the time held by most families. As a candidate for election to the Victorian Parliament, he had received the largest number of votes in Castlemaine of any candidate in the 1860s which demonstrates the widespread feelings of respect and goodwill towards him in the district. He was reputed for his unostentatious manner.

Having resigned on 23 April 1861 as Warden of the Goldfields and Police Magistrate of Victoria after eight years of unremitting work, he was elected to the Victorian

Parliament on 17 May of the same year. He was very popular, a singular thing for a goldfields officer. He was considered a substantially wealthy man by many, having a town house in Castlemaine and a homestead at Langley, a property earlier known as Langley Vale. He had purchased Langley Vale from Thomas and Charles Peevor on 6 February 1861 and was to live there the rest of his days.

The property was not far from the Campaspe River on the Kyneton-Redesdale Road and close to Murrays Road. Langley Vale, which was near Kyneton, was Gazetted on 4 October 1848 and had an area of 9,000 acres. The original owner from May 1849 had been Edward John Hogg when it had still been a part of the Colony of New South Wales in the Port Phillip District before separation.

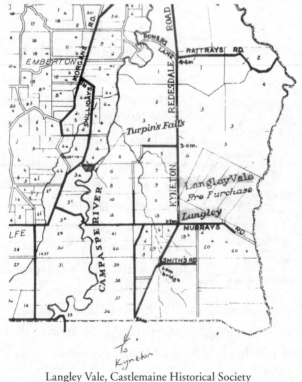

Langley Vale, Castlemaine Historical Society

Castlemaine Market Square & Mostyn Street, lithograph of photograph by Joseph Wheeler, Castlemaine Art Gallery & Historial Museum

Alexander had previously purchased a town house for his family by auction on 19 November 1858 on allotment 32 called 'Talbot' in Guildford on the outskirts of Castlemaine. He also apparently purchased other properties in the same town later on.

As a Member of the Legislative Assembly, Alexander Smith stayed at the Melbourne Club while Parliament was in session.[1]

* * * * *

Back on 21 August 1857 at The Camp, Castlemaine, Edward Bernhard Smith[2] was born to Alexander and Aubrey, their sixth child. Sadly, he died as a little boy on 19 April 1861 just before his father had resigned as Warden of the Goldfields and

---

1 Details provided in documents held by Castlemaine Historical Society Inc., courtesy of Ian Hockley.

2 Family Notes, *Argus*, 24 August, 1857, p.5.

Police Magistrate of Victoria in Castlemaine. Thus Alexander went to his first Parliamentary session a saddened man and Aubrey too had to struggle with grief at Langley while busy caring for her other children.

After Edward Bernhard was born, Maud Margaret appeared on the scene, born on 15 September 1859, their seventh and last child. She died on 3 June 1946, living to a grand old age. Alexander Henry was born while they were on their sojourn in England on 21 April 1852; he died on 6 July 1935. Edith Margaret, who was then born in Victoria after their return from England on 15 August 1854, died on 14 April 1906. So Alexander and Aubrey had four more children in the 1850s after leaving Tasmania to add to their three older daughters who had been born in Hobart in the 1840s.[3] Six of their children survived to adulthood. It should be noted that Alexander and Aubrey were buried with their infant son Edward Bernhard in the Castlemaine Cemetery. The family vault is incribed with their three names.[4]

*　　*　　*　　*　　*

The records of the House indicate that Alexander Smith was an energetic, alert Member of the Legislative Assembly for Castlemaine and, as always, took his responsibilities seriously. His attendance in the House, unlike some other members, was meticulous and he strongly supported measures that would enhance and progress the economic, social and educational development in his electorate. His particular concerns were compensation for miners where it was a just cause, the

---

3　Modified Register for Captain Alexander John Smith, pp. 1-3.

4　Ian Hockley, Castlemaine Historical Society, to John Ramsland, 7 February 2011.

extension of the railway, the reduction of rail freight charges from the district to the city and the establishment of new schools for the children of local communities.

He was forthright in asking questions of substance in the House, particularly for his own constituents. One of his first questions was to ask the government if the miners at the White Horse Gully Reservoir would receive compensation for the loss of their claims as well as the injuries they had received.[5] Alexander John Smith did not ever become a silent Member.

Dr Macadam, the other Member of Parliament for Castlemaine and a man with a showier personality, had been elected to the office of Postmaster General which had led in turn to what was described as a 'severe contest' in which 'Lieutenant A.J. Smith RN, formerly a warden in the district', had been returned as an MLA.[6]

In Parliament, Alexander Smith presented partitions on many occasions, like the petition from Edward Bell 'praying for compensation ... for the loss of office as an immigration agent, and for expenses incurred' with his work.[7] It was not long before Smith had made his mark as an upright, re-sourceful parliamentarian. He made several amendments and adjustments to new legislation before the House. From time to time, he even called attention to the lack of a quorum in the House.

He stoutly supported the official visit of the Prince of Wales to the Australian colonies (and was presented to him in full Royal Naval uniform as a Commander). He showed a strong interest in the initiatives of the government in support of the proposed Burke and Wills Expedition. He had worked

5   'The Victorian Parliament', *Argus*, 24 May 1861.

6   'Summary for Europe', *Argus*, 25 May 1861.

7   'Summary for Europe', *Argus*, 29 May 1861.

Commander Alexander Smith RN received a similar invitation
to the reception of the Duke of Edinburgh

closely with Robert O'Hara Burke when he was a district
magistrate and Burke had been head of the police force in the
Castlemaine district in the late 1850s. He strongly advocated
the development of plans by the government to provide assistance to the expedition on their homeward journey.[8]

* * * * *

When Alexander John Smith entered Parliament, politics in
Victoria while in a pioneering phase were rapidly changing
and moving towards responsible government. *The Constitution
Act of 1850* under which the colony was first constituted had
provided for a legislative council, partly nominated by the
lieutenant governor (La Trobe at the time) and partly elected
by persons having property qualification. As the population
grew with the rush to the goldfields, the membership of the
council was increased and eventually the franchise was extended to gold diggers holding licences.

In 1853, the council was invited by the Imperial government to frame a constitution for the colony on similar lines

8 *Argus*, 19 June 1861.

to that of Canada with two houses of legislature, the council and assembly, together with ministers responsible for different specialised portfolios.

Thus, the legislative council of Victoria passed early in 1856, five years before Alexander Smith was elected, the first effective provision for voting by secret ballot brought into use by English-speaking peoples. In July 1856, *The Constitution Act* received royal assent after amendment by the British parliament and, in November, the first parliament consisting of both houses (a legislative council and a legislative assembly) met in Melbourne. All this had been closely watched by Alexander John Smith in his government positions at Castlemaine.

In 1857, the Victorian parliament adopted the principle of manhood suffrage, a matter in which Victoria was a pioneer. The ground was thus prepared for a democratic experiment. Sir Charles Hotham, who had been granted the title of Governor-in-Chief before his death, was succeeded by Sir Henry Barkly who arrived in December 1856 and remained in office until 1863. The term of his governorship was marked by several attempts to deal with what had become a burning question during Alexander Smith's time in parliament – that of settling an agricultural population on the land until then so largely populated by squatters. Alexander Smith was also part of that agricultural population with his purchase of Langley Vale in 1861.

The principle of 'selection' was introduced, but there was much 'dummying' by squatters trying to maintain their old monopoly. Not until several experiments with land acts had been tried was the problem to receive a satisfactory solution.

The 1850s gold rushes themselves had caused a steep decline in the agricultural and pastoral industries in Victoria. But by 1861, Victoria was producing more wheat than New

South Wales (3½ million bushels to 1½ million). By 1865, Victoria had nearly nine million sheep, surpassing even the sheep population in the mother country.[9]

* * * * *

Alexander Smith's writing desk & bureau at Langley homestead (now housed at Bontharambo, Wangaratta)

In the legislative assembly by late June 1861, Alexander Smith had been pursuing the issue of the Robert O'Hara Burke Expedition. He asked the Chief Secretary whether the government had taken steps to procure intelligence of the Expedition and if any plans had been adopted to provide assistance to it on their homeward route, 'either northward of or at Cooper's Creek'.[10]

It is clear that Smith was drawing strongly on his own expeditionary experiences in the Antarctic under the leadership of James Clark Ross and his principles of careful planning. He was correct in his emphasis on careful planning that could save lives on explorative expeditions, whether they be on the high seas or the equally dangerous inland desert.

In the previous year of 1860, Castlemaine had witnessed a

9   Jose & Carter (eds), *Australian Encyclopedia*, pp. 621-4.

10   'The Victorian Parliament', *Argus*, 22 June 1861.

celebratory dinner at the Albert Hotel put on by eighty local notables in honour of Robert O'Hara Burke, the leader of such an expedition into the interior. Alexander Smith was one of the invitees – at the time still a Warden of the Goldfields and a local Magistrate. The assembly included those from the law (like Smith), medicine (like Dr Barker on whose property gold had been first discovered), the local clergy and representatives of leading local commercial firms, storekeepers, farmers and, 'in fact, every grade found representatives'. The enthusiasm shown by all was said to be unbounded, warm-hearted in nature and the evening passed off in a most pleasant manner. Robert O'Hara Burke had ridden over from his encampment at Mia-Mia Creek to attend.

At the gathering, the denizens of Castlemaine expressed a confidence in Burke – he was highly esteemed and had managed to charm them. They all believed (in hindsight, ironically) that he would, without the shadow of a doubt, bring the expedition to a successful outcome. The gathering met on 16 July 1860. Burke was depicted as 'the first leader whoever thoroughly penetrated the wilds of Australia, and set at rest all doubts or speculations for the future as to the interior of that vast country'.

Robert O'Hara Burke (1820-1861) was born in a manor house near Galway in 1820 and educated in Belgium. He had the appearance of a gentleman, a handsome daring Irishman with a reckless look about him, 'a fiery furnace of a man'. He had a scar across his face, caused, so the rumour went, by a sabre-cut in a duel while in the Austrian Army as a mercenary. He had entered the Austrian Army in 1840 and attained the rank of Captain, but returned to Ireland in 1848 and joined the constabulary. He was witty and immensely charming and was said to dance divinely. He had all the habits of a gentleman and, like Alexander John Smith RN, was a member of the most exclusive club (The Melbourne Club) in Melbourne. As Manning Clark put it, he was 'in the tradition of the gentlemen explorers of the Australian wilderness'.[11] Burke had migrated to Tasmania in 1853, but crossed to Victoria soon after where he was appointed inspector of police.

In 1859 while at Castlemaine as police inspector, he was chosen by the Exploration Fund Committee to lead the expedition from Melbourne to the Gulf of Carpentaria.

Burke & Wills memorial, Melbourne

The celebratory dinner was described along with the wines as *par excellence* and many speeches with toasts were enjoined to loud applause during the course of the evening. 'Bumpers' were drunk to the health of Robert O'Hara Burke. The chairman emphasised to the gathering the valuable service Burke had rendered to the community as superintendent of the police force at Castlemaine.[12]

Heralded as 'Our First Victorian Hero', Burke joined the Victorian Police in April 1853, the same year that Alexander Smith was appointed as Goldfields Commissioner in Castlemaine. He was stationed at the Beechworth diggings between 1854 and 1858 and was then transferred to Castlemaine in November 1858. He was well-built and tall

---

11 Clark, *A History of Australia*, pp. 146-7.

12 'Complimentary Dinner to R.O'H. Burke Esq., Leader of the Exploring Expedition', *Mount Alexander Mail*, 19 July 1860.

with a magnificent beard. Women seemed enchanted by this bold adventurer and he gained a reputation as a womanizer. On the surface, he seemed a man who was born to lead, although he was incapable of maintaining order in his personal affairs. While possessed of a charismatic persona, he had little knowledge of navigation, no experience at exploration and no bushcraft skill. His Anglo-Irish pedigree, however, ensured his name was put forward to lead a vast expedition to the Gulf of Carpentaria which left Melbourne on 20 August 1860, cheered on by a large enthusiastic crowd of well-wishers. As Manning Clark put it: 'Chance or the gods had planted in him an insatiable hunger for glory and public acclaim'.[13] The exploration across the desert, however, was ill-fated.

Burke & Wills funeral procession, *Australasian Sketcher* 1863

Largely owing to Burke's impatient temperament and ignorance of bushcraft, the expedition floundered hopelessly and Burke and his second-in-command William John Wills died of exposure and exhaustion on Cooper's Creek towards

13 Clark, *A History of Australia*, p.146.

the end of June 1861. It was something that Alexander John Smith had perhaps feared.

Alexander Smith's parliamentary anxieties about Burke were well-founded. The citizens of Castlemaine were honoured to lead Robert O'Hara Burke's mighty funeral procession through the streets of Melbourne on 21 January 1863.[14] A large party of residents from Castlemaine had boarded the train to Melbourne at Castlemaine Station the previous day. They were to take part in the great funeral procession that was to honour Burke. The Castlemaine Rifle Corps, Light Dragoons and Volunteer Band of twenty-five musicians in uniform were all to pay tribute to what was then regarded and what had become known as Castlemaine's great explorer and local hero – in hindsight, a reckless hero with feet of clay.

Thousands lined the streets as the cortege passed slowly by with troops and dignities in attendance from all over the Colony of Victoria. As a tribute to the thriving town of Castlemaine, it was a Castlemaine resident, Councillor Gringell, who was appointed marshal of the procession. Gingell led the procession followed by the advance guard of the Castlemaine Light Dragoons; then came a body of forty men led by Captain C. Anderson; the Volunteer Castlemaine Band came next playing the "Dead March" from *Saul*, followed by the Castlemaine Rifle Corps of fifty strong.[15]

The citizens of Castlemaine moved quickly to build their own memorial to the ill-fated expedition.

Alexander Smith pointed out on Saturday 29 March 1862 in Parliament that the people of Castlemaine would not

---

14 Geoff Hocking, *Gold, A Pictorial History of the Australian Goldrush*, The Five Mile Press, Rowville, Victoria,2006, pp. 203, 208.

15 Geoff Hocking, *Castlemaine. From Camp to City*, New Chum Press, Castlemaine, 2007, p. 105.

consent to contributing to 'a national monument' as they were establishing and contributing to their own.[16] Support by Alexander Smith RN, MLA and many other prominent locals was a cause of some controversy. Several groups had come together, all vying to be considered the one true committee that would honour the local hero.

Burke & Wills Monument, Castlemaine

There were several other monuments in various towns started, but the granite obelisk in Castlemaine, with the assistance of the Burke Memorial Committee and J.V.A. Bruce's patronage, was the one that most appropriately paid tribute to the fallen explorers. The Castlemaine Monument to Burke and Wills was a simple, but large and dignified obelisk. The massive granite block was cut in Harcourt to the north of Castlemaine from a quarry on Mount Alexander.[17]

When Alexander Smith took the oath and his seat for

16 'Legislative Assembly', *Argus*, 29 March 1962.

17 Hocking, *Castlemaine. From Camp to City*, p. 108.

Castlemaine as reported in the *Argus* on Wednesday 6 November 1861, he immediately asked whether the Minister proposed to provide a pension for John King, the sole survivor of the Victorian Expedition, to erect a memorial for the leaders and to institute an inquiry into the causes as to why relief was not afforded to the survivors at Cooper's Creek on their return journey. The reply he received was that the Minister was intending to ask for a sum for the erection of a memorial and to institute a searching inquiry as to why relief was not afforded when the relief party was near at hand.[18]

Nothing was mentioned at the time about a pension for the survivor who had been protected and rescued by Aborigines. Apart from the humane and sincere Alexander John Smith, no one showed much of an interest in the only man who had returned alive.

In Parliament, Smith showed similar concern for other individuals. For example, in early February 1862, he asked whether the government were going to settle the claim made by Alan de Lacey for the discovery of payable goldfields at the head of Sandy Creek and on Little Snowy Creek, Mitta Mitta.[19]

Later in February of that year, he asked why his friend Captain Edward Bull, a former Goldfields Commissioner and now a captain commanding the Castlemaine Volunteers, had been passed over in recent promotions to the rank of lieutenant colonel. The answer to this question was one of seniority; Lieutenant Colonel Champ and Mair were both gazetted captains in the force before Bull was appointed a captain. Therefore, Bull was their junior, but had not been passed over,

18 'Victorian Parliament', *Argus*, 6 Nov 1861.

19 'Victorian Parliament', *Argus*, 1 February 1862.

it was argued, in the sense that Smith had implied.[20] This answer Alexander Smith found unsatisfactory.

In February 1862, Smith also gave notice that he would ask the Treasurer when the salaries of the officers and men employed on the geological survey were to be paid.[21] In March, he moved that the petition of W.H. Wright, the former Chief Commissioner of Goldfields and Crown Lands of the Wimmera district (under whom Smith had worked as a Commissioner in the early 1850s), be referred to a select committee at the time sitting on claims for compensation.[22]

Alexander Smith was intrepid in following up such matters for his constituents and friends. The following day, he asked the Treasurer upon what principles were promotions in the Volunteers based. He received a similar reply to the day before.

Railway development was another important on-going issue for Smith. He was appointed to a select committee with several others to inquire into and report upon the best site for a railway station at Melbourne.[23] In early March, Alexander Smith sent a telegram to Dr Kelly, the municipal chairman of the Castlemaine district, stating that the sites decided upon for the railway station in Melbourne were the goods station in Campbell Street and the passenger train in Templeton Street, thus greatly enhancing, he claimed, the value of properties in these streets.[24]

In late April 1862, Alexander Smith was delighted with the opening of the railway to Kyneton, the town not far from his

20 'Victorian Parliament', *Argus*, 19 February 1862.

21 'Victorian Parliament', *Argus*, 27 February 1862.

22 *Argus*, 20 March 1862.

23 'Parliament Business', *Argus*, 25 February 1862.

24 Reported in *Castlemaine Advertiser*, 27 February 1862.

Langley homestead and 9,000 acre agricultural property. It was the section of the Murray River Railway from Woodend to Kyneton known widely by this time as the 'Garden of Victoria'. For the locals, it was an auspicious event to celebrate.

As was usual practice on such occasions, a local banquet was organised at which 'a large party of gentlemen from Melbourne', including members of the Victorian Executive Council and both houses of parliament, would be present. They were provided with a special train from Melbourne. The Melbourne party numbered about 200 including several ladies, the wives of notables. Their pleasant journey from Melbourne occupied about two hours and fifteen minutes before Kyneton station was reached, the line from Melbourne to Woodend having already been completed.

The rail passed over about eight miles from Woodend to Kyneton of comparatively flat country, rich in agricultural activity. This section of line had been completed comparatively rapidly. The only other noteworthy portion was a viaduct over that river – a handsome solid bridge of three arches. There were, however, two heavy cuttings on the line that required more intense work after the Campaspe River had been bridged.

Alexander Smith was among the prominent people of Kyneton and surrounding district well pleased 'to find rapid and immediate communication with the metropolis' now within their reach. It would transform their lives.

The visitors walked about a half mile from the station to the local School of Arts where the elaborate celebratory banquet was held for their enjoyment. This was a men's only affair, typical of the nineteenth-century Victorian culture; the ladies were entertained elsewhere in private homes.

About two hundred gentlemen sat down to the banquet at

the School of Arts. As was usual in these Victorian era events, there were many speakers and many toasts with many vintages. As a series of dishes on an expansive menu were heartily consumed, Alexander John Smith was one of the speakers as the Castlemaine member of the Legislative Assembly of Victoria. In full naval dress uniform, he replied to a toast by Dr Mackenzie to the 'Army and Navy and Volunteers'. As retired member of the Royal Navy, Commander Smith stated that he felt a great pride in the British military forces and this feeling had not lessened at all since his retirement from the senior service. After reading the recent military accounts from home, he felt that a war with America was imminent (because of the American Civil war that was raging between the North and the South).

He then referred to an English fleet providing for the military emergency and consisting of thirty-seven sails of the line carrying 1,273 guns of heaviest calibre – a force surpassing all the American Federal navy put together. The English fleet, he informed the audience, was commanded by Admiral Milne. Another fleet in the Mediterranean under Admiral Davies was also alerted and would double the entire American navy when it arrived in American waters in about ten days. With these facts in mind, he was confident that 'the flag of England would wave triumphantly wherever it appeared'. Smith had not lost his imperial enthusiasm for England ruling the waves.

His comments were met with enthusiastic patriotic cheers from the audience. He went on to further enumerate proudly the powers of the Royal Navy – more cheers. More patriotic speeches then followed by other leading figures at the banquet. Finally, and at long last, a toast was made to the Commissioner of Railways and the success of the rail to Kyneton.[25]

---

25 'The Opening of the Railway to Kyneton', *Argus*, 26 April 1862.

Cobb & Co light Concord thoroughbrace coach

The steam train was in the process of tethering the mighty bush to the world of the metropolis. Cobb and Co., the celebrated coaching firm founded in the Victorian Goldfields in 1854 by a young American, Freeman Cobb, a man with a large moustache and slight limp, met the competition from the advancing inland railways, like the one to Kyneton, by moving further and further inland.

In early 1853, coaching expert Freeman Cobb had brought two light Concord thoroughbrace (leather sprung) coaches with him to Melbourne from the United States and had begun daily services to and from the goldfields at what seemed at first a financially risky enterprise as good horses were expensive and so fares too had to be fairly costly. It was soon possible to travel the eighty miles from Melbourne to Castlemaine in ten hours with a change of horses at Cobb and Co. stations on the way, instead of a number of days slow journey in other types of horse-drawn vehicles.[26] The Cobb and Co. coaches were

26 Michael Cannon, *The Roaring Days*, Today's Australia Publishing Company, Mornington, 1998, p.491.

comparatively fast, but the ride was uncomfortable and could not be compared with a passenger or even a freight train. Most regular passengers almost without exception preferred the steam train to the horse coach.

In the 1860s, there had become a veritable frenzy of railway building.[27] Horse coaches began to disappear slowly on the roads leading from Melbourne to Castlemaine and return. The railway network changed everything. As Henry Lawson expressed it in 1889:

> The flaunting flag of progress
> In the West unfurled,
> The mighty bush with iron rails
> Is tethered to the world.[28]

Alexander Smith believed in such material and economic progress which he saw as the indispensable by-product of the intellectual and moral progress of mankind. Before the railway was linked to Kyneton, it took him sometimes two days or more to travel to Melbourne to attend parliament; now it would take only two and a half hours or so. The tyranny of distance was thus diminished and the train was far more comfortable in all weathers and conditions than the horse-drawn coach.

The roaring days were over. No longer would come the Royal Mail behind 'six foaming horses' dashing past the camps, the little homes of calico 'that dotted all the scene'.[29] The iron rail, the telegraph and agricultural machinery began

---

27 Geoffrey Blainey, *Black Kettle and Full Moon. Daily Life in a Vanished Australia*, Viking, Camberwell, 2003, p. 91.

28 Henry Lawson, 'The Roaring Days' in Leonard Cronin (ed.), *A Camp-Fire Yarn. Henry Lawson. Complete Works 1885-1900*, Lansdowne, Sydney, 1984, p. 68.

29 Lawson, 'The Roaring Days'.

at long last to give man mastery over the land of Australia. Such advances, Smith believed, would bring prosperity to all.

He was very proud of the new rail link between Kyneton and the metropolis as it brought with it so many benefits. Those involved in the district agricultural, pastoral, mining and commercial industries were also overjoyed. Smith maintained his focus on the issue of the railways as a local member. On 9 May 1863, for example, he asked the Chief Secretary for the free conveyancing of certain public bodies, like the army Volunteers and municipal council members and employees, so they could carry out their official work and participate in the Melbourne celebrations of the marriage of the Prince of Wales. The reply he received was that rates could be reduced, but not given free-of-charge.[30] In 1867-8, the first visit of a member of the royal family caused a sensation and an explosion of patriotic fervour in city and country throughout the colonies. In late 1868, decked out in his full naval dress uniform with dress sword, Commander Alexander Smith was presented at a special reception in Melbourne to Prince Alfred, second son of Queen Victoria, the Duke of Kent and the Duke of Saxe-Coburg and Gotha. This took place after the Prince had recovered from bullet wounds as a result of an assassination attempt by Henry James O'Farrell at a charity event at Clontarf Beach in Middle Harbour, Sydney on 12 March 1868.[31]

On the same formal visit to Melbourne, Prince Albert laid the foundation stone for the Prince Alfred Hospital. Alexander Smith was in attendance as a member of the Victorian Parliament. The Hospital opened its doors on 5 May 1871.

Apart from his parliamentary and agricultural interests,

---

30 'Parliament', *Argus*, 9 May 1863.

31 Clark, *A History of Australia*, pp. 250-5.

Alexander Smith was on the board as a director of the Australian Alliance Assurance Company by mid-1862.[32] Because of his naval background and scientific work on the Rossbank Magnetic Observatory in Tasmania in the 1840s, he also became a member of the Board of Visitors to the Astronomical and Magnetic Observatories in Victoria.[33] In early 1863, he became the Chairman of the Gold-fields Reward Board which dealt with the financial rewards for new discoveries of goldfields such as those at Walsh's Creek and Donovan's Creek. Prospectors were required to communicate with the Secretary for Mines without delay and to furnish documentary or other evidence about their claims so that the Board under Smith's chairmanship could prioritise them respectively.[34] Smith was appointed to this responsible position because of his outstandingly honest reputation as a former Goldfields Commissioner and Warden in the turbulent 1850s. Various *Government Gazette* notices on relevant matters appeared under his name and title.[35]

At times, Alexander was slightly angered in parliament when confused with other members with the same surname, J.T. Smith, L.L. Smith and W.C. Smith.[36] These were the only times he seems to have become agitated. Usually he was calm, practical and progressive in demeanour. He was not given to showy or stagey flights of political indignation.

In the House, Alexander maintained his focus on the railway question with great determination as a back-bencher. In May 1863, he moved the appointment of a select committee

32 Advertisement, *Argus*, 13 June 1862.
33 'Appointments', *Argus*, 18 June 1862.
34 'Government Advertisement', *Argus,* 6 Feb 1863.
35 For example, *Argus*, 11 Feb 1863.
36 'Legislative Assembly', *Argus*, 21 May 1863.

to inquire into the subject of the removal of the railway station from Chewton, briefly presented the case against it and nominated the full personnel of the committee. While the motion was seconded, the Commissioner of Railways successfully asked that it be postponed until a report on the subject be laid on the table.[37] The enquiry did proceed at a later stage.

Alexander was also part of a movement to petition for the establishment of the Coliban Water Supply. Others included representatives for Castlemaine, Chewton, Eaglehawk, Sandhurst and other adjacent places. Their demand was, as A.J. Smith put it, to commence the building of the Coliban Scheme. It had been ascertained that the quantity of water that would be available when the works were completed would be equal to 10,000 gallons *per diem* of which quantity 9,800 would be devoted to mining purposes, the remaining 200 gallons being intended for the domestic supply of the householders of Castlemaine and Chewton.[38] The balance of distribution of water was to change radically over time towards a much better supply to homes.

Smith remained active in his interest in the magnetic observatory. He gave notice in the House that he would move an address asking for the production of a copy of the despatch from His Excellency Sir Henry Barkly to General Edward Sabine, with any other papers to the Royal Society relating to the purchase of a telescope of greater power than any previously used in the Southern Hemisphere.[39] Edward Sabine was one of the key initiators of the 1839-1843 Antarctic Expedition and an expert on international territorial magnetism.

In early March, Alexander Smith continued the discussion

37 'Legislative Assembly', *Argus*, 29 May 1863.

38 'The Coliban Water Supply', *Argus*, 18 Feb 1864.

39 'Legislative Assembly', *Argus*, 25 Feb 1864.

in the House about the telescope for the Victorian Observatory. His attention had been drawn to it by a pamphlet published by the Royal Society. The telescope in question was the earlier invention of the French astronomer Nicolas Louis de Lataille of the Paris Observatory and was of great strength. From the correspondence that had taken place, Smith was absolutely convinced that the whole scientific world of Europe was in favour of the establishment of such a telescope in the Southern Hemisphere.

The scientific objects to be realised by its establishment, Smith hastened to point out, were of great importance. He argued for £5,000 to be placed on the Additional Estimates of the government with the purpose of defraying the cost of the telescope and its erection. He then put the following motion:

> That an address be presented to His Excellency the Governor, praying His Excellency to cause to be placed upon the table of the House a copy of the dispatch from His Excellency, Sir Henry Barkly to General Sabine, with any other papers to the Royal Society relative to the purchase of a telescope of greater power than any previous used in the Southern Hemisphere.

The motion was seconded, put and received with 'no opposition on the part of the Government'.[40] In other words, a rare bipartisan agreement on the matter was reached thanks to Alexander Smith's determination.

In early March 1864, there was excitement in the air when there was a Vice Regal visit to Castlemaine and Sandhurst that occurred on the 8th of the month. It was the first visit that Sir Charles Darling, Governor of Victoria, paid to the mining and agricultural districts and underlined their growing im-

---

40 'Legislative Assembly', *Argus*, 3 March 1864.

portance to the colonial economy. The Governor witnessed picturesque hills, wooded lowlands, 'smiling' vineyards and substantial homesteads as he passed through the two districts. Every mile travelled by train gave ample evidence of the future of such countryside. He was greeted everywhere in the towns and villages by crowds of adults and school children. Patriotic feeling filled the air.

The reception at Castlemaine was considered a remarkable affair. The streets were crowded by the denizens of the town dressed in their holiday best waving flags. Lieutenant A.J. Smith RN, MLA was on hand with the Mayor and other dignitaries as were the local rifle corps headed by Lieutenant Colonel Bull, Smith's old Goldfields Commissioner, colleague and friend. The brass band of the Castlemaine Volunteers provided a rousing welcome as did the Chinese community rich in colourful traditional costumes. At the town hall, an endless variety of speeches were made.[41]

In his parliamentary work, Alexander Smith also focused attention on the need for the Victorian Council of Education to provide new common schools in developing areas especially where such provisions had previously been neglected.[42] On at least one occasion, he seriously challenged the government policy about the matter.

He strongly supported the bill for the establishment of Reformatory and Industrial Schools for delinquent, deserted, vagrant and depressed youth. English evidence was that such measures decreased crime rates. He saw it, like others in the parliament, as a duty of the government as well as voluntary organisations of the colony. Such institutions contained the idea of rescuing youth from a life of crime through industrial

41 'Vice-Regal Visit to Castlemaine and Sandhurst', *Argus*, 9 March 1964.

42 'Legislative Council', *Argus*, 11 March 1864.

training and elementary education. He believed that more should be spent by the government on the matter. Compulsory powers were needed to ensure proper training in useful occupations that would enhance the colony's economy.[43]

Smith maintained his efforts in the House of improving the rails and the roads of the colony and, especially, of removing the inequality of rail tariffs charged between Castlemaine and Melbourne. He emphasised that the freight rates by rail from Castlemaine to Melbourne were higher than those charged from Melbourne to Ballarat. He felt strongly that the citizens of the Castlemaine district were being unjustly treated.

Several protest meetings were organised in Castlemaine to bring grievances about railway charges to the notice of the head of the railway. A delegation, including Alexander Smith MLA and other town notables like the Mayor, waited upon the Commissioner of Railways and conducted a long interview with him pressing their claims in the strongest of terms. They argued that the difference in railway charges between Castlemaine and Ballarat was about eleven per cent in favour of the latter place, not withstanding that the goods had to be conveyed about sixteen miles longer to Ballarat. The delegation contended that the tariff or transport rates should be equalised between the two contesting towns; there should be no preference over one place to the other.[44] On behalf of the people of Castlemaine, Alexander Smith presented to the House a petition from the mayor and burghers, 'praying for the assimilation of the traffic charges on the Murray line of railways to those on the Ballarat line'.[45]

In the newly-elected Victorian Parliament in late October

43 'Legislative Assembly', *Argus*, 22 April 1864.

44 'Goods Traffic on the Victorian Railways', *Argus*, 19 May 1864.

45 'Parliament', *Argus*, 28 May 1864.

1864, Alexander Smith amongst others was re-elected to the seat of Castlemaine, such was his popularity and reputation for reliability. Castlemaine, because of its population of electors (5,000) was entitled to have three members in the House.[46] Alexander John Smith headed the list with the most votes. For the first time, he was listed as Commander Alexander John Smith R.N. as he had received a promotion on the retired list. (With his new title, he was presented to the Duke of Edinburgh on the occasion of his official visit to the Colony of Victoria.)[47]

In October 1870, A.J. Smith RN of Langley, Kyneton, was gazetted as a Justice of the Peace.[48] While he continued this work for as long as he was able, his life was beginning to draw to a close. His health was deteriorating.

*   *   *   *   *

Commander Alexander John Smith RN, MLA had seen the Colony of Victoria through its turbulent years of the 'Roaring Days' of the Gold Rushes. His work as a Goldfields Commissioner and later as a Warden had been most demanding and time-consuming. Moreover, the conditions of life on the goldfields had been difficult in themselves. Supply of fresh water had become a major problem as the population had increased rapidly. The creeks had been muddied and infected by constant digging, panning and pollution from careless humans and wandering stock. Some unsuccessful miners earned a hand-to-mouth living by carting water from distant streams and selling it for a shilling a bucket. But many

---

46 'The New Parliament', *Argus*, 25 October 1864.

47 'The Duke of Edinburgh in Melbourne', *Argus*, 27 November 1867.

48 *Argus*, 1 October 1870.

people could not afford to pay for clean drinking water and dysentery spread rapidly.

Goldfields Commissioners like Alexander Smith had to do their best to prevent health problems caused by the sudden flow of population into the diggings. The water problem in the Roaring Days led Smith to be a keen campaigner for a reliable water supply for Castlemaine in the 1860s.

As Goldfields Commissioner in the 1850s, he observed and had to superintend as far as possible other conditions on the diggings around Castlemaine. The labour of the diggers was conducted in sludge, filth and confusion and sometimes in chaos. In mines close to the streams, men dug waist-deep in water until driven out by the rapidly rising water levels. Blowflies, March flies and sandflies made their serious contribution to discomfort and disease. Crippling illness was feared by miners. Their diets were poor in many cases. Typhoid, cramps, dysentery, colds, rheumatism and eye infections had to be contended with. Many deaths occurred but little record was kept of burials. Human tragedies were two-a-penny.[49]

For Alexander Smith, the work as Protector of the Chinese was equally difficult and problematic, especially in the late 1850s.

By about 1861, things had begun to settle down for Alexander Smith and he went into parliament. The economy of Castlemaine had been transformed from temporary chaotic camps with thousands of independent diggers to a prosperous, well-integrated township of diverse industries and a settled countryside of productive agriculture and grazing.

After the abortive uprising and rout of the miners at Eureka followed by the abolition of the licence fees and the removal of the most corrupt troopers, life on the goldfields

49 Cannon, *The Roaring Days*, pp. 192-4.

had become gradually less turbulent and chaotic, but also less attractive to small-scale independent miners. Progress had become the mantra. The provision of education was improved, the railways were extended and the tyranny of distance was overcome – changes that Smith played a large part in as a parliamentarian. Closer settlement took place. All sorts of enterprises boomed. Towns took on a more complex shape.

Fate decreed that Australia was about to burst headlong into the modern age. There was a new fluidity in the social structure brought on, in part, by the gold rushes themselves. The land had become unlocked. All this was witnessed with interest by Smith up until the time of his death in 1872.

Throughout the last decade of his life, Alexander Smith maintained a reasonably regular correspondence with his single sister Emma in which he demonstrates a tender interest in his extended family in England while providing a detailed picture of his everyday life at Langley, the activities of his children and grandchildren, his encounters with his friends and his visits to Melbourne. His persona emerges from his letter-writing as a kind, personable man with intense interest in a wide range of contemporary matters. His love of farming comes through. He is open about his feelings and frequently wears his heart on his sleeve, but is also astute in his observations of people and events.

He is heavily involved in the social life of his local community and shows a generosity of spirit: 'I was very busy at home preparing for a great Picnic we gave on the 25th, a delightful day and all went off to our heart's content.'[50]

At times, he writes vividly about the physical environment. On Monday, '… we had a narrow escape from fires after a Summer cool & pleasant only remarkable for the long drought

---

50 A.J. Smith to Emma Smith, Melbourne Club, 25 March 1865.

extending over a period of two months'. He recounted that, on the morning of that day, the heat was intense (94° to 98° in the shade) even on his verandah from which he could see several dangerous bushfires in the distance of about six or seven miles. A strong wind was blowing towards his homestead that sustained itself dangerously all day. By noon, they were surrounded by smoke and the situation was threatening.

At the time, the Dutch Consul and his wife were staying with them. The consul crossed to the mountain range on horseback and came back about 2pm to say that fires were rapidly approaching. By 4.30pm, the fires had crossed Smith's boundary fences about three-quarters of a mile away from the homestead. By that time, Smith had prepared a 'good strong gang of hands' and they had begun to burn a firebreak from the garden fence outwards to protect the house and to have some bare ground to retreat to while fighting the fires. They had hardly finished the firebreak in front of the house when the fires rushed up the Creek 'like a whirlwind'. The old 'venerable' gum trees along the creek became 'enormous monuments of flame'. The burning fences looked to Alexander like 'what the ending of the world' may be like if it ever came. The flames caught the ears of several hundred tons of wheat and oaten straw. The fencing of the paddock beside the woolshed, coach house and stables was burnt to the ground, but fires miraculously missed the homestead and then swept over the paddocks burning every blade of grass around.

Fortunately, rain and a change of wind at 6.30pm extinguished all of the dangerous fires apart from the old tall gums and the fencing. The trees continued to burn for days on end. Of a night, Smith viewed it as a truly grand scene, despite the destruction.

The district had suffered frightfully. The smaller farmers

The scene from the Smith homestead at Langley (Private Family Collection)

lost all their crops and were ruined. Smith did all he could to help them as a prominent community leader. In a few minutes, houses had been swept away. Together with the local clergy, Smith set up a collection in Melbourne in aid of the destitute from the fires. In one day alone, he gathered £108. People of the metropolis gave generously, but unfortunately several other parts of the countryside had also suffered similar destruction by the fires.

One estimated loss in the Kyneton District amounted to between four to five thousand pounds. Smith's cows and horses were sadly 'in want of grass', but they had had a few recent showers that began to make the 'blackened ground' on the property 'look tinged with green'. On the positive side as well, despite all the earlier dry weather, Smith's elaborate garden was showing a 'lovely abundance of grapes now ripe'.[51]

Smith's optimism and determination to keep going ring out in his letter to Emma on this occasion. It also provides a picture of the extent of his grazing and farming activities at Langley and the vigour of his endeavours.

Alexander Smith reveals everything to Emma in his letters: shopping trips for his family to Melbourne, horse riding accidents to family members, his happiness with his infant grandchildren, and so on and so forth. He speaks tenderly of them in all his letters to the home country.

He and the family attended an annual ball in the Melbourne Club at the beginning of 1867 which he enthusiastically described as the best ball ever given in Melbourne; 'I never remember a more elegant affair'. His daughter 'Fan' came out at it. He pointed out that she looked so nice and did so enjoy herself. At the ball, Smith met Sir William Montagu Manning, the leader of the 'urban aristocrats' of Sydney, and had a long chat with him. He found him a most kindly and charming person. He invited him to visit Langley at a later stage: 'I think we shall meet again'.

Manning was a member of the New South Wales Legislative Council, President of the University Music Club, Vice President of the Australian Club, large landowner, legal counsel for the Australian Mutual Provident Society and President of the Sailors' Home. He looked after the interests of the Duke of Edinburgh during his visit. After shooting the Prince at Clontarf, O'Farrell fired at Manning, but missed. Manning was a fervently patriotic Queen's man like Alexander Smith.[52]

By 1867, the letters to Emma reveal that Alexander Smith's

---

51 A.J. Smith to Emma Smith.

52 Clark, *A History of Australia*, pp. 245, 401.

health was failing:

> We have some idea that we shall leave Langley next
> winter for two months at Queenscliff. I like the idea
> and the sound of the ocean waters again will put fresh
> life in me. Aubrey and the girls quite like it and I know
> that Ally [his son Alexander Henry Smith] will. I have
> some vague notion of trying to let Langley House and
> everything, furniture, horses, cows etc. If I can get
> my price and go away for 2 years perhaps ...[53]

Clearly, he was having doubts for his future from 1867
onwards.

In 1868, A.J. Smith wrote to Emma: 'Neither of us [he
and Aubrey] can get about like we did formerly...' Still he
consoled himself with farming, gardening and domestic and
family affairs to the end of his life.

To others in the district, he stood out – he was reliable, honest, trustworthy, sympathetic and supportive – a prominent
citizen of a new colony. He and his wife led simple, exemplary
lives. Alexander planned to retire from Langley and move closer to the city to restore his health, but at the age of fifty-nine,
death overtook him instead.

---

53 A.J. Smith to Emma Smith, Melbourne Club, 23 February 1867.

11

Alexander's Younger Brother
Bernhard Smith

A person without fortune, following refined art in a
rough tricky age, a large family to support and educate
in the costliest capital in the World [Melbourne]: and
following the most unpopular art in existence has I
think you would admit a problem to solve that admits
no trifling.

Bernhard Smith to Thomas Woolner, 8 August 1880[1]

Bernhard Smith expresses here the melancholic situation facing
the creative artist five years before his tragic death in 1885. This
was especially so for a sculptor in Australia who had no family
fortune to back him and with heavy family commitments.
By the time he wrote these words to his long-time friend in
England, the eminent sculptor Thomas Woolner, Bernhard
Smith was in his sixtieth year and had been in the colony of
Victoria since 1852. There was no chance by then for him to
return to England to achieve a measure of fame as an artist.

Unlike his three older brothers, Henry Thomas, Alexander
John and William Richard, Bernhard Smith was not attracted

---

1   Bernhard Smith, MS 9963, Box 7, La Trobe Heritage Collection, State
Library of Victoria, Melbourne.

3 st Edmund's Terrace,
Primrose Hill London, N.W.
5 nov./90.

My old & very warmly regarded friend Bernhard Smith.
Few indeed have I known to match him, either in Geniality
of character & bearing, or in the striking manly mould of
his face & person. Believe me
Very truly yours.
Wm Rosetti

Extract of letter Copied by
M.B.S.

Portrait of Bernhard Smith with extract from William Rosetti's letter.

to a life at sea in the Royal Navy despite being born and raised in Greenwich with its seductive surrounds of the iconography of heroic sea exploits and British Empire patriotism. Nor was he drawn to the postal service, like his next older brother Edward James who became postmaster at Leeds. The career of his closest-born elder brother John Peter as a general merchant and banker did not appeal at all. Such occupations were not for him.

Instead, Bernhard William Smith set out from an early age with great enthusiasm and determination to become a renowned creative artist. He had inherited the artistic genes of his father Lord Henry Smith who had a flair for comic illustration and a wide knowledge of artistic and literary endeavour of all sorts. Bernhard was most certainly raised in a highly suitable cultural atmosphere to follow in adulthood a life as a creative artist.

Bernhard's birth to Lord Henry and Jane Mary in Greenwich took place on 20 November 1820. At the age of nineteen in 1840, he was accepted into the prestigious Royal Academy Antique School in London where he obtained his main formal training in the fine arts. In 1842, he came into contact with the then sculptor apprentice Thomas Woolner who had begun at the Royal Academy Schools in London that very year. The two young aspiring artists formed a strong bond of friendship and they later shared a London studio in Stanhope Street. Woolner was five years younger than Smith having been born at Hadleigh, Suffolk in 1825.

Like Bernhard Smith, Thomas Woolner had decided to become an artist at an early age. He was only thirteen years of age in 1838 when he began as an apprentice to the painter Henry Behnes, who worked under the name of Burlowe and had exhibited at the Royal Academy. Henry Behnes died at an early age in 1838 and Woolner immediately transferred as an unpaid apprentice to Henry's brother William, also a sculptor who had gained a good reputation chiefly for portrait busts between 1820 and 1840. His studio was in Regents Park, London. Woolner stayed with William Behnes for four years until 1842 when he went on to study at the Royal Academy Schools and met up with Bernhard Smith. By 1846, Thomas Woolner was still working for William Behnes on a part-time basis and also assisting Alexander Munro who specialised in portrait medallions.

Even by 1838, the eighteen-year-old Bernhard Smith was heavily and frequently involved in studying art exhibitions in London and spending many hours on a regular basis drawing the classical casts found in the British Museum. His first major sculpture was a memorial to his late sister Mary Elizabeth Smith. Mary Elizabeth had been born in 1816 in Greenwich and had died tragically and unmarried at the age of eighteen. For this memorial, Bernhard Smith modelled a full-length reclining figure with an angel whispering to her.[2]

At the time, Bernhard lived in Blackheath, then an artist's village on the London-to-Dover Road,[3] while studying at the drawing and painting school in Bloomsbury in Central London run by Richard Sass from where he was accepted into the Royal Academy Antique School on 21 April 1840. By this time, Bloomsbury had become the abode of writers, intellectuals, artists and lawyers.

By October of that year, he had travelled to Paris, intending to enter the studio or atelier of the artist David d'Angers, but

---

2   Minnie Bernhard Smith, 'Bernhard Smith and his Connection with Art or "The 7 Founders of the P.R.B".' [Pre-Raphaelite Brothers], 1917, MS 4901, Mitchell Library, Sydney, p. 1.

3   Later, a solidly elegant suburb of London.

instead he joined Etienne-Jules Ramey's studio on advice he had received that d'Angers neglected his studio and his students, being too heavily involved in radical politics in Paris.

Bernhard worked assiduously both in and outside the atelier visiting renowned galleries like the Louvre to study painting and sculpture. As well, he visited libraries like the Bibliothèque du Roi to make a close study of historical costume. He most admired the paintings of Paul Delaroche and David d'Angers as contemporaries, together with some modern German artists of his time. Ramey also encouraged his hard-working student to look at Poussin and Flaxman. John Flaxman

Plaque of James Clark Ross RN, Bernhard Smith, pic.an7743311, NLA

Joseph Dalton Hooker, Wedgewood ceramic medallioin, Frank Bowcher 1897 (Private Collection)

(1755-1826), a sculptor, was employed by the Wedgewoods to design wax models for prizes and medallions in Wedgewood ceramic ware. Flaxman was a close friend of William Blake, poet, mystic and artist, and was profoundly influenced by his art works.[4] His medallions were in the classical style that

---

4   'Flaxman, John (1755-1826)', *Concise Dictionary of National Biography*, Vol. 1, Oxford University Press, 1992, pp. 1023-4.

Bernhard Smith adapted in his medallion of James Clark Ross and others. The profile of Ross by Smith is depicted as Roman with a Roman hair style. Flaxman also influenced Smith in his much later sketches of fairies in bush or nature scenes in Australia.

In France, Bernhard Smith enjoyed sketching trips into the picturesque countryside before returning to London and his shared studio with Woolner. Back in London in 1842, he wrote a manuscript 'The World in Miniature', but there is no direct evidence that it was ever published (although it may have been in private form). No copies seem to be extant.

John Edward Gray, a relative of Smith who worked as a naturalist at the British Museum, sent two of Bernhard's medallions sculpted in 1842 to the Royal Academy. One was a portrait (apparently of Gray) and the other was *An Old Satyr Extracting a Thorn from the Foot of a Young Man*. The following year, Smith was at 10 Sackville Street, London, the address from where he sent the academy two oil paintings – *Mrs. Mackenzie of Flowerburn and John Ogilby, Esq.* – and three small sculpted medallion portraits of John Richardson, his brother Lieutenant Henry Thomas Smith (exhibited at the Royal Academy in 1844) and, more importantly, Captain Sir James Clark Ross RN, the great Antarctic explorer and mentor to his older brother Lieutenant Alexander John Smith. Smith's medallions of Ross are held by the National Portrait Gallery, the Linnaean Society and the Scott Polar Institute.

Bernhard Smith's brother Alexander had a lifelong friendship with Sir Joseph Hooker, his colleague and messmate aboard the *Erebus* for nearly four and a half years. Hooker had possession of one of Bernhard Smith's plaster casts of his medallion of Sir James Clark Ross executed in 1848. He had received it as a gift from the artist. In 1892, Hooker donated the medallion (8 inch/ 203mm in diameter) to the National Portrait Gallery of London where it is still held.

By 1851, some twenty-one works by Bernhard Smith had been exhibited at the Royal Academy. Most sculpted medallions continued to be members of his family circle or known associates. His medallion portrait of his sister Emma Smith was exhibited at the Royal Academy in 1846 and his medallion of Mrs Thomas Ringrose (his sister Fanny Voase Elizabeth Smith) in 1848. A portrait sculpture of the great naturalist John Gould was shown in 1847 as well as a sculpture listed as *Fairie* (a precursor of his later works on fairies in Australia).

The works displayed by Smith evinced self-conscious austerity and astringency in the use of line that was in close sympathy with the earliest Pre-Raphaelite style.

The evidence is now strong that Bernhard Smith, partly because of his close life-long friendship with Thomas Woolner, became a member of the Brotherhood of Pre-Raphaelites along with William Holman Hunt, John Everett Millais, the Rossetti brothers, Dante and William, and their sister Christina, and others. Both Woolner and William Rossetti were much later to acknowledge Bernhard's presence and involvement when the Brotherhood was founded in 1848. He was more certainly a close, early associate and enthusiastic member and contributor. Smith once stated the Brotherhood's early manifesto:

> The thing [the Brotherhood] arose from disgust at the sloppy way we used to see the modern painters putting out work. Our motive was to represent conscientiously what we saw... It was to draw and to paint more carefully and to avoid slummy, sloppy work, and to prove the truth of that idea, that we banded together.[5]

---

5   Cited in Juliet Peers, 'Smith, Bernhard (1820-1885)', Joan Kerr (ed.), *The Dictionary of Australian Artists*, Oxford University Press, Melbourne, 1992, p. 734.

In 1847, Thomas Woolner first met the charismatic Dante Gabriel Rossetti and soon after joined the Pre-Raphaelite Brotherhood. Drawn in with Thomas Woolner his close artist friend and studio partner, Bernhard Smith became part of the Brotherhood in a great swell of enthusiasm.

Dante Gabriel Rossetti, who was eight years younger than Bernhard Smith having been born in London in 1828, commemorated Bernhard's membership of the Pre-Raphaelite Brotherhood in his poem *St. Wagner's Eve*:

> The hop-shop is shut up the night doth wear.
> Here, early, Collinson this evening fell
> "Into the gulfs of sleep", and Deverell
> Has turned upon the pivot of his chair
> The whole of this night long: and Hancock there
> Has laboured to repeat, in accents screechy
> "Guardami ben, ben son, ben son Beatrice";
> *And Bernhard Smith still beamed, serene and square.*[6]
> By eight the coffee was all drunk. At nine
> We gave the cat some milk. Our talk did shelve
> Ere ten, to gasps and stupor. Helpless grief
> Made, towards eleven, my inmost spirit pine.
> Knowing North's hour. And Hancock hard on twelve,
> Showed an engraving of his bas-relief.

Clearly, Rossetti recounts in verse a bonding party of the brotherhood. Beer drinking is enjoyed until the 'hop-shop' is closed. Back at the co-operative's studio, Collinson drops off into a deep sleep, Deverell swings on his chair all the time and Hancock continues to talk irritatingly the rest of the night with his high-pitched accent.

Only the genial, good-natured Bernhard 'still beamed, serene and square' – a likeable character who could hold his

---

6   Italics by the author of this book for emphasis.

grog well. At eight o'clock, they all take coffee and at nine the cat is given a saucer of milk. At ten, there are 'gasps and stupor' by the more inebriated and at midnight Hancock shows off his artwork – a bas-relief sculpture.

This characterisation of Smith's personality was reinforced many years later when, in 1890, William Rossetti, Dante's brother, wrote a mini-memoir of his late friend and erstwhile member of the brotherhood and sent it from Primrose Hill in London's North-West to Bernhard Smith's daughter in Australia:

> My old and very warmly regarded friend Bernhard Smith. Few indeed have I known to match him, either in geniality of character & bearing, or in the striking manly mould of his face & person.
>
> > Believe me
> > Very truly yours
> > Wm. Rossetti.[7]

By the time this was written, the Brotherhood of the Pre-Raphaelites had long been dissolved. Dante Rossetti had died in 1882 in London. Bernhard Smith had died in Victoria, Australia, in 1885. William Rossetti had not seen Bernhard Smith since he had left for Melbourne and the Victorian Goldfields in 1852. In physical appearance, William Rossetti described Smith as 'six foot broad ... with a hearty English look and manner, and a clear resonant voice'.[8]

Although expressing an intention to migrate to Canada in 1849, Bernhard Smith remained in England for another three

---

7 William Rossetti to Minnie Bernhard Smith, 3 St. Edmond's Terrace, Primrose Hill, London N.W., 5 November 1890, reproduced as a frontispiece of Smith, 'Bernhard Smith and his Connection'.

8 Modified Register for Bishop John Smith (Merilyn Pedrick Collection), pp. 18-19.

years working at his art on a full-time basis, but with little financial success or reward. It was hard to make a living in his field of endeavour without patronage. His most developed oil painting of this period is *Puck*, Shakespeare's character from *A Midsummer Night's Dream*. His Puck is depicted as somewhat malicious and sinister, half infant, half elderly man. Bernhard's oil is similar to Thomas Woolner's 1847 statuette, which was probably used as a model.

A sketch also survives of Bernhard's oil painting *Two Water Elves* which was exhibited in the Royal Academy in 1851. It portrays two female nudes floating in a miniature boat made of a curled leaf. A number of similar sketches by Smith were later to be executed in his subsequent life in Australia (for example, fairies flying on feathers and thistledown, seated on mushrooms and in rosebuds). Clearly the tone of his Australian oeuvre continued to be set in Victorian culture on a mystic theme.[9]

In 1850, the Pre-Raphaelite Brotherhood established *The Germ*, a periodical to disseminate their ideas about art and literature. It lasted four issues between January and April 1850. William Michael Rossetti, his brother Dante Gabriel, Thomas Woolner and James Collison jointly edited the endeavour and Holman Hunt provided some illustrations. It printed contributions in verse as well as essays on art and literature from William Rossetti, Ford Madox Brown and Coventry Patmore. There were also book reviews. The title *The Germ* referred to the Pre-Raphaelite belief in the importance of nature (a *germ* is a seed) and of the human imagination as implied by the phrase 'the germ of an idea'.

The Pre-Raphaelites hoped that their magazine would be a seed from which new creative ideas would grow. The editors

---

9   Peers, 'Smith, Bernhard', p. 734.

emphasised the belief that poetry and art were closely intertwined. Such beliefs engendered themselves in Bernhard Smith's practice which expressed 'thoughts toward nature in art and literature',[10] the subtitle of *The Germ* magazine. He remained closely associated with these ideas for the rest of his life.

In 1851, Thomas Woolner was unsuccessful in a major competition for a memorial to the poet William Wordsworth which he had been very confident of winning.[11] News of the Victorian Gold Rushes reached him, Bernhard Smith and others at the same time. Disappointment was replaced by a quest for adventure and the notion of striking it rich.

In July 1852, Bernhard Smith, Thomas Woolner and Edward La Trobe Bateman, all close friends in London's art and literary world who were all strongly associated with the Pre-Raphaelite Brotherhood movement, left for Australia aboard the *Windsor*. Bernhard, displaying his innate generosity of spirit, assisted Woolner, who was down on his luck, with his passage money. The three were in search of gold to make their fortune in the goldfields. They reached Melbourne on 23 October and soon set out for the Ovens diggings after buying the essential equipment. After a short period, they moved on to Fryer's Creek and Sandhurst.[12]

'The Last of England', oil painting by Ford Madox Brown, 1855

10 <http://en.wikipedia.org/wiki/Pre-Raphaelite_Brotherhood>, accessed 3 December 2010.

11 Ken Scarlett, *Australian Sculptors*, Thomas Nelson Australia, Melbourne, 1980, pp. 708-11.

12 Peers, 'Smith, Bernhard', p. 736; Scarlett, *Australian Sculptors*, pp.709, 602.

Their farewell departure from England on the *Windsor* inspired Ford Madox Brown's painting *The Last of England* which was executed in 1855 from Brown's memory of the departure of the intrepid trio.[13]

Meanwhile back in London on 12 April 1853 at Dante Gabriel Rossetti's suggestion, the remaining members of the Pre-Raphaelite Brotherhood met for breakfast in John Everett Millais' studio. After taking a large breakfast together, they drew portraits of each other to send to their colleagues in Australia. Rossetti's drawing of Holman Hunt captured that artist's slightly solemn and earnest character. It was in pencil over a grey wash with scratching. Underneath it is Rossetti's signature. It is addressed to Bernhard Smith and the other two voyagers Woolner and Bateman.[14] This artwork provides further proof of Bernhard Smith's strong association with the early Pre-Raphaelite Brotherhood as one of its founding members (now forgotten about because of his arrival in the early 1850s and permanent residency in Australia). It is definite then that Bernhard Smith in his formative years as an artist was an original member of the Pre-Raphaelite Brotherhood and adhered throughout his life to the doctrine they espoused.

The Brotherhood's intention had been to reform art by rejecting what they considered to be the mechanistic approach first adopted by the Mannerist artists who succeeded Raphael and Michelangelo. They believed – hence the name they gave to their movement – that the Classic poses and elegant compositions of Raphael had been a corrupting model on English academic teaching and practice of art. In particular, they

---

13 Scarlett, *Australian Sculptors*, p. 709.

14 Portrait of William Holman Hunt (1827-1910) by Dante Gabriel Rossetti. Width 206mm, Height 274mm, <http://www.preraphaelites.org/the-collection/1904> , p 392, accessed 3 December 2010.

objected to the influence of Sir Joshua Reynolds, the founder of the English Royal Academy of Arts, who they lampooned as "Sir Sloshua". Their coined term "sloshy" which meant anything lax or scamped in the process of painting, broadened to mean anything or any person of a commonplace, conventional and boring kind.

In contrast, they wanted to return to abundant detail (as Bernhard was to show in his later Australian sketches), intense colours and complex compositions derived from Quattrocento Italian and Flemish art.

The Pre-Raphaelites were the first English avant-garde movement in the British art world of the nineteenth century, but some critics deny them that status as they continued to accept both the concept of history painting and mimesis (the imitation of nature) as central to the purpose of art. The Brotherhood, without a shadow of a doubt however, defined themselves as a reform movement. Their early doctrine which indelibly influenced Bernhard Smith was expressed in four declarations: to have genuine ideas to express, to study Nature closely so as to know how to express it, to sympathise with what is direct and serious and heartfelt in previous art, to the exclusion of what is conventional and stereotypic and learnt by rote, and, most indispensable of all, to produce thoroughly good pictures and statues.

As he voyaged to Australia with his two friends in 1852 at the age of thirty-two, Bernhard Smith held these principles close to his heart. On the back of the first-known sketch Bernhard Smith produced in Australia, he wrote: 'Bernhard Smith P.R.B. [Pre-Raphaelite Brotherhood]. One of the founding members of the P.R.B. with Millais, Holman Hunt, [Dante] Gabriel Rossetti, Wm. Rossetti, Thomas Woolner, and Collins[on] who left us in 1850'.[15]

The rest of the Pre-Raphaelite Brotherhood were younger than Bernhard Smith who was born in 1820 and thirty-two by the time he left for Australia. Woolner was born in 1825 and died in 1892; Collinson was born in the same year and died in 1881; Holman Hunt was born in 1827 and died in 1910 and D.G. Rossetti was born in 1828 and died in 1882. Millais was the youngest. He was born in 1829 and died in 1896. W.M. Rossetti, the secretary to the PRBs was born in 1829 and died in 1920. With William's death, the Brotherhood was no more. By 1885, their eldest member Bernhard Smith, in far-off Australia, was also dead.

William Rossetti, man of letters and art critic, held down a public service job in the Excise Department[16] as Bernhard Smith did in Australia as Goldfields Commissioner, Protector of the Chinese and Police Magistrate. Neither could make a living from art criticism or art.

Dante Gabriel Rossetti, the central most flamboyant figure of the PRB, persisted as a painter and poet by gaining the patronage of John Ruskin, a dominant and powerful art critic and sponsor who stoutly defended the Brotherhood in the *Times*. In his ambitious work *The Stones of Venice*, Ruskin reacted like the Brotherhood against industrialisation that was threatening creativity across the Western world – standardisation, mass production, derivative ideas and repetitive motifs. He loved the early Gothic style of architecture in Venice because it was irregular, asymmetrical, created by artists and craftsmen out of their own heads and, derived directly from

15 Cited in Smith, 'Bernhard Smith and his Connection', p. 2.

16 'Rossetti, William Michael (1829-1919)', *Concise Dictionary of National Biography*, Vol. III, Oxford University Press, 1992, pp. 2587-8.

the beauty of nature, it was essentially organic.[17]

Dante Rossetti became an intimate friend of both the romantic poet Algernon Swinburne and the craftsman and poet William Morris. He later lived with his brother, Swinburne and the prolific novelist and poet George Meredith at well-known Tudor (or Queen's) House, Cheyne Walk, Chelsea.[18] While he maintained his art and poetry, these life activities did not lead to financial success.

Sir John Everett Millais was the most socially and financially successful of the PRB and eventually became president of the Royal Academy. His various history paintings had great social success during his lifetime. In later life, he devoted himself mainly to portraits and landscapes and deviated somewhat from the principles of Pre-Raphaelite ideology.[19]

William Holman Hunt as a painter was consistent in carrying out Pre-Raphaelite principles until his death in 1910. He found a valuable patron in Thomas Combes, a wealthy printer and leading benefactor. He was certainly powerfully defended in the art world by art critic John Ruskin in the *Times* and became

Rosetti's portrait of Holman Hunt sent to the three members of the Brotherhood in Australia.

17 John Ruskin, *The Stones of Venice*, ed. & intro. by Jan Morris, The Folio Society, London, 2001, p.xii.

18 'Rossetti, Dante Gabriel (1828-1882)', p. 2587.

19 'Millais, Sir John Everett (1829-1896)', *Concise Dictionary of National Biography*, Vol. II, p. 2030.

a close friend. He worked with William Morris in Florence on the design of furnishings and wallpaper and visited the Holy Land to produce history paintings of impressive authenticity.[20]

Thomas Woolner, as we have learnt, travelled to Melbourne with his friends Bernhard Smith and Edward La Trobe Bateman to go to the Victorian Goldfields because he had met with little early success in London as a sculptor. They stayed in the goldfields for seven months. Before leaving England, Woolner had expressed bitter disappointment to all his friends in the art world about being unsuccessful in the public competition for the memorial to Wordsworth.

After only limited success in arduous gold prospecting, he came back to the metropolis of Melbourne where he stayed with Dr Godfrey in Collins Street for several months. He earned a living by modelling at least a dozen commissioned portrait medallions in the classical style at twenty-five guineas apiece, including one of Lieutenant Governor Charles La Trobe (Bateman's uncle) in 1853. By a strange and lucky coincidence, an earlier work of Woolner's *Red Riding Hood* was in the Governor's residence when Woolner arrived in Melbourne.

In 1854, Woolner visited Sydney in an endeavour to gain a commission for a proposed colossal statue of William Charles Wentworth. He was unsuccessful, but made about ten medallion portraits including one of Wentworth and another of the Governor General Sir Charles Fitzroy. Woolner, while making something of a name for himself in Sydney, then returned to England in the same year. His career as a sculptor eventually took off in the home country. By 1861, he was reasonably

---

20 'Hunt, William Holman (1827-1910)', *Concise Dictionary of National Biography*, Vol. II, Oxford University Press, 1992, pp. 1522-3.

wealthy and well-known. In 1874-79 in England, Woolner produced a statue of Captain James Cook for Hyde Park in Sydney through a commission (the statue was later transferred to Sydney's Royal Botanical Gardens). Woolner produced the statue in his London studio. Some other Australian commissions followed. He was well known to Henry Parkes, the frequent Premier of New South Wales who visited England on occasions. Between 1863 and 1887, Woolner also published six volumes of poetry.

In a letter, Dante Rossetti vividly recalled Woolner's departure to Australia in 1852:

> The most important event among us lately has been Woolner's exodus to the diggings. ... He was accompanied as I think you know, by Bernhard Smith and Bateman, all of them plentifully stocked with corduroys, sou'westers, jerseys, firearms, and belts full of little bags to hold the expected nuggets. Hunt, William, and myself deposited them in their four months' home [the *Windsor*] with a due mixture of solemnity and joviality. Woolner desired more than once his particular remembrances to you. All his friends congratulate him on the move, with the sole exception of [Thomas] Carlyle,[21] who seems to espy in it some savour of the mammon of unrighteousness. Tennyson[22] was especially encouraging; at his house at Twickenham Woolner spent two days of his last week. The great Alfred [Tennyson] even declares that were it not for Mrs. T. he should go himself. His expectations seem, however, to be rather poetical, as

---

21 Thomas Carlyle (1795-1881), satirist and essayist; famous for *French Revolution* (1837) which made his reputation as a historian. He lived for a time in Cheyne Row, Chelsea, in 1834 and mixed with the Brotherhood.

22 Alfred Tennyson, Lord (1809-1892), poet laureate in 1850. Famous and popular for his treatment of the Arthurian legend.

he gravely asked Woolner if he expected to come back with £10,000 a year.[23]

*   *   *   *   *

Sudden achievement of wealth for Bernhard Smith, Thomas Woolner and their colleague Bateman in the Victorian gold rush was not to be. Disillusionment set in after months of seemingly fruitless and grinding labour. They came to realise that gold prospecting was by no means a certain affair in becoming rich quick.

They noticed the behaviour of the crowds of people desperately working on the goldfields: numbers were returning to where they had come from without even earning enough to pay for their expenses; those who succeeded frequently squandered their new-found wealth 'in a most disgrace manner'. The prices of everything essential to carry out the work were very dear and little luxuries could only be purchased by 'triumphant diggers'. Even the price of an ordinary cauliflower was 3/6! The discovery of gold had made everything expensive especially in the metropolis of Melbourne.

The people they met at the diggings mostly wore beards, carried firearms with a swagger and were 'fiercely independent'. Bernhard Smith himself was 'wonderfully well' and, according to Woolner, was well up to the heavy work at the diggings. Woolner captured the atmosphere of the place on Sunday, 31 October 1852:

> The price of things here would seem fabulous if not true. Nature and Custom are topsy-turvy in this country, the reverse of England: day and springtime here when night and winter there: here the trees shed

---

23 Cited in Scarlett, *Australian Sculptors*, p. 711.

their bark instead of leaves, vegetation stops in mid summer and cherries grow with their stones outside. The man of labour only buys the luxuries of life and servants rule their masters who bow down and flatter them: such is the power of Gold ...[24]

After travelling mile after mile through the monotonous flats with trees everywhere, the three intrepid gold-seekers had finally reached the diggings. There they found the camp scene busy and wild with fires blazing, meat frying and bullocks being unyoked. Dogs barked, whips were cracked, guns banged away in all directions and heavily-laden drays were being unloaded noisily. All in all, it was a vigorous vibrant scene with bustle and excitement among men. The earth looked as if 'an earthquake had torn it up'. The numerous tents were scattered everywhere making it seem like the 'grand meeting place of all the gipsies on the earth'; indeed, all the men according to Woolner looked like gipsies.

Bernhard Smith and his friends soon discovered that digging for gold was not child's play. Woolner's hands trembled so much that he found it difficult to write. They felled trees, barked and carried bark and baled water 'the whole day'. It was extremely heavy labour for little gain. Woolner was moved to write: 'this is the hardest day's mere labour I ever did when sinking a hole five feet deep', with the water coming fast upon them. Where they were working near the creek soon filled with many people jostling each other in the search for the valuable metal.

Before the shaft was completed, Thomas Woolner gave up. He wrote that he should 'leave this place with disappointment'. Despite that, he and Bernhard Smith decided to leave for Forest Creek or even Bendigo where they would perhaps

24 Cited in Scarlett, *Australian Sculptors*, p. 712.

start again with a better knowledge.

Smith and Woolner returned to Melbourne on their way to new diggings on Saturday, 8 January 1853 and had to search through half the town before they could find lodgings which they eventually procured with a great deal of difficulty. The landlord of the Imperial Inn 'did not seem much to relish our uncouth aspect, rough from the bush life'. Mosquitoes tormented them in bed. Woolner had a particularly nasty experience: 'I felt something heavy walking over me and on giving a kick a great rat fell limp on the floor, whirled about, squeaked and scampered off with another wretch'.

They stayed a few nights in Melbourne and started off with two others to the Fryer's Creek diggings where they were a little more successful for a time. But soon that failed and they moved to Bendigo where they got little more than a speck of gold. After sinking hole after hole to no avail, they finally decided to sell their tent, tools and other equipment and break up the party of four, each to seek his separate fortune by other means.

At this point, Woolner returned to Melbourne and began to manufacture medallions in order to make a living. He found it not a bad way to earn a living in the metropolis in comparison: 'I get 25 pounds for a medallion here. In England they would not give me 25 pence [for the same]'. At the diggings, Woolner claimed to his father in a letter that he had lost a little over thirty pounds in the layout of the equipment needed. He found gold to the value of £50, but his expenses overall came to £80.[25] There was no gain whatsoever.

* * * * *

---

25 Various documents written by Thomas Woolner, cited in Scarlett, *Australian Sculptors*, pp. 711-3.

In the meanwhile, what of Bernhard Smith?

He was soon to meet up with his elder brother Alexander John Smith RN who was a help in providing his life with a different direction.

To his sister Emma in a letter dated 13 March 1853 and written at The Camp in Castlemaine at Forest Creek, Mount Alexander, Bernhard tells of his first encounter with their brother, now assistant Goldfields Commissioner of the place. When Bernhard had returned to his tent after working in the diggings all day, the man who kept the store came to say a party of ten including his brother Alexander had come looking for him. Alexander had just joined The Camp in his official capacity. Bernhard takes up the story in his letter:

> So I was disquieted all that night and killed some 19 fleas and having got up early made breakfast and washed a shirt and put on decent apparel walked over and found him installed [in the official Commissioners' Camp] ... and both of us were well pleased to see each other ...

Bernhard then came over to Alexander's camp and passed the Sunday with him from morning till night; they talked intently into the night about old times, about their memories of their family life and friends in England. He then made up his bed on Alexander's camp floor. (Usually all work stopped at the diggings on Sundays, apart from the very desperate.)

Bernhard admitted to Emma that he had got into the bad habit with his prospecting companions 'of looking at every pretty gully or fine hilly range with a wish to dig it up, and viewed all timber as good stuff to burn to make a damper with ...'

He recounted how he came up from Melbourne and rea-

The Camp where Alexander & Bernhard Smith
met for the first time (no: b28258, SLV)

ched Fryer's Creek near Mt Alexander on 19 February 1853 with three other newly-acquired companions. They sunk a hole which proved entirely worthless and from the next they at least took 40 ounces of gold. One of the companions then took off for Melbourne. The others were glad to see him go as he had never done a day's work with them. Another rough man, but a good worker, replaced him in the party.

Alexander then took over writing the same letter to Emma. He recounted how he left Hobart Town and Launceston later on 26 January 1853. On 11 February, he arrived in Melbourne 'the most disagreeable town you could wish to be in'. Bernhard had already concurred with this sentiment. He had seen thousands of tents of all sizes pitched about a mile from the "Town" belonging to crowds of immigrants. It was a chaotic, overcrowded scene.

While in Melbourne, Alexander made a formal visit to Governor Charles La Trobe, but he was out of town at the time. Shortly after, he met an old friend from Van Diemen's Land who was by this time the Chief Magistrate and who, it was claimed, had even more influence than the Governor. This old friend was very pleased to see Alexander and immediately made him several offers of employment to positions like Police Magistrate, but the stations for these positions were too far into the interior and he did not think he and Aubrey would care for them, so he refused. But he clearly accepted a posting at Castlemaine. At the same time, he considered purchasing a property called Langley Vale.

Langley Vale (later shortened to Langley by Alexander) far surpassed his expectations. In his joint-letter with Bernhard to their sister Emma, he enthusiastically described the property with great affection:

> A very pretty large Cottage with roses etc. climbing all over it, a fine garden & overlooking a fine rich undulating Country, and everything denoting that comfort was much studied it took me much of the day looking about me & the following day Sunday we [most likely with Bernhard] had a long ride over different parts of the run & adjoining stations.

Alexander was so pleased with the property that he made up his mind to take possession when the lease expired the following year. Refusing to buy it for £3,000, he eventually paid £1,200.

On Monday morning, he and Bernhard left at daylight for Geelong to give his answer about his appointment. On the Wednesday, he was informed that Charles La Trobe, the Governor, had already ordered his appointment to be made as Commissioner for the Goldfields. So without even formally accepting it, Alexander Smith had been appointed 'Commander in Chief' on a salary beginning at £400 per annum with a servant, a house, rations and other gratuities. While offered another station or position in Melbourne (well-educated civil servants were at a premium), he refused because of the huge expense of living there and accepted instead the station at The Camp in Castlemaine at first as assistant Goldfields Commissioner and then as full Commissioner.[26]

The *Government Gazette* noted that, with two others, Alexander John Smith (his given names printed as John Alexander) was appointed to be Commissioner of Crown Lands of the Goldfields of the Colony of Victoria by His Excellency's Command.

Bernhard was to follow in his elder brother's footsteps. Disillusioned with gold prospecting with so little return, he joined the staff of the Gold Commissioners on 17 May 1854 as Assistant Commissioner for the Westernport district. By 1854, he was at Ballarat. In 1856, he visited his married sister Mrs Maria Wise in Sydney.[27]

After returning to Victoria, Bernhard Smith was appointed on 5 January 1858 along with Alexander as Wardens of the Goldfields – a new but similar position to Commissioner. The two brothers were appointed later in the year on 7 May 1858 in addition to their Warden's positions as Protectors of the Chinese. In 1858-59 while carrying out his duties to a

26 Bernhard and Alexander Smith to Emma Smith, The Camp, Castlemaine, Forest Creek, Mount Alexander, 13 March 1853.

27 After migrating to Australia, Maria Bate Smith married Edward Wise in the presence of her two brothers at Kyneton near Langley on 1 January 1856. The couple went to live at Edgecliffe House Wollahra, Sydney. Wise, already eminent, arrived in Sydney from England in February 1855 & was admitted to the Bar that year, a month after their marriage, he was appointed to the NSW Legislative Council and soon became solicitor-general. In 1859, he became attorney-general for NSW, was appointed a judge of the Supreme Court in 1860. He was a strong supporter of the underprivileged in Sydney. J.A. Ryan, 'Wise, Edward (1818-1865)', *ADB*, Vol. 6, 1976, pp.427-9.

miscellaneous, unsettled population of a temporary nature at the diggings, Bernhard Smith compiled a book of natural history records (no longer extant). The writing of this book occupied his evenings under canvas while, during the day, he collected material while engaged in his official duties on horseback.

Bernhard resigned from government service in March 1861 to join his brother Alexander on Langley Vale Station near Kyneton and was then reappointed Warden of the Goldfields and Commissioner of Crown Lands.

A gum-blossom drawn for his sister now held in the La Trobe Library Collection suggests that his earlier Australian drawings were somewhat weaker than his more confident works of the 1870s, although an extant drawing of 1861 already displays the precise line work and decorative, even Baroque invention that characterised his more mature work of the last few years of his life. His manuscript 'Notes of growth' (1866) held in the Victorian State Library contains a tiny drawing of a lyrebird. A scrapbook of natural history drawings including studies of moths, butterflies, kangaroos and flowers begun in the 1870s is also held in La Trobe.[28] There are sketches of gravestones in country cemeteries made while he was carrying out his civic duties on various journeys as a circuit magistrate.

Bernhard Smith entered the marriage stakes at the age of forty-two. He married Olivia Frances Josephine Boyes of Richmond on 12 February 1863 in Melbourne at St Paul's Church of England. Olivia was about twenty-two years younger than Bernhard. At the time, Bernhard was staying at the Port Phillip Club Hotel for the wedding. His usual official residence was in Stanwell where he was Police Magistrate and

---

28 Bernhard Smith, MS 9963; Peers, 'Smith, Bernhard', p. 735.

Warden of the Goldfields. He had been first appointed at Stanwell in 1860.[29]

Bernhard and Olivia produced nine children, the first six being born at the couple's official residence at Stanmore: Bernhard Alexander Smith, named after his father and uncle, was born on 4 December 1863. Ethel Mary was born on 1 March 1866; William Boyes on 22 September 1867; Sophie Alice on 12 April 1869; Minnie Ellen, who became her father's family biographer, on 3 December 1870 and Frances Josephine on 11 March 1873. They were all baptised at Christ Church, Stanmore.

Next, Emma Maria was born at Ballarat on 9 July 1874, but died the next year on 4 March 1875. She was buried in the New Cemetery, Ballarat. The next child also died in infancy within a year: Francis Edward born on 20 March 1882 at Hawthorn, died on 26 March 1883 and was buried at Borondara Cemetery, Kew. The ninth child George Noel Bernhard was born on 21 December 1883 and survived to adulthood. Like Francis Edward, he was born at Hawthorn.

In 1874, Bernhard Smith was made Police Magistrate at Smythesdale and it was there he was summarily dismissed by the Berry Government on 'Black Wednesday', 9 January 1878, together with hundreds of other Victorian civil servants. When reinstated, he was transferred to the new district of Alexandra in the

Portrait of Bernhard Smith
(Merilyn Pedrick Collection)

29 Certificate of Marriage, Bernhard Smith and Olivia Boyes, 12 February 1863, St. Paul's C of E, Melbourne, District of Bourke.

mountainous east of Victoria, far from his adored family and home. Financial need forced him to take up this position in a remote locality.

Bernhard Smith's death was a heroic one. He died of pneumonia at Alexandra on 7 October 1885 after attempting to rescue two children from a flooded stream. His health had been undermined by travelling through unusually heavy snowfalls on horseback during the extremely severe winter of 1885.[30] Only a few of us are allowed a hero's death and Bernhard Smith was one. His attempt to save the two stricken children not only showed his courage, but his genuine generosity of spirit.

*   *   *   *   *

At the time of his death as a hard-working civil servant in Australia, Bernhard Smith was to some degree a frustrated, unfulfilled artist. And yet he achieved great respect as a Police Magistrate. Working extremely hard on the circuit and moving from place to place, he still found time in the summer evening to sketch from nature butterflies, moths and wildflowers and to produce delicate watercolours. Commissions in art were rare and he was unable to make his living as an artist in the backblocks of rural Victoria.

But he never abandoned art as a vital life interest. He persisted in honing his skills night after night in lonely wayside travellers' hotels or under canvas. While never a celebrity as an artist, his work in Australia was highly original and reflected the core values of the Pre-Raphaelite Brotherhood to the end. He was true to authentic organic detail in nature drawing and provided a balance of complex imagery across the canvas or

30 Peers, 'Smith, Bernhard'.

sketch book. Unfortunately, however, few of his works have survived, at least in the public arena.

His single daughter Minnie Ella Bernhard Smith spent a lifetime seeking recognition of her father's connection with the Pre-Raphaelite Brotherhood and his artistic achievement. She died in a nursing home on 6 July 1942.[31] Minnie fondly remembered that her father at Smythesdale used to slave away at a lovely garden 'all the hot broiling day long'. Like his brother Alexander, he loved gardening and producing beautiful gardens.

Five weeks before his death, Bernhard Smith began work on a connected series of pictures of Macbeth in the Pre-Raphaelite style. They were never completed. In his last affectionate letter to Minnie from Alexandra, he described his efforts to rescue two children from a flooded creek. He told her lightly that only a severe cold was the result. This was soon to lead to pneumonia and sudden death. His widow and seven young children survived him. Bernhard had been the youngest boy of his family of orientation and the most artistic.[32] He is buried at the Alexandra cemetery.

Despite his seeming obscurity as an artist, his portrait medallions of Sir John Richardson and Sir James Clark Ross, his brother's mentor, are held in the prestigious National Portrait Gallery in London.

There is a tendency among Australian art critics in recent years to hail Smith's art as a spontaneous and isolated neo-surrealist phenomenon, yet his later drawings had a wider public life than their twentieth-century obscurity suggests. The famed opera singer Madame Tosca exclaimed on viewing

---

31 Notice of death, of Minnie Ella Smith, Mental Hospital, Mont Park, Bernhard Smith, MS 9963, Box 1.

32 Smith, 'Bernhard Smith and his Connection', p. 5.

them in an exhibition that, until that moment, she had despaired of Australia ever producing beautiful art and Georgiana McCrae, a prominent artist, wrote glowingly of them. The architect Joseph Reed and the well-known colonial painter Louis Buvelot both admired the artistic merit of the drawings. Other contemporaries spoke of him highly. At that time as an artist, he was not an unknown.

For the last seven years of his life, Bernhard Smith was moving slowly but surely towards full-time professional art practice. The 1880 Melbourne International Exhibition provided a venue for his public 'coming out' and the drawings that he exhibited were awarded a second-class order of merit. These drawings were highly original and mystic. Sadly, it was a false dawn.

In 1885, he built a house at Elgar Park, Box Hill, where he later hoped to spend his retirement and concentrate on his art.[33] But even that was not to be.

Sketches of fairies by Bernhard Smith, MS 4901 ML

33 Peers, 'Smith, Bernhard'.

The drawings he made towards the end of his life stand out. They show an innate sense of composition and structure achieved solely by a thin nervous line. The subjects have a lyrical quality that marks them off from other works of their time in Australia. They have a Blakean mysticism and possess surreal qualities, according to art expert Ken Scarlett. They attain a peculiar value as they approximate to the surrealist approach of the twentieth century. There was nothing like them in nineteenth-century Australian art.[34]

---

34 Scarlett, *Australian Sculptors*, p. 602.

12

Epilogue & Epitaph

Sarah Aubrey Smith
(Private Collection)

Commander Alexander John Smith RN, second son of Lord Henry Smith, gentleman, and Jane Mary (née Voase), in his fifty-nine years of life – packed with extraordinary experiences – made important contributions to Imperial England and to the development of the Colonies of Tasmania and Victoria. He was born on 20 December 1812 at Greenwich in the reign of George III, King of Great Britain and Ireland who, in 1810, suffered a recurrence of a mental derangement and the Prince of Wales was made Regent by the parliament. The year Alexander was born saw Napoleon Bonaparte forced into a costly retreat from Moscow and the beginning of the end of French domination of Europe. The Battle of Trafalgar of 1805, seven years before Alexander's birth, began to give England supremacy of the high seas that was to play a significant role in his adolescent and adult life.

Educated as a gentleman primarily at home in a large exuberant and cultured family environment and surrounded by the iconography of patriotic heroes like Admiral Sir William Sidney Smith, Lord Horatio Nelson, Admiral Sir James de Saumarez and Admiral Sir William Cornwallis, it seemed entirely natural and almost inevitable that Alexander Smith would join His Majesty's Navy as a volunteer midshipman First Class with aspirations for a place at a higher level on the quarterdeck. He aspired to be an officer and a gentleman and achieved both in a lifetime into which many adventures and responsibilities were woven.

He served his first assignment on the frigate HMS *Thetis* signing on and going aboard at Portsmouth. The *Thetis*, named after the sea nymph in Greek mythology, was sent, with Alexander on board wearing his new midshipman's blue jacket and white ducks with obvious pride as a fourteen-year-old, to the Royal Navy's South American Station. The frigate was frequently based in the splendid harbour of Rio de Janeiro, visiting from there Buenos Aires, the Falkland Islands, Valparaiso and other South American spots on military patrol at sea.

Nearly four years later, the *Thetis* was shipwrecked on 5 December 1830 at Cape Frio, Brazil, in a violent storm soon after leaving the harbour of Rio de Janeiro bound for England and home leave for Alexander Smith at the age of eighteen. At the time, the monarch was George IV, King of Great Britain and Hanover, the eldest son of George III. George IV took the throne in 1820 and soon became a leader of taste, fashion and the arts and gave his name to the Regency period, synonymous with elegance and style.

Twenty-eight crew including three officers died in the violent collision with a storm-swept cliff face. Others were seriously injured; several had to have legs or arms amputated. Alexander made a miraculous escape with only superficial injuries. He was very fortunate to have survived by making a daring escape from the wrecked frigate under a cliff face. He later wrote to his family: 'I sprang from the Ship as far as I could, and at the same time a heavy sea took me & landed me safely [on a half submerged rock] with the exception of a few bruises'.

Eventually, he was rescued from there by the remnant of the crew who had reached higher ground above the cliff face. They threw him an improvised rope made up of seamen's stout duck trousers tied together. By this means, he was hauled to safety.

The adventure did not end there. After surviving for some time with little food in abandoned fishermen's huts of a local but absent native tribe, he and the surviving members of the ship's company were finally rescued on 18 December 1830 when several men-of-war arrived from South American Station headquarters. Alexander had had to spend his eighteenth birthday almost like Robinson Crusoe with his four-year-old uniform in tatters.

After the *Thetis* disaster, Alexander returned to England on the frigate HMS *Druid* for a well-earned but very short leave. He was then appointed to HMS *Warspite* on which he wrote a vivid account of his shipwreck adventure in a long letter to his family dated 23 December 1830. His next assignment and adventure was as a midshipman on HMS *Harrier* which was sent to the remote East Indian Station of the Royal Navy in the Indian Ocean. He was now quite accustomed to the wooden world of the navy and the sea which was shaping his youthful character and persona.

Sailors like Alexander always dwell on the fringes of settled stationary society. The shipboard world is a mystery to the majority of landlubbers. The popular impression was a stereotype quite removed from reality. Shipboard society was a complex world in which each person's place was defined by many invisible and subtle distinctions. Age for example divided and united a ship's company. A midshipman like Alexander Smith was in reality like an apprentice officer facing a steep and rough-hewn learning curve.

As midshipman, Alexander attended the captain, observed him at work, learned from him and carried his messages. There were many minor and occasional risky tasks, sometimes aloft. It was a matter of learning the ropes and the effectiveness of the strict chain of command. There was a lot to learn and all had to be fully mastered before there was any possibility of promotion which was gradual anyway, particularly in peacetime. His every action was being carefully observed by superior officers. He was expected to show courage in difficult situations and to maintain a high morale among the crew. The quarterdeck was his domain, but only for his training – an uncertain one at that. While a midshipman, he was only considered as a naval cadet, there to learn by practical experience.

On the *Harrier* in the Indian Ocean, Alexander visited such exotic places as the Cape of Good Hope, Trincomalee, Madras, Ceylon, Bengal, Prince of Wales' Island, Batavia, Singapore and Bombay, all with different fascinations. The *Harrier* was actively employed in the suppression of piracy in the Straits of Malacca and Mauritius, a dangerous set of tasks during Alexander Smith's tour of duty. He took part in two severe conflicts which ended in the destruction of the pirate settlements at Paulo Arroa and Paulo Sujre – great but risky adventures for a young man. Such experiences provided Alexander with a distinguished war record that he never boasted about, but saw as being in the line of duty to the Imperial homeland and the monarchy. It is a pity that there is no extant document that describes his adventures in the Indian Ocean in more detail.

In the navy, he was bound by mutual ties of dependence and obligation to others resting on a fundamental stability. He belonged to a naval code and tradition of behaviour, the real, natural discipline of the Service, something that was inherent in the nature of seafaring and common to wooden ships and seamen everywhere. It involved a collective understanding and collective forms of skill and action.

A ship at sea depended utterly on disciplined teamwork and any good seaman like Alexander knew without thinking that sea orders had to be obeyed for the safety of all. He well understood too that intelligent co-operation as well as initiative led to survival. Such discipline was functional and existed only to preserve the ship's company in safety.

As a member of the Royal Navy, Alexander Smith remained part of British society and partook of its ideas and ideology. A young recruit in the navy was at first brought up in the strictest obedience to authority, but one that rested on unstated consent not force. Alexander had been with such a regime since the age of fourteen.

After passing his examinations as midshipman at the age of twenty-one, he returned to England on HMS *Harrier* and was paid off. Alexander Smith was then appointed as a mate aboard HMS *Cove* in 1835 and, for the first time, served under the famous polar explorer Captain James Clark Ross. In January

1836 at the height of winter, Alexander left England aboard the *Cove* when Ross was sent on a special urgent mission to find and convey relief to some missing whalers who had been frozen in the ice in Baffin Bay.

Smith was to learn much under Ross' astute and determined captaincy and mentorship that was to radically change the direction of his future career in the Royal Navy. On the voyage of rescue, they encountered dangerous wild storms with force 10 and 11 winds that had the likelihood of destroying HMS *Cove* but for Ross' seamanship and leadership. In the process, Ross became Alexander's lifelong mentor and patron. They formed a warm and close friendship despite required status differences aboard ship. Alexander was often called to Ross' cabin for private and personal conversations.

Soon after, Smith gained further experience for a couple of months by serving as mate aboard HMS *Salamander*, a steamer on patrol on the north coast of Spain and then, through Ross' influence, for two years amongst the Orkneys off Scotland as an extra mate on HMS *Mastiff*, a surveying vessel where he acquired scientific skills and knowledge. Ross was obviously grooming him for more important things.

In November 1837, Alexander had taken charge of HMS *Cutter Woodlark* as its commanding officer for a period until he joined HMS *Mastiff* as mate under the charge of the experienced George Thomas. Captain James Clark Ross understood Alexander Smith's potential as a seaman who needed experience in leadership and kept him in mind for the future. From 1837 too, a new monarch was to be served as Queen Victoria had taken the throne. Alexander was to serve her faithfully to his life's end. His patriotism never wavered.

When Alexander sailed with Ross on the *Cove*, his captain was already a renowned and experienced polar explorer. By

1826, James Clark Ross had already spent nine summers in the Arctic sailing with his uncle Sir John Ross and Sir William Edward Parry as commanders. James Ross, who started as a midshipman like Alexander, had an aptitude for scientific magnetic observation well above the ordinary. In November 1827, he was promoted to Commander; in October 1834, he gained promotion to Post Captain.

James Clark Ross' opportunity for more national fame came when he was offered the command of a large-scale complex and expensive British Expedition to Antarctica primarily to locate the true position of the magnetic South Pole. On the way to the Southern Seas, he was required to set up a full series of magnetic observatories in the southern hemisphere and to carry out other important scientific discoveries. He was the right man in the right place at the right time. Moreover, he stood head and shoulders over everybody as far as polar exploration in wooden ships was concerned.

Ross was able to choose the officers and crew for the two ships of the expedition under his command, HMS *Erebus* and HMS *Terror*, both former bomb ships. Without, hesitation, he selected Alexander John Smith as his senior or first mate aboard the *Erebus*, the flagship of the expedition. Alexander joined the *Erebus* on 17 April 1839 in a state of great excitement. By that time, he was a mature experienced and accomplished seaman, (but young and unmarried at the age of twenty-six). Ross would not have chosen him if he wasn't.

Both the *Terror* and the *Erebus* were sturdy but ungainly ships that Ross was careful enough to reinforce structurally and add double-coppered hulls. They were suitably degaussed in the River Medway. Ross made every provision for the crews' welfare: the ships' interiors were maximised for warmth and comfort that would be needed in Antarctica. An unusually large supply of food was taken on board, including, as a new innovation in ship supplies, a variety of tinned meats and vegetables.

Ross enlisted scientists under the guise of ship surgeons. For one example, the botanist Joseph Dalton Hooker, later to be internationally famous but then only a young man about the same age as Alexander, was appointed assistant surgeon aboard the *Erebus*. Hooker became a lifelong friend of Alexander Smith and corresponded with him for many years both in Tasmania and Victoria. (The unfortunate aspect of this highly personal correspondence was the expectation that Ross would patronise both of them after the Antarctic Expedition was over and seek further promotion in the Royal Navy for them both. There was a bad feel about some of Hooker's more sarcastic comments about their erstwhile leader, together with a hint of jealousy about the fame and adoration that Ross received from the scientific and naval elite of England when he returned from his great Antarctic voyages. Hooker need not have worried. He was to achieve widespread fame as a naturalist of the highest order.)

Each of the ships had a company of sixty-four, all especially chosen by Ross for their talents and experience. Smith had had at least twelve years intense and valued experience at sea in all zones and climates. Many of the men were unmarried, including Ross.

Alexander Smith aboard the *Erebus* saw the last of the Cornish coast on 5 October, with the *Terror* close behind. With heavy loads, they had struggled ungainly through the English Channel. Successively, they visited the Canaries, the Cape Verde Islands, the islands of St Paul, Trinidad and Martin Vaz and, after a meandering cruise, reached St Helena on 31 January 1840 where they established the first observatory. During this leg of the journey, First Mate Alexander Smith turned twenty-seven on 20 December 1839. No doubt, there was a small celebration over dinner in the officers' mess and several toasts were made to his good health over a few bottles of red wine and port.

From St Helena, the expedition pressed on across the Atlantic to the Cape of Good Hope for a respite. They departed from there on 6 April 1840 as autumn was beginning to settle in. They headed southeast into much colder and windswept regions. Thus began the grand adventure to the mystical Lost Continent for Alexander Smith and his stalwart comrades.

The two ships arrived at Kerguelen Island amidst thick fog, squalls, snow and heavy seas where they anchored in Christmas Harbour on 15 May 1840. They stayed there for sixty-eight days. For forty-five of those days, the winds were gale force – a realistic foretaste of Antarctica and its weather conditions. Despite the weather, scientific experiments were carried out on a daily basis making a series of complex magnetic readings with care, but with great difficulty and discomfort. Smith worked on many of these days in the makeshift magnetic observatory on the windswept beach. It snowed or sleeted on sixty-one of those days.

To the south of the intrepid windswept voyagers was *Terra Antarctica*, *Terra Incognita*. These words were synonymous; and for nearly two thousand years they had been spaced out across every world map of substance and imagination.

On Kerguelen, James Clark Ross had tirelessly and continuously made accurate recordings. As an explorer, he was determined to see the job through without a break. Alexander Smith, inspired by his leader and mentor's capacity, worked just as hard. He became conversant with aspects of the scientific research in the process. It was mid-July before they left 'this most dreary and disagreeable island' and set a course for Van Diemen's Land. It was a difficult stormy crossing.

The *Terror* arrived in Hobart Town on 15 August 1840 and the *Erebus* arrived the next day. Both the officers and the crews were glad to find their land-legs again. They were greeted with wonderful enthusiasm by Lieutenant Governor Sir John Franklin, himself a famed polar explorer and scholar as well as a good friend of James Clark Ross. Almost the entire population of Hobart Town turned out to greet the adventurers. The people there were fascinated with the possibility that the British Expedition would solve the age-old mystery of *Terra Incognita* despite the fact that its main mission, according to the dour Admiralty, was to 'make an extensive series of magnetic observations in the high latitudes of the south, and to determine, if possible, the position of the magnetic pole'. These were its strict orders and the reason its commander had been chosen and the ships requisitioned.

For the crews of the *Erebus* and *Terror*, Hobart Town, a short way up the estuary of the Derwent, was a most pleasant and agreeable change from Kerguelen. It was much more like paradise for the weather-worn exhausted sailors. As well, the welcome they received was overwhelming. The ten weeks of interlude was delightful for Alexander and his seafaring companions. The expedition spent ten weeks in Hobart, establishing an observatory and caulking and repairing the ships.

Franklin went out of his way to give the expedition all possible help and hospitality. The Hobart community supported wholeheartedly. Franklin had used two hundred convicts to make the necessary preparations for a fixed observatory. They finished its erection in nine days. Observations were begun by the intrepid Ross on 27 August 1840 with Alexander Smith and a selection of others to assist. Later in the 1840s after the expedition had finished, Alexander Smith was appointed to a senior position of what Franklin had named Rossbank Observatory after his friend James Clark Ross.

After much local celebration, the expedition departed Hobart on 12 November 1840 under a gentle breeze. Making good headway, the voyagers arrived at the Auckland Islands a week later, before going on to Campbell Island the following day. There Alexander Smith was commissioned by Ross to make extensive observations around the harbour the two ships sheltered in.

They sailed south on 17 December 1840. The weather was favourable. Three days later, Alexander celebrated his twenty-eighth birthday. On Boxing Day, they sighted their first iceberg. They crossed the Antarctic Circle on 1 January 1841 – icebergs and floes which were larger than the first ones sighted began to multiply and the weather became more unsettled. Nevertheless, Ross decided to push further south after celebrating New Year's Day. New warm clothing was issued to each man: a boxcloth jacket and trousers, a pair of water boots, two pairs of warm woollen hose, two comforters, a red frock and a Welsh wig or knitted cap. All such gear was to maintain their body warmth in the freezing conditions.

Next morning, they sighted a bar of yellow across the southeastern horizon. The old hands with polar experience in the Northern hemisphere recognised it as an iceblink or a barrier of pack ice which they were about to reach and enter. At this moment, the weather worsened. A northern gale brought snow and high seas and forced the *Erebus* and *Terror* to shorten sail and haul away from the ice. Visibility was dangerously bad during the night, so the watch was doubled – there were many dangerous life-threatening icebergs about. By dawn, the weather had cleared.

Ross, demonstrating his brilliant seamanship, guided the expedition safely through the pack ice. On 5 January 1841, he decided firmly to push on south. Four days later, they were in the open water of what was to become the Ross Sea. They were the first known human beings to do so. It seemed as though they had already found the Golden Fleece.

Ross had hoped that they would find the magnetic pole beneath the sea, but this was not to be. On 11 January, land was sighted ahead – the ice-sealed coastline of what was called Victoria Land. Its range of mountains was named Admiralty Range.

On 12 February, the Union Jack was raised on Possession Island and land was claimed for the new young Queen who had taken the throne in 1837. No doubt Alexander swelled with pride.

Magnetic readings, however, indicated that the magnetic pole was still 800 kilometres away. Ross decided to follow

The *Terror* & *Erebus* amongst the ice floes in a gale, January 1841
(Private Family Collection)

the coast to the south. On 22 January 1841, they reached a latitude higher than the previous record set by the whaler James Weddell.

Alexander Smith and the rest of the two crews again found themselves in a spot where human beings had never before been. It was something of an awesome experience for the more reflective personalities like Alexander.

Franklin Island was discovered, named and thus formally possessed by Imperial Britain on 27 January. The following day, an active volcano was sighted to the south and named Mount Erebus. A smaller volcano to the east was then called Mount Terror. The south magnetic pole was estimated to be about 70° S, 256 kilometres into the interior to the west – a disappointment for Commander and Post Captain Ross. Obviously, they could not reach it by sea. They had unexpectedly encountered a continental land mass that had previously been thought of as pure ice like the Arctic.

The expedition found that further penetration south was blocked by a seemingly endless majestic perpendicular ice-cliff that Alexander Smith marvelled at and never forgot for the rest of his life. His dreams were to be full of it.

Ross named **Smith Inlet** in Victoria Land on 21 February 1841 after, and in honour of, his first mate on the *Erebus*. It appears in Ross' map of the area in his 1847 publication.

Ross had decided sensibly that any further attempt to penetrate the ice shelf was as likely 'as sailing a ship through the white cliffs of Dover'. The land continent was impenetrable with mere wooden ships.

By 15 February, they had returned to Franklin Island. The sea was beginning to freeze over. Winter was coming on fast. A prompt departure north was by that time absolutely necessary, otherwise they would be trapped in the ice for the whole of winter.

Exit through the ice pack proved more difficult than the entry. The loss of wind at times left the ships at the mercy of strong and dangerous swells. Eventually after reaching Balleny Island, Ross took the ships west for a while to carry out further scientific investigations.

The *Erebus* & the *Terror* reach the Great Ice Barrier

They then turned back for Hobart Town for the winter. The ships were refitted on the Derwent and more provisions were put on board. While in Hobart, Ross wrote to his friend Rear Admiral Phillip Parker King: 'our voyage has been successful … but we still hope for much more … they say d'Urville [leader of the French Expedition] was incorrect, this is untrue … The Yankees [under Captain Wilkes leadership and the ships of the American Expedition] have made a sad mess of it'.

Alexander Smith had just experienced the voyage of his lifetime which he would always remember vividly in his waking hours and in his dreams. In a real sense, it was the peak of his naval career. He and the other members of the two crews were fêted in Hobart as heroic celebrities of Ancient Greek proportions. As sea gods, they were invited to dinners, balls, receptions and picnics – admired by all men, and adored by all women.

Alexander Smith wrote home that 'on the Evening of the 7 April to our great Joy we once again dropped 𝄢 [anchor]

in the Derwent having been out 146 days & not a man in the sick list & in as good health & Spirits as when we left – and last night about 25 of them had comfortable lodgings in Jail having nearly taken the Town owing to the too great hospitality of the inhabitants'. The several brothels nearby the Hobart docks had done a roaring trade with men who had been contained for many days in a cold wooden world in stormy unknown seas. The drunk and disorderly had been placed in the lock-up overnight.

By this time, Alexander, always conscientious, had gained a fine reputation amongst his polar colleagues. Much later, his naval friend John Davis recalled that, throughout the voyages in the Antarctic Circle, Alexander was clear-headed, even-tempered and resourceful. His fine qualities as First Mate had maintained a high and vital level of morale amongst the crew aboard the *Erebus*: 'his genial disposition helped us through many a danger, many a tedious hour …'.[1] He had a great skill, not sometimes possessed by others, to adapt to circumstances.

While in Hobart Town, Ross wrote in his journal that society there was both English and agreeable. Alexander especially found it so – he became engaged to Sarah Aubrey Read who he described enthusiastically to his family in England by letter as 'very pretty, petite and vivacious'. She had won his heart. Very clearly, he had met the love of his life. She was the daughter of a Sydney currency lass, Elizabeth Driver whose parents had both been transported convicts

Ross and his loyal men had stayed in Van Diemen's Land until July 1841, some making excursions inland and collecting specimens. It was more likely that Alexander was ensuring

1 J.E. Davis to Aubrey Smith, 19 November 1872, Hydrographic Office, Admiralty.

success in his love life. The sojourn in Tasmania was a golden opportunity to do some courting. But by the end of June, the ships were ready for a second Antarctic voyage. They sailed from the Derwent on 7 July 1841 with provisions to last three years.

Since the *Erebus* encountered inward-going ships as it headed out on its second voyage of discovery, Alexander was able to dispatch a letter to Sarah **Aubrey** Read who lived with her family in New Town, Hobart. Gossip travelled fast in those days. The Lieutenant Governor's aide-de-camp came knocking on the Read family door with a request 'that Miss Read would graciously give any information of interest' with regard to the expedition to Lieutenant Governor Sir John Franklin. No doubt she blushed as the letter was of a passionate personal nature. Sir John Franklin was anxious for another type of information.

They first headed for Port Jackson, Sydney, where an observatory had already been established independently of Ross. After some magnetic observations on Garden Island, they headed for the Bay of Islands in New Zealand on 5 August. On 23 November 1841, they sailed south again and met their first iceberg on 15 December 1841. Two days later, they re-entered the pack ice where conditions were far worse than on their first journey. In dismal conditions aboard the *Erebus* on 20 December, Alexander celebrated his twenty-ninth birthday.

Christmas Day was spent shrouded in fog with both ships hemmed in by pack ice. Early January storms forced Ross into a meandering course across the Antarctic Circle. On 19 January 1842, the *Erebus* and *Terror* were pounded continuously by large rolling fragments of ice, causing severe damage.

It wasn't until 2 February that the two ships broke through to more open waters. By then, the temperatures were so low

Re-entering the Antarctic Circle, the ships were pounded by large rolling fragments of ice, 19 January 1842 (Private Collection)

as to cause sea water to freeze as it splashed over the decks of both ships.

At last on 22 February, they arrived at the eastern end of the Ross Ice Shelf in 78° 11' S/167° W. They turned east. Two days later, the ice shelf veered northwards. It became clear to Ross that no closer approach could be made to the South Pole than they had achieved in the initial voyage from Hobart.

Profoundly disappointed, James Clark Ross gave orders on 24 February 1842 to retreat to the north and head for the Falklands where Alexander Smith had previously visited as a much younger midshipman aboard the *Thetis* while on duty in the South American Station.

On the way there, a serious accident occurred. In heavy stormy seas on 12 March, in attempting to avoid an iceberg in poor visual conditions, the *Erebus* swerved suddenly into the course of the *Terror* which could not help but plough straight into the other vessel in front. The *Erebus* was badly disabled and extensive damage was caused. Ross' superb seamanship and the calm heroism of the crew led by First Mate Alexander Smith got them through. The two ships were eventually parted and, in three hectic days, received frantic but efficient emergency repairs of a temporary nature. Rounding Cape Horn, they arrived safely into Port Louis in the Falkland Islands on 6 April 1842.

The crews were in good health thanks to Ross' planning, but they had been together on high and difficult seas through many life-threatening dangers for much too long. It had been like a battleground. Psychologically, the expedition was beginning to fracture at the edges. They had been confined together for too long in the most of difficult of circumstances and conditions.

Life in the Falklands proved disappointing and particularly depressing for the crews. The human experience was totally unlike Hobart where they had been merrily fêted by the locals and treated like heroes. Port facilities were poor. There were no brothels to speak of, few pubs and inadequate shore accommodation for the able seamen. Alexander, however, was overjoyed as he found himself promoted to Lieutenant from First Mate. He joined the officers' mess.

Some disagreements had broken out amongst a few of the officers. Ross and Francis Crozier, the captain of the *Terror*, found something positive for them to do while the ships underwent extensive repairs. They carried out a survey of the Falkland Islands, suggesting that Port William (later re-named Port Stanley) was a better harbour for shipping than that of Port Louis. They also continued magnetic observations that Alexander Smith took part in. These were completed by 4 September.

The two crews found themselves happy enough to leave the Falklands on 19 September 1842 for Tierra del Fuego for an interlude of magnetic research that Ross wanted to complete on Hermit Island. After completing observations there, they returned to the Falklands until mid-December.

On 17 December, Ross plunged his expedition south again deep towards the Antarctic Circle, this time intending to penetrate the Weddell Sea. In the South Shetland Islands, they carefully charted what was to become James Ross Island. They claimed Cockburn Island for the British Crown, but by this time the voyagers were exhausted from arduous travel and returned north soon after finding themselves in the pack ice at 64° S.

Ross turned his expedition east, but did not cross the Antarctic Circle until 29 February 1843. As the summer season was closing fast, Ross decided that, as far as new exploration was concerned, the expedition was now at an end.

Eventually and at last, they dropped anchors at Simon's Bay, South Africa. After refitting and loading provisions onboard, they proceeded to St Helena, the Ascension Islands and Rio de Janeiro. From Rio en route to England, Alexander Smith was terribly ill and seemed to be almost at death's door, but recovered around about the time they sighted England. It is possible that his health in his later years could have been affected by this episode.

The *Erebus* and *Terror* anchored off Folkestone while Captain Ross went ashore and travelled immediately to London by coach to report his findings to the Admiralty. The two ships of the expedition were then paid off on 23 Sep-tember 1843. The two ships' companies had been away on the expedition for almost four and a half years, mainly on the high seas. Alexander Smith by this time was well into his thirtieth year and soon to turn thirty-one on 20 December while on home leave.

He had been an essential part in the last of the great voyages of discovery made wholly under sail in wooden ships – a great achievement in itself. Antarctica had been discovered by the *Erebus* and *Terror* under sail. For five thousand years, sailing vessels had brought grace and beauty to the oceans of the world. They only just penetrated to the last of the continents before giving way to steam.

D'Urville, Wilkes and Ross captained the last of a series of great expeditions towards the South Pole that never fully succeeded. A century of feverish activity ceased and the Antarctic lay quiet and undisturbed. It was the end of an epoch. South Polar exploration was not revived until towards the end of the nineteenth century.

As the expedition's leader, James Clark Ross was showered with accolades and much spun off onto Alexander Smith and the rest of the officers providing them with unique and life-lasting identity and celebrity. They had all become national heroes and, at the same time, heroes of the Empire. Ross was awarded medals from the Royal Geographic Society and the Royal Geographic Society of Paris. He was knighted a year after the expedition returned and was awarded an honorary degree from Oxford University.

All of this acclaim rubbed off on those that had lived for more than four years aboard the *Erebus* and the *Terror*. They were collectively considered grand and intrepid voyagers.

Meanwhile, Alexander Smith's life at thirty-one years of age spun into a more personal, romantic context. It was plain he wanted to leave his sea adventures behind him, while they still clung to him in terms of remembrance of things past. Marriage was the new brighter destiny.

Sarah Aubrey Read, the Hobart-based daughter of Captain George Frederick Read and Elizabeth Driver, married

Captain Alexander John Smith RN, son of Lord Henry and Jane Mary Smith, on 12 October 1844 in St John's Church, New Town, Van Diemen's Land. It was to be a most happy and fruitful union. Alexander took up a land-based Royal Navy appointment at the Rossbank Magnetic Observatory to carry out scientific observations pioneered and commenced by James Clark Ross. Alexander was, therefore, entrusted with the golden fleece of the James Clark Ross odyssey, nearly the last long adventurous voyages in sailing boats.

After about eight years of meticulous work in pleasant, quiet surroundings of Hobart, Alexander resigned his appointment in 1852. After a sojourn in England to visit his family, he proceeded with his wife and children to Victoria to bring his naval career to its end in terms of retirement.

The Victorian gold rushes had already started. The following year, 1853, he was appointed Commissioner of Crown Lands for the Goldfields stationed at Castlemaine and appointed directly by Lieutenant Governor Sir Charles La Trobe. His rank in the Royal Navy had carried him into such an important position of leadership and authority within the government employ. One of his many duties was to issue licences to gold diggers and arbitrate often violent disputes between them. He sat on the bench in legal and criminal cases which were almost daily occurrences on the chaotic goldfields.

He gained a soaring reputation for even-handed fairness, honesty and solid determination in the rapidly-growing community and town of Castlemaine where great wealth was being torn from the ground. His younger brother, the Pre-Raphaelite artist Bernhard Smith, joined him as an assistant Goldfields Commissioner and later became a prominent Victorian Police Magistrate.

By 1861, Alexander resigned his government employ to

become an elected member of the parliament of the young Colony of Victoria. At the same time, he took up farming at Langley, a homestead property of 900 acres. Farming was his second love to the sea. Alexander performed well as a parliamentarian supporting economic and social progress and growth in his district, especially the expansion of the railway, the founding of new schools, the improvement of road conditions, assisting the development of the mining industry and achieving fairness for individuals and local communities.

He and Aubrey welcomed visitors from England, especially colleagues from the Royal Navy. They both became highly regarded in local district circles and supported many rural activities and events.

But by 1868, the couple were finding ageing a difficult matter, especially Alexander, despite close joyful family ties. Alexander Smith's health was fading and failing fast.

On 3 July 1867, he had a legal document drawn up stating:

> This is the last will and testament of me Alexander John Smith of Langley near Kyneton in the Colony of Victoria Esquire, a Commander in Her Majestys Navy. I devise and bequeath the real and personal Estate of or to which I shall be possessed or entitled at the time of my decease unto my dear Wife Sarah Aubrey Smith absolutely but as to Estates vested in me Upon trust or by way of Mortgage subject to the Trusts and Equities affecting the same respectively I appoint my said Wife Sarah Aubrey Smith Sole Executrix of this my Will and Guardian of my infant children [meaning grandchildren] And I revoke all former Wills and declare this only to be my last Will and Testament.[2]

---

2   Copy supplied by Hockley, Castlemaine Historical Society.

This is the paper writing marked A being the original Will of Alexander John Smith deceased mentioned and referred to in the annexed affidavit of Sarah Aubrey Smith sworn this twentieth day of November One thousand eight hundred and seventy two –

Before me

Commissioner of the Supreme Court of the Colony of Victoria for taking affidavits

In a real sense, this was his last love letter to Aubrey – a tribute to their life together.

In the last decade of his life, Alexander John Smith devoted himself to farming and domestic and local concerns. He died in his married daughter's home in Sandhurst of heart failure and inflammation of the lungs at the age of fifty-nine on 7 September 1872,[3] having received, amongst his many other accomplishments, the retired rank of Commander in the Royal Navy. He had been suffering from ill health for several years. He was survived by his wife Sarah Aubrey, son Alexander Henry, and daughters Mrs (H.M.) Emma Chomley (in whose home he died), Mrs (P.H.) Georgie [Georgina] Parker, Lady Manifold [Fanny], Edith Margaret, wife of Dr Thomas Gray, and Maud Margaret, wife of James Read Officer.

Alexander's well-loved Aubrey died on 21 June 1900 at Toorak in Melbourne. His younger brother Bernhard, who was also born at Greenwich (on 20 November 1820), died of pneumonia on 7 October 1885 in Alexandra, Victoria, after a heroic attempt to save two children from drowning.

* * * * *

Many of Alexander Smith's surviving letters to his family in

---

3   Death notice, *Mount Alexander Mail*, 10 September 1872.

the Imperial motherland were sent, especially in later years, to his single younger sister Emma Ann Smith who like him was born at Greenwich. She kept him posted on family news. His letters to her reveal a great love and respect for his family of orientation. Alexander also wrote to his mother Jane Mary (née Voase), who died on 18 December 1845 when he was at the Rossbank Observatory in Hobart, and to his father Lord Henry who died on 7 February 1855 while he was a Goldfields Commissioner in Castlemaine, Victoria.

Less than a month before his death on 13 August 1872, Alexander John Smith wrote his final letter to his sister Emma.

> My dearest Emma
>
> You will wonder at the above address, but I must tell you we have been away from Langley over three weeks. I was feeling ill when the last mail left [the colony] and a few days after I got knocked up & had to send to Kyneton for the Doctor who at once saw I was in a bad state with inflammation of the Lungs & much disturbance about my Heart in fact I could hardly breathe had no rest or sleep, constant violent spasms; he treated me promptly but as we had to send in 9 miles for Medicine & 9 miles to return & having got wandering in my mind Aubrey did the best thing by having the Horses put in the Buggy in bringing me to Melbourne. I fancy notwithstanding the long cold journey that change worked wonders. A Dr. Tracey came who confirmed Dr. Gray of Kyneton's opinion. We stayed a week at the Port Phillip Club Hotel & as soon as Aubrey could get me away we came here where I am now I am glad to say all but well in health & Aubrey could leave me without any anxiety... We have made up our minds to leave our dear old Langley & come and live in Melbourne for all the medical

men say the Elevation and the Cold climate there I could no longer stand now... Having filled my paper & feel rather tired so with much Love to you all My Dear Sisters &c. Ted, John & your belongings Ever my Dearest Emma

Your affectionate Brother
A.J. Smith[4]

The last resting place of Alexander & Aubrey Smith & their infant Edward in a family vault at Castlemaine Cemetery (with inscription). Photo by Ian Hockley, Castlemaine Historical Society

Sacred
to
The Memory Of
EDWARD BERNHARD
THE BELOVED CHILD
of
ALEXANDER JOHN
AND
SARAH AUBREY SMITH
WHO DEPARTED THIS LIFE
APRIL 19TH 1861
AGED 3 YEARS AND 8 MONTHS
Let not your heart be troubled
neither let it be afraid
ALSO
TO THE MEMORY OF
ALEXANDER JOHN SMITH
COMMANDER IN THE ROYAL NAVY
WHO DEPARTED THIS LIFE
SEPTEMBER 7TH 1872
AGED 59 YEARS
ALSO
TO THE MEMORY OF
SARAH AUBREY
HIS WIFE
WHO DEPARTED THIS LIFE
21ST JUNE 1900
AGED 79 YEARS

As time went on after Langley was abandoned in 1872, the property was sub-divided to become urbanised as a suburb of

---

4 Alexander Smith to his sister, 13 August 1872, Spring Hurst St. Gr Melbourne. His sister, Emma, has written on page 1, 'Dear Alick's last letter to me'.

Kyneton. The traces of Alexander Smith's work as a gardener and a farmer no longer linger.

To the last, Alexander Smith was truly stoic, unostentatious, a heroic gentleman of the scientific enlightenment of the Royal Navy and the British Empire. He was widely respected and known. He served with distinction from midshipman volunteer first class to lieutenant, as a seaman, an Antarctic explorer, an astronomer, a goldfields commissioner, a magistrate, a pioneering parliamentarian, a naturalist and agricultural producer and farmer. He was also to become the 'long time past' of the origins of the Victorian town of Castlemaine where he was very popular – a singular thing for a former goldfields officer.

All of these things, but the James Clark Ross Antarctic Expedition remained the greatest adventure of his lifetime.

Model of HMS *Erebus*, 1826, D9479, NMM, Greenwich

In the Wake of the *Erebus*, — a dynasty...

Commander Alexander John Smith RN and Sarah Aubrey Read

In the wake of the *Erebus* and the great Ross Antarctic Expedition of 1839-1843, Commander Alexander John Smith RN and Sarah Aubrey Read produced seven children, six of whom survived to adulthood and married. Thus a family dynasty began to take shape. Five of those children have left progeny to the present day.

AUBREY SMITH

The first, **Aubrey Emma Elizabeth**, born on 24 August 1845 in Hobart Town, Van Diemen's Land, married Hussey Burgh Malone Chomley (1832-1906) at the age of twenty-one on 3 December 1866 at Scots Church in Collins Street, Melbourne. Hussey Chomley, who was born in Dublin but came to Port Phillip as a child, became Chief Commissioner of Police in Melbourne on 20 March 1882. They had previously lived in Sandhurst, Bendigo where Alexander Smith died in 1872 while he was convalescing from a serious breakdown in health. Hussey held office as Police Commissioner until June 1902 when failing health forced him into retirement. He had started as a Police Cadet in September 1852 and was soon promoted to an officer. He spent his early years in the Victorian police patrolling the diggings at Ballan and Ballarat. Later, he was stationed at Inglewood, Swan Hill, Jericho and Benalla. He went from there to Bendigo in 1862 and became superintendent in charge of the Bendigo, Bourke and Geelong districts. He was gazetted as a first-class superintendent in 1876. When promoted to Chief Inspector in 1881, he was given charge of re-organising the entire Victorian police force to stamp out corruption and make it more efficient. During his fifty years as a police officer, his record was without blemish. A tall, bearded and robust presence, he was noted for his courage, honesty, devotion to duty and his partiality. Under his command, the Victorian force reached a high level of efficiency and became a respectable, smoothly-run organisation. Hussey Chomley died at Malvern in Melbourne on 12 July 1906. His marriage to Aubrey Emma was a happy and fulfilling one. They had two sons.[1]

---

1   A.F. Kimber, 'Chomley, Hussey Malone (1832-1906)', *Australian Dictionary of Biography*, Vol. 3, 1969, p.393.

Alexander Francis Chomley was born in 1867 and followed in his father's footsteps (and those of his grandfather Alexander John Smith) as a Victorian public servant. He eventually became Chief Surveyor of Melbourne's Board of Works. Alexander Chomley was one of the founders of the Victorian Lawn Tennis Association and became a Board member of the South Yarra Tennis Club. Arthur Aubrey Chomley was born in 1870. He was educated at Trinity College and the University of Melbourne. Through their marriages, Alexander and Arthur were to leave many descendants in the following generations.

Their mother, Aubrey Emma Elizabeth (née Smith) died on 26 October 1914.

GEORGIE SMITH

Alexander and Aubrey Smith's second child, **Georgina Jane** known as **Georgie**, was born in Hobart Town, Van Diemen's Land, on 8 June 1847. She married Captain Philip Reginald Hastings Parker RN, Commander of the Royal Yacht *Victoria and Albert*. They had three sons. Philip Morley Parker was born at Greenwich in 1872, the birthplace of his grandfather, Alexander John Smith, ironically in the year his grandfather died. Philip did not marry. He died in Kuala Lumpar in Malaya.

Their second son, Aubrey Hastings Parker, was born in 1873 at St Helier in Jersey in the Channel Islands. During the Great War, Captain (later Major) Aubrey Parker was twice mentioned in dispatches and was awarded the Military Cross (MC) for bravery in the field. He was invested by King George V in Buckingham Palace. Educated at Trinity College, Melbourne, he subsequently became a member of the Punjab Civil Service in India. During leave in London and with the approval of the Indian Government, he offered his services to the War Office and was accepted, first as an observer in the Royal Flying Corps. He rose in the ranks during the course of the war to a Commander of the Royal Flying Squadron. He married Margaret, the daughter of Major G.F. Bartrop VDF.

The son of Major Aubrey Parker and Margaret, Reginald Hastings Parker, was born in 1903. He was killed in action at Mudanya, Turkey, in a British Expeditionary Force in the Royal Navy as a midshipman on 25 June 1920 at the age of seventeen. He was shot in the back by a Turkish trooper just as he was returning to his ship.

Georgina Jane and Philip Reginald Parker's third son, Hastings Theophilus Parker, was born on 14 April 1875 and baptised in the Old Charlton Church in Kent, England. He died in England from wounds received on active service in India. As a result, the direct line of Georgina Jane Smith and Captain Philip Reginald Hastings Parker sadly died out with the seventeen-year-old grandson who had followed in the tradition of his great grandfather Commander Alexander John Smith RN who also began his naval career as a midshipman.

Georgina Jane (née Smith) Parker died in India on 31 May 1899.

FAN SMITH

The third child of Alexander and Aubrey Smith was born on 8 July 1849 also in Van Diemen's Land just before it became Tasmania. She was **Frances Maria**. At the age of thirty-six on 23 April 1885, she married Walter Synnot Manifold (1849-1928) who was the same age. She became

Frances Maria Smith

Lady Frances Manifold when her husband was knighted in 1920. Walter Synnot Manifold, a prominent pastoralist and Victorian politician, was born at Grasmere, Warrnambool, Port Phillip District (later Victoria), on 30 March a few months before Frances Maria. He was the second son of Thomas Manifold and Jane Elizabeth, daughter of Captain Walter Synnot.

Walter Synnot Manifold was educated in Germany and at Melbourne Church of England Grammar School. He signed the roll as a Victorian solicitor in 1875 at the age of twenty-six but did not practise. With his elder brother James, he bought Pine Grove West station near Echuca. After visiting Europe again, he purchased Sesbiana (1,800 square kilometres) in Queensland entering into a partnership with his uncle Peter Manifold. He managed Sesbiana between 1878 and 1884, then sold it and returned to Warrnambool to take up his inheritance of Wollaston Station. By late April 1885, he was married to Frances Maria. They had no children. Manifold bred cattle, but turned most of Wollaston over to dairying on a share-and-tenant basis. This left him time to devote to his favourite hobbies, modern machinery and breeding cattle. By 1904, he had installed an electrical plant there. After World War I, Wollaston was broken up for soldier settlements.

Walter was elected to the Victorian Legislative Council for Western Province in June 1901. He eventually became a prominent, but unofficial leader of the Council through his thorough examination of legislation and his amiable tempe-rament. In 1919, he became (the first native-born) President of the Council. As recounted, he was knighted in 1920, but forced to retire in 1923 because of ill health. He resigned from his seat in January 1924.[2]

Walter and Frances travelled widely, especially in Asia where they purchased many splendid pieces of furniture and pottery. Walter was President of the Melbourne Club in 1908. He undertook public work as a duty, imposed by his position as a leader of society and a member of the pre-gold upper-class. Frances Maria died on 7 April 1921 and her husband on 15 November 1928, a widower at Toorak. They are both buried at St Kilda Cemetery. His estate was sworn for probate at £83,356.

Alexander Henry Smith

ALEX SMITH

Alexander Henry Smith, the only surviving son of Alexander and Aubrey and their fourth child, married Emily Josephine Clarke, dau-ghter of Mary Jane Docker and her first husband Thomas Clarke of Gooramadda Station on the Murray about twenty miles south of Albury. Alexander Henry was born in Blackheath in London on 21 April 1852 while his father Alexander John Smith was on leave there.

Mary Jane Docker, Thomas Clarke's wife, was reputed to be the first white child to cross the Murray River when it was known as the Hume. She was the daughter of the Reverend Joseph Docker and his wife Sarah (née Bristow) who over-

2   P.H. de Serville, 'Manifold, Sir Walter Synnot (1849-1928)', Bede Nairn & Geoffrey Serle (gen. eds), *Australian Dictionary of Biography*, Vol. 10, Melbourne University Press, Carlton, 1986, pp. 390-1.

landed stock from Windsor in the west of Sydney, New South Wales, to Wangaratta in Victoria on the Ovens River, a major tributary of the Murray. They got there by following the cart-tracks of the famous explorer Major Thomas Mitchell, the Surveyor General of New South Wales. Joseph Docker and his wife were amongst the first settlers in Wangaratta in 1838.

Thomas Clarke

The Reverend Docker's cavalcade of overlanders included his wife Sarah, their six children and his young adult niece as well as their household possessions, farming equipment, food stores, clothing, bedding and more than 3,000 animals – mainly sheep, twenty milking cows and a mob of horses. With them were men – shepherds, drovers and rouseabouts – and women employees. They had to move slowly with bullock wagons, carts – some covered with canvas on hoops – and horse-drawn drays over the rough and rugged track. One wagon carried a boat they used to cross the mighty Murray (then the Hume), the greatest obstacle on their journey. Even crates of chickens and ducks were lashed to the sides of the drays. The shepherds' dray moved ahead of the large flock of sheep and sheep dogs.[3] All in all, it was a complicated epic journey full of incident and adventure.

Docker took over the Bontharambo run for his stock. It was a thickly grassed plain ideal for grazing and suited his enterprise. While there was trouble between settlers and Aborigines elsewhere on the Ovens River, Joseph Docker was particularly and successfully conciliatory to the original inhabitants and

---

3   J.M. McMillan, *The Two Lives of Joseph Docker*, Spectrum Publications, Melbourne, 1994, pp.129-38.

The old and new at Bontharambo, sketch by N. Chevalier

achieved peace and goodwill with them. For many years, they held a corroboree on the island on the lagoon a little way from the homestead. In 1840, Docker began to employ Aboriginal stockmen and gained their trust. In 1843, he set about building a second homestead named after the run: Bontharambo. The property was situated in the north of Wangaratta with the Ovens River as one border. Docker moved his family there ten years after his arrival in the Australian colonies.[4]

In developing the Bontharambo run, Docker built successive slab, but comfortable homesteads. He was content to add one bark hut annex after another as his family increased. The rooms were joined to each other at 'all sorts of strange

---

4   Due to a major disagreement with his superior in Sydney, Archdeacon W.G. Broughton, over a complaint by a local magistrate that it was alleged he was intoxicated at a dinner, Joseph Docker, then Vicar of St Matthews, Windsor, resigned as one of His Majesty's chaplains in a letter of 1 August 1833. Having cut his ties with the established church in the penal colony of New South Wales, he decided to leave Windsor and head south to the Ovens River in the Port Phillip District (later Victoria). Many of his former parishioners regretted his going. He chose not to take up another appointment in the Church.

and nondescript angles'. Chimneys were erected all over the place.

Docker then employed the architect Thomas Watts to design a mansion which was built in 1857-9 after Docker had been granted his pre-emptive right to the run in 1855. Much of the surrounding landscape was developed into lush parkland. Various agricultural industries were developed on the property at the same time during the 1860s.

Bontharambo is a picturesque two-storey Italianate asymmetrical brick and stone building with a dramatically prominent square tower. A complex of outbuildings surrounded it including the remains of the 1843 second slab homestead, a Chinese gardener's cottage built in the late 1850s and stables built in 1855. A private family cemetery was established on the property in 1843 and now contains memorial headstones of family members.

In 1873, Bontharambo with its gardens and mansion were highlighted and colourfully described by Edwin Carton Booth in *Australia in the 1870s*:

> Honeysuckle, and jessamine, and sarsaparilla so crowded and crushed the wisteria and other foreigners, that they had in self-defence to grow beyond their ordinary luxuriance and beauty, in order to hold a position with the natives they endeavoured to displace. All round the house, and indeed at some points almost within it, there lay a garden full of wonderful flowers and sweet smelling herbs. Roses grew in such plenty that at the fall of the leaf the garden looked like a gigantic *pot-pourri*. Fruit trees grew on every side, and vines took advantage of the projections of the house to rest bunches of luscious fruit thereon. The banks of the [Ovens] river in front bore melons in abundance, whilst all around the soft velvety turf

made walking a positive delight. … the old cluster of huts still stands, but it is overshadowed by a grander dwelling-place. Just beyond the boundary of the old garden a mansion has been erected. It has terraces and corridors, magnificent entrance-hall and handsome rooms. Plate-glass glistens in the windows, whilst London and Paris-made furniture garnish the rooms. Everywhere the signs of graceful luxury abound, and the new palace of Bontherambo [*sic*] has taken the place of the old but most comfortable hut.[5]

The gravestones of the Rev. Joseph Docker and his wife Sarah at Bontharambo (photo by Marie Ramsland)

Alex (Alexander Henry) Smith came to North East Victoria in 1873 and bought a property, Mundara at Laceby, ten miles from Wangaratta. He was twenty-one at the time and his father Alexander John had died the preceding year. Alex made several improvements to the property by draining low-lying swampy areas, eradicating noxious weeds and boring for underground water supplies. He kept fine horses that did not escape the attention of the famous bushranger Kelly Gang. Legend developed that Ned Kelly 'borrowed' horses from Mundara from time to time, but always returned them after he had used them. It's more than likely, however,

5   Edwin Carton Booth FRCX, *Australia in the 1870s*, Summit Books, Paul Hamlyn, Sydney, 1979 – facsimile of *Australia*, illustrated with drawings by Skinner Prout, N. Chevalier *et al.*, Virtue and Company, London, 1873, pp. 60-1.

that he returned them worn-out only to replace them with fresh ones.

Like his father, Alex was active in community affairs over an extended period of time. In 1882, he became a member of Oxley Shire Council and remained so for thirty-seven years. On eight occasions, he was President.

Alex and his wife Emily had three daughters; two have left descendants. The eldest daughter, Emily Irene (1879-1946), married Dr Leslie Henderson who practised at Wangaratta. The other two daughters were twins, Lillie Muriel (1880-1961) and Amy Maud (1880-1965). Lillie married Charles Graham Weir Officer (known as Graham) in 1909 in Holy Trinity Cathedral, Wangaratta. After Graham graduated with a Bachelor of Science degree having been educated at Toorak College and Edinburgh and Melbourne Universities, he became a Mining Engineer in Western Australia and Tasmania. He then managed the pastoral property Kallara Station in New South Wales with his brother Suetonius Henry Officer. Graham died two years after his marriage and sadly would not have known that a daughter would be born eight and a half months later. In adulthood, this child would be the mother of Merilyn Pedrick.

In 1922, Lillie married Campbell Meredith Ffloyd Chomley, thus reuniting the Chomley and Smith families. Campbell was a nephew of Hussey Chomley who had married Alexander and Aubrey's eldest daughter Aubrey Emma.

EDITH SMITH

The other children of Alexander and Aubrey Smith were not born in Tasmania, but in England, in the case of Alex, and in Victoria. This was their fifth child **Edith Margaret** born in 1854. She became a talented nature artist and catalogued and classified a comprehensive study of Tasmanian shells. Her illustrated book is held in the British Museum. On 23 October 1889, Edith married Dr Thomas Gray of New Norfolk, Tasmania. They had two sons and two daughters; they have descendants to the present day.

EDWARD SMITH

The sixth child **Edward Bernhard Smith** did not survive infancy and died on 18 April 1861 aged 3 years 8 months having been born in 1857 in The Camp, Castlemaine.[6]

MAUD SMITH

The seventh and last child of Alexander and Aubrey Smith was **Maud Margaret**, born in 1859 in Castlemaine. She married James Read Officer of Rocklands near Balmoral in Victoria. He was educated at Wesley College, a prominent pastoralist who, between 1910 and 1921, owned a series of properties in western New South Wales, including Billilla homestead. He retired to Worrough near Seymour in 1921 and died in 1927. Maud survived to 1946. They had two sons and two daughters. The first son Mervyn was born in 1888 and died in infancy. The second child, a daughter, Eila Aubrey, married her first cousin once removed, Henry Suetonius Officer. They had no issue. Maud and James' third child Lorraine Maude was born in 1891 at Hermitage Plains, Nymagee in New South Wales and died in 1963 at Wangaratta. She married Hubert Spencer Docker, the grandson of the Reverend Joseph Docker and Sarah (née Bristow). Their descendents still live at Bontharambo, Wangaratta.

Their fourth child was Philip Langley Officer born in 1894. He served in the First Australian Imperial Force (AIF) in the

---

6 'Family notices', *Argus*, 23 April 1861.

artillery and was commissioned a lieutenant in the field. After the Great War, he became the managing partner for many years of Billilla on the Darling River. Philip never married.[7] He died in Wilcannia in 1963.

*   *   *   *   *

From one female, the daughter of transported convict parents, Elizabeth Driver, a currency lass, who married Captain Read and bore Sarah Aubrey, the bloodline has continued through to the present day, initiated by the fruitful and happy marriage of Sarah Aubrey to an English naval officer Alexander John Smith RN of the *Erebus*. Sarah Aubrey's mother died when she was scarce an infant. They are truly in the wake of that worthy vessel that survived the voyages into the fabled Antarctic under the command of Sir James Clark Ross, only to be lost forever in the North West Passage together with its commander Sir John Franklin and its entire company. Had Lieutenant Alexander John Smith been in England at that time and not in Van Diemen's Land, he surely would have been the first chosen to be on the vessel and this particular dynasty would not have occurred.

The complex dynasty as it is now has interwoven the Smith, Chomley, Docker and Officer family members in both warp and weft.

---

7   'And what of Alexander's descendants?', notes to author from Merilyn Pedrick, June 2011.

Bontharambo graveyard

Family gathering at Bontharambo, July 2011 (photos by Marie Ramsland)

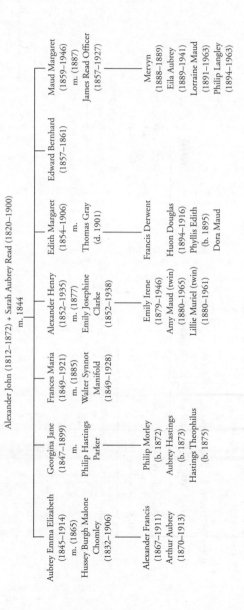

The Smiths of Australia

Alexander John (1812–1872) + Sarah Aubrey Read (1820–1900)
m. 1844

Aubrey Emma Elizabeth (1845–1914)
m. (1865)
Hussey Burgh Malone Chomley (1832–1906)

Georgina Jane (1847–1899)
m.
Philip Hastings Parker

Frances Maria (1849–1921)
m. (1885)
Walter Synnot Manifold (1849–1928)

Alexander Henry (1852–1935)
m. (1877)
Emily Josephine Clarke (1852–1938)

Edith Margaret (1854–1906)
m.
Thomas Gray (d. 1901)

Edward Bernhard (1857–1861)

Maud Margaret (1859–1946)
m. (1887)
James Read Officer (1857–1927)

Alexander Francis (1867–1911)
Arthur Aubrey (1870–1913)

Philip Morley (b. 1872)
Aubrey Hastings (b. 1873)
Hastings Theophilus (b. 1875)

Emily Irene (1879–1946)
Amy Maud (twin) (1880–1965)
Lillie Muriel (twin) (1880–1961)

Francis Derwent
Huon Douglas (1894–1916)
Phyllis Edith (b. 1895)
Dora Maud

Mervyn (1888–1889)
Eila Aubrey (1889–1941)
Lorraine Maud (1891–1963)
Philip Langley (1894–1963)

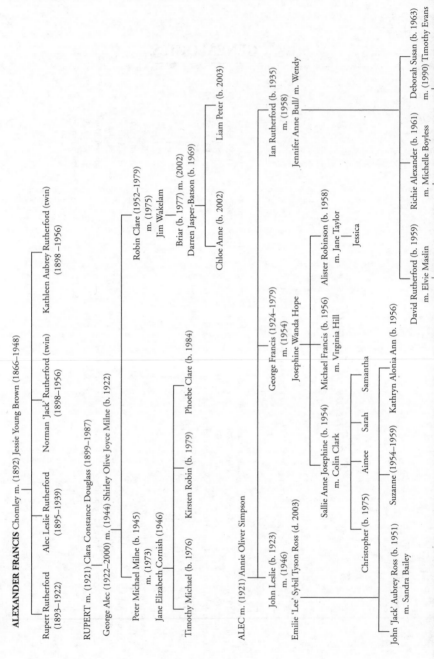

CHOMLEY FAMILY

ALEXANDER FRANCIS Chomley m. (1892) Jessie Young Brown (1866–1948)

Rupert Rutherford (1893–1922)

Alec Leslie Rutherford (1895–1939)

Norman 'Jack' Rutherford (twin) (1898–1956)

Kathleen Aubrey Rutherford (twin) (1898–1956)

RUPERT m. (1921) Clara Constance Douglass (1899–1987)

George Alec (1922–2000) m. (1944) Shirley Olive Joyce Milne (b. 1922)

Peter Michael Milne (b. 1945) m. (1973) Jane Elizabeth Cornish (1946)

Timothy Michael (b. 1976)

Kirsten Robin (b. 1979)

Phoebe Clare (b. 1984)

Robin Clare (1952–1979) m. (1975) Jim Wakelam

Briar (b. 1977) m. (2002) Darren Jasper-Batson (b. 1969)

Chloe Anne (b. 2002)

Liam Peter (b. 2003)

ALEC m. (1921) Annie Oliver Simpson

John Leslie (b. 1923) m. (1946) Emilie 'Lee' Sybil Tyson Ross (d. 2003)

John 'Jack' Aubrey Ross (b. 1951) m. Sandra Bailey

Christopher (b. 1975)

Sallie Anne Josephine (b. 1954) m. Colin Clark

Aimee

Sarah

Samantha

Suzanne (1954–1959)

Kathryn Alonia Ann (b. 1956)

George Francis (1924–1979) m. (1954) Josephine Wanda Hope

Michael Francis (b. 1956) m. Virginia Hill

Alister Robinson (b. 1958) m. Jane Taylor

Jessica

Ian Rutherford (b. 1935) m. (1958) Jennifer Anne Bull/ m. Wendy

David Rutherford (b. 1959) m. Elvie Maslin

Richie Alexander (b. 1961) m. Michelle Boyless

Deborah Susan (b. 1963) m. (1990) Timothy Evans

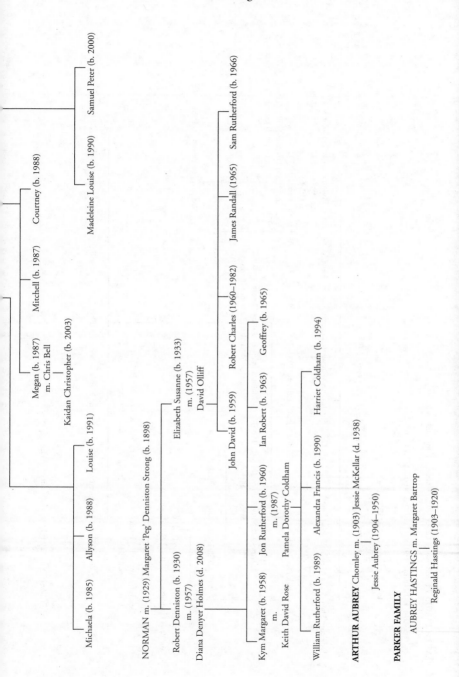

Michaela (b. 1985)

Allyson (b. 1988)

Louise (b. 1991)

Megan (b. 1987)
m. Chris Bell

Kaidan Christopher (b. 2003)

Mitchell (b. 1987)

Courtney (b. 1988)

Madeleine Louise (b. 1990)

Samuel Peter (b. 2000)

NORMAN m. (1929) Margaret 'Peg' Denniston Strong (b. 1898)

Robert Denniston (b. 1930)
m. (1957)
Diana Denyer Holmes (d. 2008)

Elizabeth Susanne (b. 1933)
m. (1957)
David Olliff

John David (b. 1959)

Robert Charles (1960–1982)

James Randall (1965)

Sam Rutherford (b. 1966)

Kym Margaret (b. 1958)
m.
Keith David Rose

Jon Rutherford (b. 1960)
m. (1987)
Pamela Dorothy Coldham

Ian Robert (b. 1963)

Geoffrey (b. 1965)

William Rutherford (b. 1989)

Alexandra Francis (b. 1990)

Harriet Coldham (b. 1994)

ARTHUR AUBREY Chomley m. (1903) Jessie McKellar (d. 1938)

Jessie Aubrey (1904–1950)

PARKER FAMILY

AUBREY HASTINGS m. Margaret Bartrop

Reginald Hastings (1903–1920)

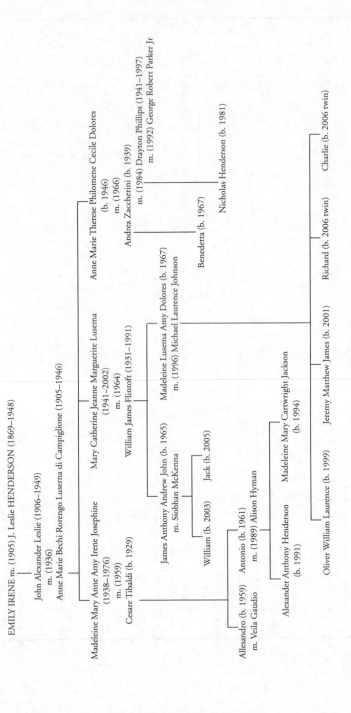

SMITH FAMILY / Henderson / Gayer / Weir Officer / Ffloyd Chomley

EMILY IRENE m. (1905) J. Leslie HENDERSON (1869–1948)

John Alexander Leslie (1906–1949)
m. (1936)
Anne Marie Bechi Rorengo Luserna di Campiglione (1905–1946)

Madeleine Mary Anne Amy Irene Josephine (1938–1976)
m. (1959)
Cesare Tibaldi (b. 1929)

Mary Catherine Jeanne Marguerite Lusema (1941–2002)
m. (1964)
William James Flintoft (1931–1991)

Anne Marie Therese Philomene Cecile Dolores (b. 1946)
m. (1966)
Andrea Zaccherini (b. 1939)
m. (1984) Drayton Phillips (1941–1997)
m. (1992) George Robert Parker Jr

James Anthony Andrew John (b. 1965)
m. Siobhan McKenna

Madeleine Lusema Amy Dolores (b. 1967)
m. (1996) Michael Laurence Johnson

Benedetta (b. 1967)

Nicholas Henderson (b. 1981)

William (b. 2003)   Jack (b. 2005)

Allesandro (b. 1959)
m. Veila Gaudio

Antonio (b. 1961)
m. (1989) Alison Hyman

Alexander Anthony Henderson (b. 1991)

Madeleine Mary Cartwright Jackson (b. 1994)

Oliver William Laurence (b. 1999)

Jeremy Matthew James (b. 2001)

Richard (b. 2006 twin)   Charlie (b. 2006 twin)

AMY MAUD m. (1938) Oswald Ventry GAYER (d. 1946)

354

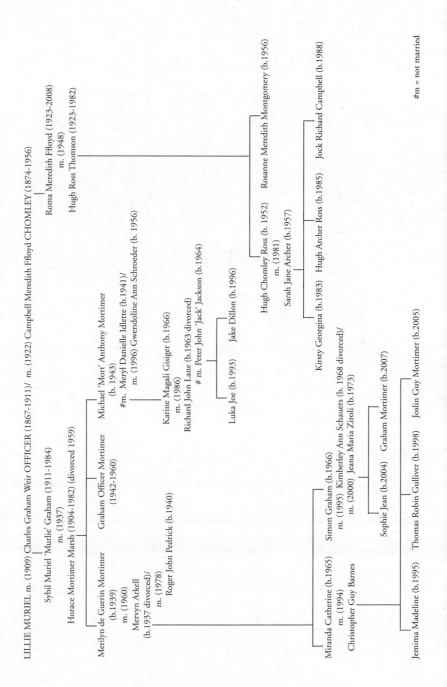

LILLIE MURIEL m. (1909) Charles Graham Weir OFFICER (1867-1911)/ m. (1922) Campbell Meredith Ffloyd CHOMLEY (1874-1956)

Sybil Muriel 'Murlie' Graham (1911-1984)
m. (1937)
Horace Mortimer Marsh (1904-1982) (divorced 1959)

Roma Meredith Ffloyd (1923-2008)
m. (1948)
Hugh Ross Thomson (1923-1982)

Merilyn de Guerin Mortimer (b.1939)
m. (1960)
Mervyn Arkell (b.1937 divorced)/
m. (1978)
Roger John Pedrick (b.1940)

Graham Officer Mortimer (1942-1960)

Michael 'Mort' Anthony Mortimer (b. 1943)
#m. Meryl Danielle Idlette (b.1941)/
m. (1996) Gwendoline Ann Schroeder (b. 1956)

Karine Magali Gisiger (b.1966)
m. (1986)
Richard John Lane (b.1963 divorced)
m. Peter John 'Jack' Jackson (b.1964)

Luka Joe (b.1993)

Jake Dillon (b.1996)

Hugh Chomley Ross (b. 1952)
m. (1981)
Sarah Jane Archer (b.1957)

Rosanne Meredith Montgomery (b.1956)

Kirsty Georgina (b.1983)

Hugh Archer Ross (b.1985)

Jock Richard Campbell (b.1988)

Miranda Catherine (b.1965)
m. (1994)
Christopher Guy Barnes

Simon Graham (b.1966)
m. (1995) Kimberley Ann Schauers (b. 1968 divorced)/
m. (2000) Jeana Maria Ziroli (b.1973)

Sophie Jean (b.2004)

Graham Mortimer (b.2007)

Jemima Madeline (b.1995)

Thomas Robin Gulliver (b.1998)

Joslin Guy Mortimer (b.2005)

#m = not married

355

GRAY FAMILY

FRANCIS DERWENT m. Edith Muriel Bayley
|
Huon (b.1923)

PHYLLIS EDITH m. Reginald Baker
|
Michael (b.1929)

OFFICER FAMILY/ Docker

LORRAINE MAUD m.(1919) Hubert Spencer Docker (1881-1965)
|
Stanley Spencer (1920-2007)
m. (1949)
Patricia Howard Earp (1920-2007)
|
John Spencer (b.1950)   Anne Louise (b.1952)   Mary Lorraine (b.1957)
m. (1977)   m. John Paul
Peter Stewart Pennington (b.1944)   Guy (b.1997)

SELECT BIBLIOGRAPHY

Books

Bartlett, Norman, *The Gold Seekers*, Jarrolds, London, 1965.

Blainey, Geoffrey, *A Land half won*, Macmillan, Melbourne, 1980.

Blainey, Geoffrey, Sea of Dangers. *Captain Cook and His Rivals*, Penguin, Viking, Camberwell, 2008.

Blainey, Geoffrey, *Black Kettle and Full Moon. Daily Life in a Vanished Australia*, Viking, Camberwell, 2003.

Bomann-Larsen, Tor, *Roald Amundsen* (translated by Ingrid Christophersen), Sutton Publishing, Stroud, 2006.

Bowden, Tim, *The Silence Calling, Australians in Antarctica 1947–97*, Allen & Unwin, Sydney, 1997.

Bradfield, Raymond A., *Castlemaine. The North-End, Some Early History*, Castlemaine Mail, Castlemaine, 1978.

Bradfield, Raymond, *Castlemaine. A Golden Harvest*, Castlemaine Mail, Castlemaine, 1993.

Cameron, Ian, *Antarctica: The Last Continent*, Little, Brown & Company, Boston, 1974.

Cameron, Ian, *Lodestone and Evening Star*, Hodder & Stoughton, London, 1965.

Cannon, Michael, *The Roaring Days*, Today's Australia Publishing Company, Mornington, 1998.

Clark, G.M.H. *A History of Australia Vol III. The Beginning of Australian Civilization 1824-1851*, 1973, and *Vol. IV The Earth Abideth for Ever 1851-1885*, Melbourne University Press, Clayton, 1978.

Clodd, E., *Thomas Henry Huxley*, William Blackwood & Sons, London, 1911

Davis, Captain J.E. RN, *A Letter from the Antarctic*, William Clowes & Sons Ltd, London, 1901.

Descriptive Catalogue of the Portraits of Naval Commanders, Representations of Naval Actions and of the Relics, &c. Exhibited in the Painted Hall and the Royal Naval Museum at Greenwich Hospital, printed for her Majesty's Stationery Office, Eye and Spottswoode, London, 1900.

Dodge, Ernest S., *The Polar Rosses. John and James Clark Ross and Their Explorations*, Barnes and Noble, New York, 1973.

Frame, Tom, *Evolution in the Antipodes. Charles Darwin and Australia*, UNSW Press, Sydney, 2009

Grenfell- Price, A., *The Winning of Australian Antarctica*, Angus & Robertson, Sydney, 1962.

Hocking, Geoff, *Early Castlemaine Part 1*, New Chum Press, Castlemaine, 1998.

Hocking, Geoff, *The Red Ribbon Rebellion. Decade of Dissent*, New Chum Press, Castlemaine, 2001.

Hocking, Geoff, *Gold. A Pictorial History of the Australian Goldrush*, The Five Mile Press, Rowville, Victoria, 2006.

Hocking, Geoff, *Castlemaine, From Camp to City 1835–1900*, New Chum Press, Castlemaine, 2007.

Hodge, Brian, *Major Controversies of the Australian Goldrush. Contenders, Pretenders and Prevaricators*, Tambaroora Star Publications, Tambaroora, NSW, 2003.

Hudson, Mike (designer/illustrator of *Household Words* by Charles Dickens, 2 June 1855), *Bound for the Goldfields: a true account of a journey from Melbourne to Castlemaine by a carrier of supplies to the goldfields*, The Wayzgoose Press, Katoomba, 1990.

Hunt, Susan, Martin Terry & Nicholas Thomas, *Lure of the Southern Seas. The Voyages of Dumont d'Urville 1826-1840*, History House Trust of New South Wales, Sydney, 2002.

Huxley, Leonard, *Life and Letters of Sir Joseph Dalton Hooker*, Vol. 1, John Murray, London, 1918.

Jose, A.W. & H.J. Carter (eds). *Australian Encyclopedia*, Vols I & II, Angus & Robertson, Sydney,1926.

Kerr, J.H. ("Resident"), *Glimpses of Life in Victoria*, Edmonston & Douglas, Edinburgh, 1872.

Lambert, Andrew, *Franklin. Tragic Hero of Polar Navigation*, Faber and Faber, London, 2009.

McGonigal, David (Chief Consultant), *Antarctica. Secrets of the Southern Continent*, Simon & Schuster, Australia, 2008.

McMillan, J.M., *The Two Lives of Joseph Docker*, Spectrum Publications, Melbourne, 1994.

Markham, Sir Clements R. K.C.B., F.R.S., *The Lands of Silence. A History of the Arctic and Antarctic Exploration*, Cambridge University Press,1921.

Martin, S., *A History of Antarctica*, State Library of New South Wales Press, Sydney, 1996.

Mill, Hugh Robert, *The Siege of the South Pole*, Alston Rivers Ltd., London, 1905.

Nicholas, F.W. & J.M. Nicholas, *Charles Darwin in Australia*, Cambridge University Press, Melbourne, 2008.

Nicholson, Ian Hawkins, *Shipping Arrivals and Departures Tasmania Vols I & 2, 1834-1842*, A Roebuck Book, Canberra, 1985.

O'Brian, Patrick, *Master and Commander*, Folio Society, London, 2008.

O'Brian, Patrick, *Desolation Island*, Folio Society, London, 2009.

O'Brian, Patrick, *The Surgeon's Mate*, Folio Society, London, 2010.

Owen, Russell, *The Antarctic Ocean*, Whittlesey House, London and New York, 1941.

Rodger, N.A., *The Wooden World. An Anatomy of the Georgian Navy*, Folio Society, London, 2009.

Ross, M.J., *Ross in the Antarctic. The Voyages of James Clark Ross in Her Majesty's Ships Erebus & Terror 1839 – 1843*, Caedmon of Whitby, Whitby, 1982.

Ruskin, John, *The Stones of Venice*, ed. & intro. by Jan Morris, The Folio Society, London, 2001.

Scott, Bill, *Complete Book of Australian Folklore*, Summit Books, Sydney, 1978.

Serle, Geoffrey, *The Rush to be Rich. A History of the Colony of Victoria 1883–1889*, Melbourne University Press, 1980.

Simons, John, *Rosetti's Wombat*, Middlesex University Press, 2008.

Sobel, Dava, *Longitude. The True Story of a Lone Genius who solved the Greatest Scientific Problem of His Time*, Fourth Estate, London, 1996.

Synge, M.B., *A Book of Discovery*, T.C. & E.C. Jack, Edinburgh, 1912.

Tingay, Stan, (ed.), 'Bolivia Bonanza', *Goldfields Reminiscences. Castlemaine's Golden Era*, (facsimile), reprint, *Castlemaine Mail*, 1977.

Tooley, R.V., *The Mapping of Australia and Antarctica*, Holland Press, London, 1979 1985.

Articles and Entries in Journals and Books

Attwood, Gertrude M., *The Wilsons of Tranby Croft*, Hutton Press, Beverley, East Yorkshire, 1988, pp.20–37.

Australian Dictionary of Biography, Vols 2 (1967); 3 (1969); 4 (1972); 6 (1976); 10 (1986), Melbourne University Press, Clayton.

Ayto, John & Ian Crofton (compilers), *Brewer's Britain & Ireland*, Weidenfeld & Nicolson, London, 2005, pp. 492-3.

Bach, John, 'The Royal Navy in the South West Pacific: the Australia Station 1859 – 1913', *The Great Circle*, Vol. 5, No 2 (October 1983) pp. 116–32.

Benezit Dictionary of Artists, Vol. 12, Entry on 'Smith, Bernhard', Gründ, Paris, 2006, p.1358.

Bertie, Charles H., 'Old Castlereagh Street', *Journal of the Royal Historical Society*, Vol.22, Pt 1, 1936, pp. 42-66.

Bowden, Tim, 'Antarctic Links with Tasmania' in Alison Alexander (ed.), *The Companion to Tasmanian History*, University of Tasmania, Hobart, 2005, pp. 18-19.

Cannon, Judith, 'A Glint in the Eye of the Artist', *National Library of Australia News*, December 1999, pp. 7–9.

Clacy, Ellen, 'A lady on the goldfields', *Australian Heritage* (spring 2008), pp. 31-35.

Concise Dictionary of Biography, Vols I, II & III, Oxford University Press, 1992.

Cowburn, Philip M., 'The British Naval Officer and the Australian

Colonies', *Journal of the Royal Australian Historical Society*, Vol. 54, Pt. 1 (March 1968) pp. 1–21.

Durey, Michael, 'Exploration at the Edge: Reassessing the Fate of Sir John Franklin's last expedition', *The Great Circle*, Vol. 30, No 2, 2008, pp. 3–40.

Earl of Ellesmere [Francis Egerton], 'Voyage to the Antarctic Regions', *Essays on History, Biography, Geography, Engineering &c.*, John Murray, London, 1858, pp. 324-5.

Howgego, Raymond John, *Encyclopedia of Exploration 1800 to 1850*, Hordern House, Potts Point, 2004, pp. 514–6.

Kerr, Joan (ed.), *The Dictionary of Australian Artists*, Oxford University Press, Melbourne, 1992, Juliet Peers, 'Smith, Bernhard (1820-1885)', pp. 733-5.

Lee, Sidney (ed.) *Dictionary of National Biography*, entry 'Ross, Sir James Clark (1800-1862)', Vol. XLIX, Smith, Elder & Co, London, 1897, pp.265-6.

Martin, Stephen, 'Sir Joseph Dalton Hooker. The Botany of the Antarctic Voyage of H.M. Discovery ships 'Erebus' and 'Terror' in the years 1839–1843', *Upfront*, November 2004, pp. 6–7.

McCalman, Iain, 'New Currents in Australian maritime history', *History*, No 102 (December 2009), pp. 6–7.

McCulloch, Alan, *Encyclopedia of Australian Art*, Vol. 2 (Entry on Bernhard Smith) Hutchison, Australia, 1984, p. 1129.

Moore, Bruce, 'Gold! Gold! Gold! The Language of the Nineteenth-Century Australian Gold Rushes', *National Library of Australia News*, October 2000, pp. 7–10.

Pierce, Peter, 'White Warfare' (Reviews of three books on Antarctica), *Australian Book Review*, February/March 1997, p. 20.

Proudfoot, Helen Parker, 'Botany Bay, Kew and the Picturesque: Early Conceptions of the Australian Landscape, *Journal of the Royal Australian Historical Society*, Vol. 65, Pt 1 (June 1979), pp.20–45.

Savours, Ann, 'Sir James Clark Ross, 1800-1862', *The Geographical Journal*, Vol. 128, Pt 3, September, 1962, pp. 325-7.

Scarlett, Ken, *Australian Sculptors* (Entry on Bernhard Smith), Thomas Nelson, Melbourne, 1980, p. 602.

Wood, Tom, 'Early charitable naval pensions, *Practical Family History*, No 64 (April 2003), pp.5–7.

Wynn, Graeme, 'Life on the Goldfields of Victoria: Fifteen Letters', *Journal of the Royal Australian Historical Society*, Vol. 64, Pt 4 (March 1979), pp. 258–268.

Published Primary Sources

A Description of the Royal Hospital for Seamen at Greenwich, W. Winchester and Sons, London, 1820.

Boumphrey, R.S., 'Alexander Smith's Account of the Discovery of East Antarctica, 1841', *The Geographical Journal*, Vol. 130, No 1 (May 1964) pp.113–15.

Government Gazette, Victoria.

Hooker, Joseph Dalton, *The Botany of the Antarctic Voyage of H.M. Discovery Ships* Erebus *and* Terror *in the Years 1839 – 1843*, facsimile J. Cramer, Weinheim, NY, 1963.

Kingsford, William H.S.K., *Blue Jackets or Chips off the Old Block*, Grant and Griffiths, London, 1854.

Richardson, Sir John & John Edward Gray (eds), *The Zoology of the Voyage of HMS Erebus and Terror under the command of Sir J.C. Ross during 1839-1843*, Reeves Bros, London,1844-5.

Ships Erebus and Terror, Returns to an Address of the Honourable The House of Commons, 26 August 1841; – for Copies of such extracts from the despatches of Captain James Ross from Van Diemen's Land, as will show the nature and extent of the brilliant discoveries which are said to have been made in a high Southern latitude by her majesty's ships Erebus and Terror, Admiralty, 28 August 1841.

Ross, James Clark, *A Voyage of Discovery and Research in the Southern and Antarctic Regions during the years 1839-43*, Vols 1 & 2, John Murray, London, 1847 (facsimile by David & Charles Ltd, Devon, 1989).

Sainty, M. & K.A. Johnson, *Census of New South Wales November 1828*, Library of Australian History, Sydney.

The Tasmanian Journal of Natural Science, Agricultural Statistics &c., Vol. 1, James Barnard, Govt. Printer, Hobart, 1842.

Unpublished Sources

Ahnentafel Chart for Sarah Aubrey Read, Merilyn Pedrick Collection, Aldgate, South Australia.

'Castlemaine (including Barker's Creek)', Castlemaine Historical Society (typed notes).

Modified Register for Captain Alexander John Smith, Merilyn Pedrick Collection, Aldgate, South Australia.

Modified Chart for Bishop John Smith, Merilyn Pedrick Collection, Aldgate, South Australia.

Smith, Bernhard, MS 9963, Box 7, La Trobe Heritage Collection, State Library of Victoria, Melbourne.

Smith, Minnie Bernhard, 'Bernhard Smith and his Connection with Art or "The 7 Founders of the P.R.B."', MS 4901, Mitchell Library, Sydney.

Transcriptions & photocopies of letters between Alexander Smith and Joseph Dalton Hooker, October 1848 to October 1852; miscellaneous correspondence and documents, Merilyn Pedrick Collection, Aldgate, South Australia.

Transcriptions &photocopies of letters by Alexander Smith sent to family and friends in England, December 1835 to August 1872; Merilyn Pedrick Collection, Aldgate, South Australia.

Newspapers & websites

Argus

Castlemaine Advertiser

Herald (Melbourne)

Launceston Examiner

Melbourne Morning Herald

Mount Alexander Mail

Naval Database, <www.pbenyon.plus.com>

A.J. Harrison, 'Lt Joseph Henry Kay RN', <www.users.on.net/~ahvem/page3/page2/page31/page31.html>

PICTURE CREDITS

Permission to use pictures in this book has been granted (under license) from various authorities as indicated in the caption:

National Maritime Museum, Greenwich (NMM); Australian National Maritime Museum, Sydney (ANMM); National Library of Australia (NLA); La Trobe State Library of Victoria (NLV); Mitchell Library, State Library of New South Wales (ML); Allport Library and Museum of Fine Arts, Tasmanian Archive & Heritage Office; State Parliamentary Library Collection, Victoria; Castlemaine Art Gallery & Historical Museum; Merilyn Pedrick Collection; Various Private Collections & Occasion Studios, Wangaratta.

As well, the author and publisher wish to acknowledge several pictures from other sources, largely from:

James Clark Ross, *A Voyage of Discovery and Research in the Southern and Antarctic Regions during the years 1839–43,*

John Murray, London, 1847; M.J. Ross, *Ross in the Antarctic The Voyages of James Clark Ross in Her Majesty's Ships Erebus & Terror 1839 – 1843*, Caedmon of Whitby, Whitby, 1982; Leonard Huxley, *Life and Letters of Sir Joseph Dalton Hooker*, John Murray, London, 1918; Sir John Richardson & John Edward Gray (eds), *The Zoology of the Voyage of HMS Erebus and Terror under the command of Sir J.C. Ross during 1839-1843*, Reeves Bros, London,1844-5; J.D. Hooker, *The Botany of the Antarctic Voyage of H.M. Discovery Ships Erebus and Terror in the Years 1839 – 1843*, 1844/5; J.E. Davis, *A Letter from the Antarctic, 1901; Illustrated London News*; *London Punch*; *Australasian Sketcher*

And for particular pictures as indicated below:

p.15 Royal Hospital for seamen, Greenwich, *Practical Family History*, April 2003, no 64, p.6

p.16 Plan of Royal Greenwich Hospital, *A Description of the Royal Hospital for Seamen at Greenwich*, W. Winchester and Sons, London, 1820

p.41 Sir James Clark Ross, watercolour c. 1830, artist unknown, H.R. Mill, *The Siege of the South Pole*, Alston Rivers Ltd., London, 1905, facing p.250

p.47 James Clark Ross engraving, Henry Cook from original painting, J.R. Wildman, 1840, Ian Cameron, *Antarctica: The Last Continent*, Little Brown & Co, Boston, 1974, p.106

p.49 Roald Amundsen, photographer unknown, Ian Cameron, *Antarctica: The Last Continent*, p.163

p.66 Charles Wilkes, David McGonigal (consultant), *Antarctica. Secrets of the Southern Continent*, Simon & Schuster, Australia, 2008, p.282

p.84 Discovery of Antarctica, James Clark Ross, adapted from Ian Cameron, *Lodestone and Evening Star*, Hodder & Stoughton, London, 1965, p. 221

p.183 Lieutenant Joseph Kay as a fourteen-year-old midshipman, A.J. Harrison, 19 Firth Road, Fenah Valley, *Lieutenant Joseph Henry Kay RN*

p.210 On the road to the diggings, pen & ink by W. Matherell

p.222 Successful diggers examine the day's yield, Michael Cannon, *The Roaring Days*, Today's Australia Publishing Company, Mornington, 1998, p.193

p.223 Chinese gold seekers on the road to the diggings, Michael Cannon, *The Roaring Days*, p.245

p.227 Chinese Joss House, Castlemaine, Michael Cannon, *The Roaring Days*, p.228

p.230 Gold Commissioners Camp, Castlemaine. The escort leaving camp June 1853, drawing, Commr G. Rudston Read, Raymond A. Bradfield, *Castlemaine The North End*, unpaginated

p.235 Gold Escort leaving Mt Alexander, "Bonanza" (S.W. Jones), *Goldfields Reminiscences Castlemaine Goldfields*, 1884, p.14

p.236 Castlemaine Commissioners Camp 1852, sketch, Clarke Ismir, "Bonanza" *Goldfields Reminiscences*, 1884, p.18

p.237 Sunday washing at the diggings (right), Michael Cannon, *The Roaring Days*, p.106

p.242 Top: Chinese at the diggings (left), Chinese on the goldfields, *Illustrated History of Australia*, Hamlyn, p.587; Chinese gold washing (right), engraving from Frederick Christmann, *Australien*

Bottom : Sly grog shops, Castlemaine in the early 1850s: Sly Grog at the diggings (right), Geoff Hocking, *Early Castlemaine*, New Chum Press, Castlemaine, 1998, p.66

p.248 Diggers relaxing on a Saturday afternoon, Michael Cannon, *The Roaring Days*, p.196

p.258 Burke & Wills memorial, Melbourne, Edwin Carton Booth, *Australia in the 1870s*, title page

p.266 Cobb & Co light Concord thoroughbrace coach, Michael Cannon, *The Roaring Days*, p.492

p.291 'The Last of England', oil painting, Ford Madox Brown, 1855, Wikipedia p.330 (bottom) The old & new at Bontharambo, sketch, N. Chevalier, Edwin Carton Booth, *Australian in the 1870s*, btwn pp.60 & 61

INDEX